Weaving Sunlight

Weaving Sunlight

God's Tapestry of Two Lives

By Tony & Marsha Woods

Weaving Sunlight: God's Tapestry of Two Lives

Copyright 2019 by Tony & Marsha Woods

Marton Publishing
ABN 28 768 241 762
martonpublishing.com

ISBN: 978-0-9944034-8-3

Requests for more information should be directed to
info@martonpublishing.com

Foreword

In digging around for material for this book, I came across an old heirloom that had been packed away since the 1960's when my parents' house was closed down. In his grief after Mother passed away, my Daddy placed everything carefully in boxes and then moved on to prepare for widowhood, a new chaper and eventually a new marriage.

The heirloom is called a weaver's shuttle, and it makes a great toy. I remember playing with it when I was very young, pushing it around the room and imagining threads all coming together with a twist of the wrist, mimicking the motions I'd seen when it was explained to me how it worked.

And then somehow, as we were packing Mother's things away, I knew that this had meaning in my life somehow. I kept it, and we've lugged it around the world with us ever since. From time to time I've even picked up others, which, I believe from looking at the marks on them, have their own stories to tell.

But let me tell you about the story behind this particular shuttle. There's an old and faded piece of paper glued to the bottom, and it reads like this: "My Maternal Grandpa Henry C. Best whittled this weaver's shuttle with his hunting knife for Polly Bess, his bride, in 1819 in Madison County, Missouri." In a side note it says that Polly wove all the clothing for her, her husband and their nine children, much of it accomplished, I'm sure by this shuttle I'm holding as I write. I've tried to figure out what 'Grandparent' this is to me in the list of 'Greats", but at this point I'll have to leave it to you future readers to figure it out.

What this reminds me is that God has been 'Weaving' in our lives for a very long time, using the bits of sunlight and shadow that have made up who we are. In the pages to follow, I hope you will catch a glimpse of the Master Weaver at work. I'm looking forward to seeing the finished product when He displays it in His Kingdom. And I'm anticipating the day when you can show me your own work of art. In the meantime, let's enjoy the days, knowing that the shuttle is traversing back and forth, back and forth through the threads of the loom. What a legacy!

Marsha

Preface

August 3rd, 1969. A bright, cloudless day in Wyoming, with the sky so blue you'd think it was brushed velvet pasted above a green backdrop of the heavily forested mountains of Yellowstone National Park. But the sun was about to touch the highest peaks on its way down, and Tony and Marsha knew they would have to find a place to camp soon.

It was the peak of Yellowstone's tourist season, so they were not surprised to find the designated campsites crowded, and after nearly an hour of searching, they had yet to find a place to pitch a tent. It was the third night of their honeymoon, complicated by having to buy a new tire for their '64 Falcon, the budget was already showing signs of depletion. Camping seemed an economical way of making the most of their time, but if they didn't find a campsite soon they would have to start searching for more expensive accommodations.

Then, almost as if in answer to their unspoken prayers, they came around a corner and found a campground that seemed to have available spaces. In fact, as they turned in and started driving through the sites, they saw that there were a lot of available spaces. In fact, there was no one there. It was almost as if aliens had abducted the entire camper population leaving no trace except for a few smoking fireplaces.

Rather than consider the alien abduction possibility, the newlyweds were overjoyed at their good fortune. Driving back to the farthest site in the campground, they found an ideal spot nestled between the trees on what looked like a game trail opening out onto a meadow. Tony switched off the Falcon's engine, and as the twin Glasspack mufflers cooled into silence, he turned to his bride and with his best Charles Boyer accent said, "Alone at last."

Marsha gave him a quick kiss in response and together they unloaded their camping gear. The tent was a hand-me-down from his folks, an old canvas "umbrella" type with a center pole that supported four cross pieces, one to each corner. It didn't look like much, but it had served the Woods family for many years. With walls nice and tight, they hauled in their sleeping bags and a few snacks left over from the wedding as well as a carton of orange juice and some breath mints picked up along the way. They were just standing back to admire their work when a big motor home with Texas license plates rolled in and parked right next to the tent.

Dang!

As the busy sounds of dinner preparations drifted outside, the door opened and the Texan stepped down to say "Howdy". It wasn't long before the fact was established that Tony also claimed Texas roots and the accents between the two got steadily broader and more laced with cowboy-isms than a John Wayne movie. The contest was soon interrupted though when the Park Ranger drove up.

"You've noticed that no one else is camped here, right?" When they both agreed that it was in fact unusual, the Ranger continued, "I was about the close the campground because there's a marauding bear in the area. I'll let you stay if you must, but you'll have to be extra cautious."

The Texan pitched in at once with, "Wahl, Ah ain't scared of no bear. Ah'm stayin."

Tony by unspoken decree, joined in the one-man chorus. "Yeah, me too. Ah'm stayin." Even as he spoke, his eyes fell a little too quickly on the Texan's motor home and compared it to the canvas umbrella tent he and Marsha would be sleeping in. Being a good wife of three whole days, Marsha said nothing.

They built a fire, roasted a hot dog and listened to the sounds of the night. Finally, Tony spoke up. "Would it … well, would it be okay with you if we slept in the car tonight? We can slip back into the tent first thing in the morning so our neighbor won't draw any opinions about us."

That earned him the second kiss of the evening, and together they built up the back seat of the Falcon, laid a single sleeping bag across the top and admired their handiwork. Never mind that the car was a convertible with a well worn cloth top; it still seemed better than a canvas tent in the middle of a game trail.

"I'm so glad I'm married to you," he said, squeezing her hand. "If I was with the guys, we'd all have to be brave. But now I can just say I'm committed to protecting my wife."

They got through the night okay and jumped out of the car at first light, dragging the sleeping bag back to the tent and sniggering at this very first secret they would be holding together as man and wife. Tony stopped suddenly and Marsha ran into him, dropping the sleeping bag on the ground. There in front of them lay what little remained of the tent. Only a few scraps of canvas, a broken center pole and a trace of guy rope that gave evidence of what it once was.

The crime scene became obvious in light of the remnants. A bear had indeed come along during the night, and following his nose made his way into the tent. "So all those stories about not leaving any food out were true," they thought with some embarrassment. There was the carton of orange juice, smashed flat by a huge paw and one end chewed open for easy access. As for the rest of the food, only a sliver of green foil was left of the breath mints.

Once inside, the bear had then started to leave, but being rather big and hefty, he failed to turn around without breaking the center pole. The tent had come down on the marauder like a well-set bear trap, and the bear reacted accordingly. Several new doors were now available in the canvas. As Tony and Marsha sifted through the remains of their camping gear, the door to the motor home swung open and the Texan stepped out. "Whut the hell happened to yew?" he nearly shouted.

"Oh, We had a bear in the tent last night," Tony said without looking up.

"You had a ..." the Texan stood speechless, looking at first one, then the other, then down at the debris field. "Wull... what about yew? Are yew okay?"

At that moment, Tony and Marsha's very first "Husband and Wife Secret" got ramped up a couple of notches. Still looking down at the ground, with an occasional glance off toward the majestic Grand Teton mountain range, Tony coughed quietly then said,

"Yeah, we're okay. No problem."

We're going to go back to the beginning now, starting with Tony, then Marsha, piecing together a few decades of what has become our story. It is said that most people are three generations from extinction, but that's not supposed to make you depressed – really! Instead, just think of the rich experiences that have made up your life, both good and bad. If future generations are going to benefit from any of those experiences, someone needs to write them down. So that's our first motivation.

Also, you know how sometimes you have to step away from a painting before you can focus on the picture? That's what we're seeing as we look back over our lives. What up close seemed to be random pieces of thread are now revealing themselves to be a mind-boggling tapestry, skillfully crafted by the Master Weaver. One day, when we arrive at the Savior's feet, I'm pretty sure He will take us aside and say, "Come over here; I've got something to show you." And there, perfectly framed and exquisitely lit will be the artwork that was us. All those events, chance meetings, life-changing decisions, darkest valleys and highest mountaintops ... everything will have been woven together into something both absolutely unique and absolutely precious.

Today, in the sunset years of our lives, we're beginning to get one of those "through the glass darkly" glimpses that the Apostle Paul wrote about in I Corinthians 13:12. We want to assure you, Dear Reader, that your own tapestry is being woven at this very moment. Everything that has happened or will happen in your life is being used with great care in order that something truly beautiful will come to light one day.

And finally, there's that "Bear in the tent". If he hasn't made himself known to you already, know for a fact that he will. Every time you hit a wall, or lose a loved one or find yourself face to face with a mountain that seems impossible, just say to yourself, "The bear is back."

Knowing your enemy, in this case Satan, is the first step to resisting or even defeating him. Understand that he is not all-powerful, nor is he all-knowing. Someone has described him as a bad dog on a short leash. We might add that he's a marauding bear that's just been darted and tagged. His end is sure, but he doesn't plan to go down easily. But go down he will.

Don't forget that truth. Enjoy the journey.

CHAPTER 1

The Journey Begins

My mother was screaming as Dad pushed and pulled her from the Studebaker. The sound was enough to bring the hospital doors swinging open followed immediately by three nurses in white starched uniforms.

"Oh Mrs. Woods, you're finally here. Let's get you ready."

"It's coming it's coming it's coming! I want to push!" she yelled as they settled her onto a gurney and wheeled her into the maternity section.

"Oh no, Mrs. Woods, you can't do that. Remember what the doctor said?"

It had already been decided that a Cesarean section would be necessary, owing to my Mom's history of rheumatic fever followed by Rheumatoid Arthritis. The fact that she was even anticipating imminent childbirth was something that not many had foreseen. A doctor had told her father years before that she probably wouldn't survive more than a few months, and even if she did she certainly would never walk.

But here she was, and as the nurses began to prep her for surgery, one of them produced a clipboard. "Gonna need some names here," she said, applying the tip of a pencil to the tip of her tongue.

"Oh for Heaven's sake! You know my name. Let's get on with it!"

"No, not your name, silly. Names for your baby. One for a boy and one for a girl. We have to have something to put on the Birth Certificate".

"Now??? I don't know… we didn't have time to decide. Can't I tell you later?"

"Sorry Mrs. Woods," the nurse said, hold the ether mask tantalizingly close. "Rules are rules. Boy's name?"

"Oh, oh, oh….. Tony!"

"Is that short for Anthony?"

"No! Just Tony. Can we please…"

"Middle name?"

"Mid…. Do you really need that now?"

"Sorry Mrs. Woods. Rules are.."

"I know!! Ah…. Ray!"

"Tony Ray Woods. There, that wasn't so hard, was it? Girl's name?"

But this time the nurse leaned in just a fraction too close. Mom shot out an arm and grabbed the poor woman by her starched collar. Looking her straight in the eye with an unmistakable glare of menace, she enunciated every word so as not to repeat, "It's… not … going …to …be …a ….. girl."

And so the play was set. January 30th, 1948. Enter Tony Ray Woods, stage left.

In many respects, 1948 was a year to be remembered. The entertainment industry rocked the world with the 33 1/3 long playing (LP) records, giving music lovers an unprecedented 25 minutes of constant music; quite a jump from the old 78s, which were doing good to squeeze in one rendition of Arthur Godfrey's "Too Fat Polka". Television sets invaded the American home in 1948, jumping to over a million from less than 5000 just three years previously.

Life wasn't all fun and games, though. Just when we thought World War One and World War Two were enough to end all, the Cold One began heating up in North Korea, while back in Berlin, Russia decided to isolate the East side, complete with wall and barbed wire to keep everyone in from going out. It didn't work, by the way.

But as far as I'm concerned, the biggest event in 1948 (besides my birth, of course) was the birth of Israel. Following Rome's destruction of Jerusalem in 70AD, the Jewish Diaspora wandered the world with nothing but God's promise of a homeland. And this is why I consider 1948 such a significant year. While Jesus is comforting His people with the promise of His return, he talks about the blossoming of the fig tree as an important sign, saying in Matthew 24:34, "Truly I tell you, this generation will certainly not pass away until all these things have happened."

Fig tree, symbol of Israel… blossoming, the return to Jerusalem as a nation? Okay, so it's open to theological discussion, but I'm sticking to the very real possibility that MY generation, began for me in 1948, will live to see the return of Christ. Could happen.

Life for me began in Texas. My mother, Joann Cannon (or Jody as she was called) was a product of all that a West Texas town like "Levelland" could promise, her father a tough, no nonsense sheriff and part time oil man. Jody typified the West Texas spirit, not letting something like rheumatic fever and the ensuing rheumatoid arthritis slow her down much. She probably never enjoyed a single day without pain, but you'd never know it by talking to her. Even when her doctor told her father that Jody would probably never walk again, she just brushed it off and went on to the business of play (on her feet, I might add).

These days, my Dad, born the much later third son and named 'Elmon Lloyd" by a kindly aunt, would be termed a "latchkey kid". His parents loved him, to be sure, but it was the Depression and they both had to work just to get by. Even as a first-grader, he would often be left alone to get himself up in the morning, fix breakfast, make a lunch and get to school, then find new and imaginative ways to entertain himself after school and Saturdays until someone came home. For more on those misadventures, be sure to read the book, "*Uncle Buddy*".

The first thing he had to do was to get rid of that dreaded given name, Elmon Lloyd. A neighbor helped with that, always referring to him as "my little Buddy". The handle stuck, and the official name was never spoken of again, except when something more legal was needed, and then was usually written as "E.L. (Buddy) Woods".

Buddy was one of the last in his generation to participate in World War II, so as a result was on the trailing edge of the Fathers of the Baby Boomers. When I came along in 1948, I think that may help explain why most of my peers were a year or two older than me, a situation that did a lot toward shaping my life, as well as turning it around as a teenager.

Growing up, I was blessed with the best of both worlds, namely, a farm to grow up on and a set of parents determined to leave that farm. My grandparents had a small bit of acreage just south of Mansfield, Texas where they raised a few crops, had a few cows, some turkeys and chickens, and lived the kind of life most boys in my generation dreamed of. My parents built a small house on one corner of the property, and to me that will always be the old home place. There was plenty of space out back to run with the dogs and find more than enough adventure, both real and imaginary. As I grew older, I was part of the Future Farmers of America, which meant I was taught how to raise cows for profit, drive a John Deere tractor and tell the difference between sweet Coastal Bermuda grass and the cattleman's' curse, Nutall Deathcanus.

My folks didn't quite share that dream, and that was another life-shaper. Dad was born with a knack for selling, and most of his life was spent looking to make the "perfect deal." He sold everything from street maps to shaving cream, copying machines to steel buildings, AND the up and coming "Addressograph/Multigraph", a confusing mass of gears that would be the forerunner of modern Xerox machines.

 And that was the problem, I suppose. It seems that Dad would get into a company, start to really make his way up the ranks, and then the company would hit the wall. Farther down the road, GPS would be the death knell for street maps. Drum based spirit copiers would be replaced by mimeographs, which were in turn replaced by computer technology. The steel company that Dad worked for offered the best promise for promotion until one day when he was out of state on a business trip. He called the head office to check in and discovered that the company had gone belly up, the boss running off with the assets.

What that meant was that my folks were almost constantly on the move from job to job. Sometimes I would stay with Grandparents while they got settled, sometimes I would go with them. At least part of every school year I spent in a totally new situation, having to make new friends and find my niche among unknown tribes of potential peers.

I think that contributed to the fact that I developed a stuttering problem. Saying my name was the toughest challenge of all (not the best problem to have when you're trying to make a good first impression), and just about any hard consonant was even harder to say. How I wished my name started with a nice vowel sound, like Anthony, instead of T-T-T-T-T-Tony!

Grandpa Cannon, I have to say, didn't help much. He decided to take on the problem like any good West Texas sheriff, leading me out behind the barn to make it clear in no uncertain terms that this foolishness would stop, and it would stop NOW! And it did stop, at least as far as Grandpa Cannon was concerned, since I hardly ever spoke to him after that, about anything. It's a shame, really, because I know he was just a product of his own generation who felt like there was nothing that couldn't be whipped into shape. I'd love to talk to him now, and hear his stories of the Wild West; something I could do now, by the way, since the stuttering problem was cleared up miraculously after I got to college. But more about that later.

I mentioned that, in the Grand Scheme of Things, my peers invariably seemed to be a year or two older than me. In typical group dynamics, that meant that I normally fell into the role of mascot. My friends were not mean to me, not at all; but they didn't expect much of me either. My opinions were rarely asked for and serious discussions were nearly always led by the older boys. I didn't mind, especially since any wrong doing in the group was never my fault. I was just the kid, after all.

All that changed in 1964, when my family moved to Colorado (in search of a better job, naturally). This was the beginning of my junior year in high school, by the way, and the move was a real eye opener for ALL of us, my folks included.

I say this with a certain amount of shame, but with a reminder that all of us were products of our generation, and in Texas in the 50's and 60's, segregation was a way of life. The white folks lived on one side of town and the black folks lived on the other. I can remember as a young teenager a church business meeting when the topic of the evening was, "What do we do IF a black person comes to church?"

I'm happy to say that the church concluded that a person of any race would be welcome to worship with us, so long as he behaved. I'm also happy to say that, by the time the first black families began attending First Baptist Mansfield, attitudes had changed so much that, rather conveniently, no one remembered that business meeting discussion.

But for Mom, Dad and myself, the move to Colorado changed all of our attitudes and demolished a lot of our preconceptions. I'll never forget going to a restaurant in Denver and seeing a black family eating at a booth nearby. My parents were not offended at all, but they were flabbergasted! Back in Texas in those days, a black person would have been ushered out of the restaurant immediately, and in some cases to the nearest hanging tree. But this was the dawn of a new day, and the first rays of light were shining on Denver just a bit before they hit Texas.

It didn't take long to realize how different I was in high school either. I still sported the traditional "flattop" hair cut: easy to care for and no problems with "hat hair" after spending the day in a cowboy hat. It took several comments before I realized that mine was the only flattop in school.

Tony with Big Red, the sale of which financed his first car

And for that matter, comments in my direction were few and far between. I wasn't inclined to start any conversations because of the stuttering issue, and that only served to bolster the image that I was some kind of tough guy from out of state. Rumor had it that I had served time in Juvenile. The crime wasn't specified, but murder was one of the top suggestions.

I wasn't even aware that this image was growing until one day when I ventured to speak with a girl in my English class who was crying. She explained that her boyfriend had made some disparaging remarks about her, ruining her reputation. Keep in mind that I was a Texas farm boy, and shy or not, guys just didn't go around bad-mouthing the ladies! I assured her that I would have a talk with the young man (who by the way was a year older than me) and help him understand the error of his ways.

I didn't intend for it to get physical, honest. Where I came from, usually all a guy needed was to be reminded of the need for propriety around women. I knew that he had an after school job at the local grocery store, so I went down to have a talk with him. Asking one of the employees where I might find him, she went to the back, then came out to tell me that, for some reason, he had run out through the loading dock and it didn't look like he was planning to return.

That was a milestone in my life. As far as the school was concerned, the rumors of my convict past were all true. As far as my peers were concerned, I was the newly-elected leader of the pack. Suddenly, people were asking my opinion about everything from homework assignments to car parts. It was a developing process to be sure, but over time I found myself growing into an attitude of leadership that I had never experienced back in Texas. Without a doubt, God was preparing this quiet, stammering group mascot for a life of ministry I could never have imagined.

And maybe that helps explain my actions that fateful Sunday night when I did something so bold and daring that it changed the course of my life forever. Keep reading.

A year and a half passed, and my parents, true to their nature, had moved yet again. But this time I fully supported the decision. Denver was a great place, but we loved the mountains. It wasn't long before Dad began talking about living up in the foothills near Evergreen and commuting into Denver every day for work. For a Texas farm boy in search of a farm, this was music to my ears. The mountains of Colorado had everything to offer a young man in search of adventure, and it wasn't long before I had traded my cowboy boots for lace up "waffle stompers" and my pickup-wannabe-'55 Chevy for an old army surplus Jeep. Blizzards? Hah! I laughed in the face of adversity, welcoming the opportunity to plow through the snow and rescue fair damsels in distress. Bears and mountain lions were an occasional menace, even near Evergreen, and

I soon traded my .22 rifle and 410 shotgun for an 8mm Mauser, a 270 Remington and a 20 gauge shotgun with adjustable choke. You can never have enough firepower, I reckoned.

About the guns… reading my own words here, I have to realize that such a lifestyle has become more and more a negative image in light of the tragic increase of gun-related incidents in America. Each heartbreak brings on even more talk about gun control, and I suppose eventually things will tighten up out of necessity. But it seems to me the genie is out of the bottle, and getting him back inside may prove a bigger challenge than anyone can imagine. I could take a faith-view of it all and simply say that the world is regressing just like the Bible promised us that it would, but that wouldn't make things any easier when the next victims fall.

Or I could join the crowds demanding the disarmament of America, although I'm afraid all that would accomplish would be to give the bad guys an edge over society since they of course would manage to keep their own guns.

Or, I could look to my law-abiding, God-fearing extended family in Texas who sees all the insanity going around as a proof text for *increased* gun ownership with tougher penalties for those who mess up.

It's not an easy challenge, I'll admit, and I conclude this topic with some trepidation as I mention that I used to walk through the woods on my way to school, accompanied by my dogs who dutifully waited in the trees near the spot where I had hidden my shotgun. After school, we hunted all the way home, often bringing a squirrel or a rabbit to add to the pot. Such actions would have undoubtedly gotten me incarcerated in today's world.

I soon learned that Colorado is blessed with 52 "Fourteeners", mountains which rise more than 14,000 feet (4267 meters) above sea level; so naturally I set out as one of my life goals to stand on the top of all 52. Our first summer in Colorado, I managed to conquer two of them, Pikes Peak and Mount Evans. Of course those have roads to the summit, so I drove to the top, but it was a start!

The next summer, my friend Dave Cook and I tackled number three: 14,259 foot Longs Peak, near Estes Park. It was a real mountain, complete with a moderate degree of rock climbing, a narrow traverse 800 feet above certain death, an ice storm halfway across the traverse and enough lightning nearby to make my hair stand straight out.

After an alpine rescue team had to be called to help us down, I quietly determined to let the other 49 Fourteeners alone.

In the spring of 1966, I graduated from high school, and when I began to look around at colleges, the choice was simple: Colorado State University had an excellent forestry program, and as far as I was concerned, I was destined to be a forest ranger. When fall came, I packed up the jeep and headed 90 miles north to the town of Fort Collins. Going against my guidance counselor's advice, I signed up for nothing but forestry courses, except for a required English class (that would prove to be decisive later) and so I concentrated solely on forestry for the next two years, and then I got a summer job as a forest ranger in Estes Park.

It was a great time, living in a bunkhouse with hard livin', hard drinkin' fellow rangers, maintaining trails, fighting forest fires and oh yeah, building and then cleaning a few campsite outhouses. By September, I was tough as leather, hard as nails, and a little smarter than I had been in June. However, I realized, all the fun forestry work was being done by kids like me. The ones who went on to finish their degrees soon found themselves back in a Denver office, calculating board feet and discussing the advantages of Forest Service versus National Park Service polices and their impact on environmental issues.

Returning to CSU in the fall, I went to my guidance counselor and, trying to avoid eye contact, said,

"I don't want to be a forest ranger anymore. Can I change my major?"

Mercifully, he moved quickly past the "I told you so" talk and moved on to options.

"Well," he said, "you have two years of forestry courses under your belt. Oh wait, here are two English classes! How about changing your major to English with a teaching degree?"

Nothing sounded less appealing at the moment, but I was desperate to finish college in my lifetime, so I agreed. Altogether, I managed to squeeze a four-year college program into seven, but I don't really want to talk about that anymore.

$$\gtrless$$

And Now a Word From Marsha:

Marsha with big sister Sherry, family cat Hoot and the infamous
wrought iron fence in the backbround

I suppose my very first memory in life is hanging upside down on
the wrought-iron fence that separated me from my home in Idaho
Springs, Colorado and what I had supposed was true freedom
beyond the gate. I couldn't have been more that three years old at the
time, and in fact not far removed from two. I don't remember many
of the details surrounding the escape attempt, only the outcome. It
seems that I had successfully negotiated the ascent – no small feat
for one so young – and had managed to get one leg up and over that
cursed barrier to all that I ever truly wanted in life. At that point,
gravity took over, and I started to fall. I vaguely remember the sight
of approaching doom as the sidewalk rose to meet me. But then I
was rescued by the very thing that had been designed to keep me in
my proper place: the sharp point of a black wrought iron spear (see

photo above), one of many forming the fence, caught on my long and magnificent dress, holding me inexorably and keeping me there until my sister Sherry came to my rescue.

Thinking back to that time, and especially as I try to put a lifetime of vignettes into some kind of meaningful order, I believe that first vivid memory illustrates something within and around me that has since helped define Marsha Glee (Smith) Woods.

After that, there was the bee sting when I would have been about three or four. My grandmother was visiting so I got a lot of extra attention regarding the tragedy. I liked that. My mother was a hard working rather pragmatic woman. Thinking back, if my paternal grandmother who chose to be called "Mother Gay," hadn't been there I probably would have been nursed and then told 'little girls don't cry, so get over it'.

As I think of my mother in retrospect, none of us knew at the time that she would get breast cancer a couple of years later which would eventually take her life when I was 14. Maybe she knew her life was not going to be a picnic……..and it wasn't, but somehow I feel that she did everything she could (along with Daddy and my older sister Sherry whom I adored,) to assure me I felt loved even if times were occasionally tough.

The next thing that is still with me was my entire kindergarten class 'escaping' and running en masse to the big playground. I can't remember whether we had the nerve or luck to achieve going down the towering slide before we were corralled back where we belonged. I'm pretty sure I would not have tried such an achievement even if given the opportunity. Being the baby in the family, I was very timid about most things, happy to let my sister take the first step and often the spanking.

Then came first grade, and while nowadays kids by the first grade are usually almost literate, I remember the teacher explaining rather roughly, I thought, that no matter how I protested, I would NOT be allowed to write my name from right to left! I was shattered. After all, I discovered much later, that Leonardo de Vinci was able to capitalize on his left-handedness by writing backwards (I can still do pretty good even today but find little need for it)!

Moving on through grade school I enjoyed a fair amount of success, being around the 'B' level. So after the first big bump of having to rearrange my writing to left to right, school was easy and I was happy.

One day in the second grade, we were taking a spelling test and I decided to try something new. I had an imaginary friend. Sadly I can't remember his name, but he was a *he* and he and I got along fine. One day he seemed to indicate to me that he would like a stab at the spelling test.

"No" I said vehemently, "What if you get caught"?

"Oh please, please, just let me try. I'll tell you my answers and you can write them for me, here on the floor"

Well, that seemed like a good idea, especially since he was willing to let me take care of him, which wasn't always the case. And so it began. When the word was called out, I would write it carefully on my paper, using extra care to print legibly. Then I would bend from the waist, never moving from my seat, to the floor and scrawl (he had bad handwriting) the word, again correctly, on his paper that I'd carefully prepared for him. All this while carefully avoiding the teacher's wandering glances.

All went well till the test was over. We'd both done magnificent work. That was, until, Mrs. Mackenzie, a teacher I adored, strolled to my desk and saw the paper sticking out from under it.

"What's this, she glowered as she picked up 'his' copy".

"Uhm, uh.........I hesitated between blaming HIM, or taking the blame myself in a altruistic effort to protect him. I chose the latter and let her assume that I'd been cheating. Pain in the second grade......life lessons learned, do you stand up/cover for a friend and take the fall.... or?

Mrs. Mackenzie agreed to test me privately after class and perhaps she was able to understand what had really happened. As I write this, I still remember her with fondness for the kindness she offered me.

Unfortunately, a few weeks later I caught the mumps, which led to Rheumatic fever. I was more blessed than Jody, my mother in law to be, in that Penicillin had been discovered by 1957 and I was only in the hospital for a few weeks. I was then forced to stay in bed for six months. As a result I survived without any side effects, including having no scarring or heart murmur, which was the norm at that time after the disease.

 I think a tutor came around occasionally, but my much loved aforementioned grandmother also came up from Texas and sat with me while my parents worked. I remember I wasn't even allowed to go downstairs to my bedroom, but had a bed in the living room.

Fortunately I can't remember what I did for the toilet, because it was also downstairs, but we'd only had plumbing for a year or so, so I imagine they dusted off the good ol' potty that we'd used before. It was a good time because Mother Gay, was a teacher by trade and she and I dreamed up a whole city and built it out of carefully decorated milk cartons and boxes spread across the living room floor, complete with streets and trees. Years later she told me she had dabbled with "Montessori" learning. Maybe that's when I became a kinesthetic learner.

I finally did go back to school, but I was stick thin and had to have 'supplements' to get some weight on my bones (not a problem now).

My mother, who constantly worried about my health, insisted that both my sister and I wear thick leggings under our dresses (a girl's only option for clothing in the 50's) to walk to and from the bus stop that was at the bottom of our hill, about 500 yards. I was mortified to be seen amongst my peers in such a fashion disaster but gutted thru every morning and evening the wearing of the extra warmth. Not my soon to be teenaged sister........she smiled and went out the door every morning, assuring my parents of her love and devotion..... then pulled off the leggings and stuffed them in our mailbox before boarding the bus. Such a clever girl, except that often my parents discovered them if they happened by the mailbox during the day. I think now that perhaps if she'd have been truly smart, she would have used someone else's box!

It wasn't' until the 4th grade that I met the unmovable obstacle called Math. I had a young, seemingly unhappy or maybe just inept, teacher. I was seated directly in front of a boy named Marshall, and for whatever reason, we began to design houses. We would work fervently every moment we could get away with, drawing house plans; round rooms, many stories, elaborate and imaginative details. Presumably this was during the time when we were supposed to be learning our times tables......because to this day I can make myself almost sick facing a math problem! When I think 'Math' I have strong associations with great joy (architecting) and sudden inadequacy! Alas, if only Miss 'mismatched to teaching' could have captured our attention with architecture and won us over to the necessary math involved........

By the 6th grade however, a teacher DID capture my imagination. For whatever reason he saw my need to color outside of the lines and made me the school newspaper editor. I have no record of what we finally produced, if anything at all, but I remember running the halls with my best friend and full permission, doing our very best to get the 'paper' out. I have no idea what I learned that year but I put in hours and hours of research and review, lugging home books to work further on whatever it was... I believe somehow I graduated grade school at the top rank, even though I was seldom in class.

Junior high school went by quickly. By now my mother was frequently sicker than well, we continued to live in an unfinished house that my parents were building as they had money or could find materials. I think I remembered something about them finding out that because they'd started construction before they got a builder's permit, they couldn't get a loan. It's of some comfort to me now that even great wise people, as I pictured my parents, could make rookie mistakes.

Don't get me wrong, the house provided me shelter and some degree of warmth, but there was insulation showing on the walls because Mother wanted beautiful wood paneling and was willing to wait till we could afford it. I seldom had friends over, and as I began to think about boys, wondered what excuse I could offer my shining steed about the cinderblock front step he would have to step up on to knock on the door.

In addition to a questionable dwelling, I wasn't allowed to go to dances or even join a tap dance class, because my mother thought those things were 'nasty'.

Somehow I did manage to have some good friends and an average girl based social life and for that I'm thankful.

We as the Smith family, had a TV from about my 6th birthday or so, but we only watched "The Flintstones" for 30 minutes on Friday night and "Lawerence Welk" on Saturday night IF our hair was washed and in curlers ready for Sunday morning. The Macy's Parade on Thanksgiving Day and the Rose Bowl Parade on New Year's Day were a HUGE treat! We were members of a tiny Baptist church in Evergreen and when I was about 11, I won a beautiful Bible in a sword drill! If you're reading this generations away from the writing, a 'Sword Drill' is an activity where everyone holds their 'Swords' or Bibles over their heads, a verse is read out and the first person to find the verse and stand to read it, wins. To achieve this ability, one had to memorize the books of the entire Bible in order and know basically where they were in relation to the others.

By now my sister had been shipped off to a Christian boarding school 500 miles away. I believe she was just a little bit too big of a challenge for them......(leggings in the mailbox sort of stuff) and this school came highly recommended. After some initial adjustments, she came to love it and I looked forward to the day when I could also attend.

I even had a boy friend! His name was Bruce and sometimes we
sat together on the bus. That was it. Once we said "I like you this
much" indicating the level of our feelings for each other on the back
of the seat in front of us"…..I think his 'like' was higher than mine.

Then one Christmas, he raised the bar somewhat by showing up
at my house with a Christmas present. I didn't have anything for
him but shrugged my shoulders and, not inviting him in, took the
present with a satisfied grin and put it under the tree. Later, while
I was alone, I decided to sneak a peak and carefully unwrapped it.
There was the ugliest locket/music box bracelet I had ever seen. I
might have made a nice collar for a junkyard dog, but seriously??

It was a real challenge to ride the bus with him as usual. From there
the relationship did not prosper and I was off to Sherry's boarding
school the next year, much relieved to be leaving him behind.

The other reason I was 'relieved' to go away to boarding school was
that I was ready. Mother was getting sicker and sicker and I worried
continually both about her health and that I might do something
'wrong' in her eyes. Because she'd had a very 'unchristian' life
before she became a church going Christian, she was constantly on
the prowl for 'something nasty'. Most of my moral compass was
governed by horror stories of girls who danced or heaven forbid
'looked at the boys'. Maybe some of this over vigilance on her part
was a growing premonition that she'd be leaving us soon and couldn't
raise me to maturity. Clearly in retrospect it was going to be
difficult for both of us as I began to mature.

Many, many years later when I had two boys of my own, I realized the dangers of raising them exactly the same way, one being a rebel and the other one a bit quiet. This was Sherry and Me. You couldn't beat it into Sherry and I was beginning to wither just because I was so timid, always imagining that I might be in trouble somehow.

When I was 13, Sherry married her High School Sweetheart, Maynard Yutzy. She had really enjoyed her time at Central Christian and always told me hilarious stories from life in the dorm. Things were looking good all around and I loved being with Sherry and Maynard, seeing them as newlyweds made me happy. On the home front Mother was dying, but that had been the norm for years so I went off to school.

In October my parents came to see me at school and I could tell that things were not good. Mother looked horrible and was using a walker but was cheerful and upbeat. They had just travelled from Colorado to Chicago to get a 'miracle drug' for her cancer and were quite hopeful. Unfortunately I learned much later from Daddy that it was all snake oil and cost them quite a lot of money, but they had to try.

Unfortunately when Thanksgiving came I was excused from school a few days early to be by her side. She was already comatose but seemed to know I was there. She had told Sherry earlier that her only regret was that she hadn't seen grandchildren from Sherry or a husband for me. She passed away in the early morning before we could get there and I remember Daddy coming out of her room with a troubled smile, saying softly, "She's already gone".

I didn't cry. Looking back I think it was because at 14 I don't think I really ever knew her very well...I was typing a letter to someone the afternoon she died and Sherry came in and was upset because I had written, "I'm glad she's not suffering any more". I guess I'd been on the scene with the confusing years where she'd be good one day and sick the next more than Sherry but also Sherry was a woman who had lost a friend. Quite obviously they had their issues, but I think in a lot of ways they were so alike that they understood each other better than I did, me being 6 years younger. On the other hand I was still a kid. I loved her and knew I was greatly loved by her, but now that was over and I was ready to get on with it.   I remember suggesting to Daddy a few days after the funeral that we go see a movie……..yep, still a kid.

As I'm writing this as an adult my heart goes out to the 44 year old who had missed even saying good bye to his wife.

My life at school carried on almost without a bump. After a few weeks Daddy wrote me a letter that said, "I know you'll miss your mother and there will be some things you'll feel more comfortable asking your sister"………the shy scientist's poorly disguised plea to not ask HIM! So funny, so Daddy, who took another 10 years and a heart bypass operation that almost cost him his life to learn to be more obvious showing his love to his daughters.

Later that year on Christmas break, Daddy picked me up in Kansas and we drove to Texas to be with his family. While he was driving he explained to me that while he loved my mother very much, he'd like my permission to date. I think after struggling with her 10 years of cancer he was ready to move on. He was only 44.

I loved living in the dorm. I think I was born to 'run the show' and now I could. I could spend what I wanted, go where I wanted, do what I wanted....or at least I felt that I could.

The truth be known, it was one of the most rule rigid places I could have ever been, but I didn't know that. All I understood was that now I could participate in everything (everything that a Christian school would allow which was basically nothing except prayer meetings and basketball games). At any rate, I was allowed to be a 'cool kid' like the others without my conservative Mother's fear of 'something nasty' I might find in the public schools'. I felt free now.

Towards the upper end of my 4 years there, I even became adept at breaking the rules and going to movies and parking (that means kissing a boy in the back seat if the telling of this story becomes too dated and the reader doesn't know what that means).......we were always well behaved, partially as we were usually on double dates). These shenanigans never progressed beyond kissing, thankfully. I'm not sure why, but I'm grateful and would prefer to think God just made us dumb and protected all of us silly 60's generation girls. We'd tell our dorm mother we were at a 'prayer meeting'. I guess the unseen rule at the dorm was "don't ask don't tell" because we always got away with it.

During my senior year at Central, the High school principal announced to a writing class that I was to be the Editor of the 1968 High School Annual. I could have dropped my teeth. I wouldn't have thought that he even knew my name and here he was giving me this high honor! I didn't feel that I had a choice to refuse but at the same time was overwhelmed and frightened by the challenge. It's true that with great power comes a need for gentle leadership and I had to learn that the hard way.

Just like my 4th grade teacher, you can't motivate out of fear and browbeating.

Fortunately I realized this one day when I opened the office door and the whole team of about 10 kids, who were happily chatting, froze and looked up at me with both loathing and fear. I knew then it was my job to make our team a team instead of a stable. I hope I can say we did, I know for me it was a fun and fruitful experience and some said that the annual was the best yet…and I believe we (finally) all had fun putting it together!

About that time Daddy remarried a lady named Orva Moon. Sherry and I were pretty suspect of her, but she wore nice clothes, and liked to eat out (being a professional for many years since she had been widowed) so we were in. I was 17 and a bit of a stinker when the two of them talked about selling their respective houses and buying a new one. I stamped my 17-year-old foot and said that they couldn't move me from my family home.

So they didn't. Orva moved into Jenny's house, her only demand was that Daddy at least cover the insulation on the walls (which he did quickly and cheaply with sheetrock and ugly avocado paint). Years later when I was a married woman, I apologized but "Mom", which we had finally acquiesced to calling her, said that she felt it was only fair to get a new mother and keep your childhood home! ha I'm glad to say that the 30+ years she was married to Daddy before he died were happy ones for us all. While she never became my Mother, she was a friend and we loved her.

Chapter 2

And the Two Shall Meet

Tony's Side of the Story:

Let's go back to the time when I found the courage to tackle the "bold and daring" life changing challenge mentioned above. I was in my first year as a college student, and since Mom and Dad lived only 90 miles away, it was quite convenient to come home most weekends, do my laundry, stock up on food and keep up with Evergreen friends. By then, my parents were leading the youth at the local Baptist church, so I would often stay for services before heading back to Fort Collins Sunday night. I have to say, they were very good at what they did, and the youth group was flourishing. I also enjoyed singing in the choir because, oddly enough, I discovered that I didn't stutter while singing. Don't get me wrong though; I wasn't about to start singing all my conversations opera style, but it was fun to sing along with a group where the only worry was hitting the right note. This also led to a semi-successful quasi career in music, and I've always enjoyed playing the guitar and singing whenever I get the opportunity.

So there I was, sitting up in the choir loft on a Sunday night, checking out the evening crowd. As my eyes drifted over the congregation, suddenly they fell upon a vision. I had seen her earlier at my parent's house where she'd come for 'Training Union', the youth meeting held before church on Sundays, but somehow I didn't get around to talking to her. Now, there she was again, she was blonde, she was cute, and she was demurely looking at me! Many thoughts raced through my mind in those few short seconds, but one thing screamed through them all: this girl is awesome. This chance may never come again. DO SOMETHING! So I did, and I need to make it clear that I had never done anything even remotely like this before, nor have I since. But desperate times call for desperate measures, so I did the only thing I could do, given the situation. I *winked* at her.

Now here is a bit of wisdom for all you young ladies who may be reading this: what that girl did when I winked at her set the course of history. I winked, she blinked, then her face turned as red as a beet and she quickly looked away. As far as I know, our eyes never met again the rest of the evening, but the message had been sent and received. I think if she had looked me straight in the eye and winked back, I would have melted into the floor in sheer terror. But instead, I was left with a sense of wonder. Just who was this modest young girl? I had to know more about her, and the more I learned, the more I liked.

They say most marriages in America are not arranged, but I'm not so sure. I soon knew the girl's name: Marsha, but not much more. After all, I was away to college all week, and didn't get back every weekend. But for some reason, my Mom and Marsha's older sister, Sherry, got it into their heads that we should be "arranged". School was out for the summer, and I was helping Mom in the kitchen when out of the blue she asked, "Do you know that girl from the youth group, Marsha?" My heart skipped a beat, but I managed to get out some kind of one-syllable answer in the affirmative.

"She's a cute thing, isn't she?"

"Yeah, I guess so."

"You should give her a call."

"You think?"

"Sure. Why not?"

"Well, I think maybe I will. I'll have to find her phone number."

"Here it is," she said, passing me a piece of paper from her pocket. "I just happen to have it."

Unbeknownst to me, a similar conversation was going on at Marsha's house, but I'll let her talk about that. That evening I screwed up my courage, called the number and tried to sound casual.

"Is this Marsha?"

"Yes."

"Hi, this is Tony Woods. You probably don't remember me..."

"I remember you. I really like your folks."

"Oh, well, anyway, I'm home now, and was just wondering if maybe you'd like to go to Elitch's tomorrow night?" That was an amusement park in Denver with everything from Ferris wheels to cotton candy.

"Yeah, I guess so."

"You would? I mean, great! I'll pick you up about 5:00, okay?"

"Okay."

Now, keep in mind that I was a freshman in college, while Marsha was still in high school. I'm just saying, there's a big difference in maturity level there, and I may have come across as a little ... "mature"? Let's just say that my first attempts at "moving up the scale" in our relationship were met with a certain amount of "coldness". I accept that; she had good reasons for being reserved, and one in particular was a real deal breaker that I'll let Marsha elaborate on. But the rest of that summer was spent in total awkwardness, with me trying to get to know her better and her acting as though she knew enough about me already.

September came at last. I went back to Fort Collins and she went back to Hutchinson, Kansas, where she attended high school. I had a few girlfriends, she had a few boyfriends, and life went on. But once in awhile our paths would cross during school holidays, and the knots would return to my stomach. Who WAS this girl of mystery, and why couldn't I get closer to her?

I'll let Marsha tell it from her side:

By now I had met a boy.........His parents came to Evergreen Baptist from Texas, saying their son was in Italy for the summer. The way they said it I figured he was somehow doing hand-to-hand combat but I was wrong...

By the weekend he returned home from his study abroad with a group of High School graduates, I was smitten with his parents, Buddy and Jody Woods. They were beyond cool, even hosting the young people's 'Training Union' at their house on Sunday nights before the evening service at church! That was so 'out of the box' thinking, I loved going there and usually was treated to pie or cake, which of course added to the thrill.

It was the summer of my junior year in High School and I was working. I appeared each morning at the mansion of some very rich pig farmers from Missouri, the Schuesters, who summered in Evergreen. I was never certain what my job was but they paid me $1.50 an hour, so I was delighted. When I think back, I think I was there mostly to hear Mrs. Schuester tell me how rich they were.

Back to church. I walked into the Woods's living room and there, in a rocking chair, sat a very cute boy. He smiled and I was interested. I don't remember much about the study that followed, and we proceeded without speaking to each other on to church.

When we settled in, I was happy to notice that this mystery boy was sitting in the choir where I'd have the perfect opportunity to 'study' him without him seeing me. Imagine my surprise when he WINKED at me! I was so mortified that I ducked out of church when it was finished and went home.

Little did I know that my sister and Jody were exchanging phone numbers, and Tony called me later that week for a date. We went to Elitches amusement park and I remembered we had a good time, he even caught my hand as we were going up some stairs and that was sweet, but I wasn't used to such 'smooth operators'.

We sorta dated on and off all summer, but he always pointed out that he was a sophomore in college and I was just a lowly high school girl who had so much to learn. To that end, we decided (me more than him) to go our separate ways as we were preparing to leave Evergreen for our schools. As it turned out, I had another more long-standing boyfriend and he more or less laid down the ultimatum that it was him only or not at all. I remember I wrote Tony (and another boy as well, while I was at it) to break up, supposing there was anything to break up. After a week, I got a letter and I'll never forget what it said. After pointing out that I was still in High School and clearly didn't understand the intricacies of dating, he then finished with a curt, "No girl's ever cracked my shell, so don't consider yourself unique." Ouch!!

I didn't see Tony again till Easter of 1968. A team from our school was out in Evergreen from Kansas doing some evangelistic work in Evergreen Baptist and we all went 4 wheel driving one day, with the Woods family, of course, since they were the youth leaders and he was home for the holidays.

I was so proud of my driving skills in snow (unlike Kansas where the snow blows flat and nothing else). Before I knew it, I had driven a bit too confidently and landed myself as well as my unimpressed passengers in a snow bank and boy was I ever stuck. I'd tried every clever trick of double clutching, gunning the engine, etc, but to no avail. Then, looking up, I was mortified to see Tony come bounding over. He hooked a chain to my bumper, gave a Texas style chortle, and used his Jeep to pull me free. In a few minutes he came up to my window smiling and handed me a block of snow with a perfect imprint to the Jeep's oil pan. "You made quite an impression back there," he joshed.

I braced myself for the ribbing and teasing about my inferiority that I was used to from others, even as some of my friends began to laugh at me. But Tony just kept standing there and finally said kindly, "Never mind, it could have happened to anyone!" My head was beginning to turn!

I returned to high school, graduating a couple of months later. Then I came home again. After a few days Jody, Tony's mom, called me and asked if I'd like to go with her up to Colorado State University to get Tony and all his stuff for the summer. We'd be driving the family car with an attached trailer, but Tony, she explained, had just acquired a convertible and she and I could drive that home; wouldn't it be fun?

Although I had just talked my daddy into letting me attend Grace Bible Institute (with my boyfriend at the time) in Omaha, I didn't mind seeing the campus of CSU and besides, I really liked Jody, so away we went.

We arrived in Fort Collins two hours later, happy and ready to pack up Tony. We got a tour of the Baptist Student Union where Tony and his friends lived and saw the campus, then Jody and I positioned ourselves in the convertible and off we went.

After about two blocks Jody honked for Tony to stop and literally RAN up to his window, this in itself a bit miraculous as she was practically crippled with arthritis, shouting back to me as she exited the car that the wind was blowing her hair too much so she'd have to switch! I shot daggers at her retreating figure as Tony, who I'd spoken to less than a few times since the break up, came back to his car to drive........for the next two hours!

I didn't die; in fact, after a few minutes of awkwardness on my part at least, we fell into a friendly camaraderie. When we pulled up to his house where I'd left my jeep, he said casually, "How about a date sometime?"

"Oh I KNEW this would happen," I thought with disgust. So I popped back snidely,

"Ok, but just as friends you know" (he'd have to know since my BOYFRIEND was going to be staying at our house on the weekends for the summer while he worked as a camp counselor nearby).

"Oh, of course, I wouldn't have it any other way," he quipped back. He told me later he was dying inside, but was determined not to show it.

And so began the summer I like to think of as the summer of "Falling in Love".

I got another 'maid job' and he was resurfacing bowling alleys, but two or three nights a week we were 'hanging out' here and there, usually with some of his friends. He treated me like one of the gang, slapping my back and not opening doors for me….and perhaps in doing that, he gave me the space to get to know him better, because gradually I began to dread the weekends with the boyfriend and long for the time together with an emerging friend!

One evening as Tony was roaring up the mountain in his convertible to get me, Mom said, "Here comes your Knight in Shining Armor", to which I countered, "Oh, no, we're just friends!"

She looked at me and smiled knowingly………so much that I began to wonder myself what was happening.

And now Tony again, tugging at my arm wanting to say something.

≈

There is another incident that I must include, since it helps to define the tapestry that was coming together during those "awkward" two years of off and on dating. As I said before, the more I got to know Marsha, the better I liked her, while from her point of view, it seemed like greater familiarity was breeding greater contempt. What was I doing that pushed her away? How could I change to make myself more acceptable in her eyes?

In frustration one night, I turned to prayer. Maybe GOD could help me through this! I prayed and I prayed, but there was no message written across the sky, no seven-foot angel appearing to answer my questions. Now, I admit that I was young and foolish, but there was no excuse for my attitude. I found myself growing more and more frustrated, and that led to anger. "God," I cried out, "why won't you help me here? Can't you see I'm hurting? Do you really not want to see me happy? I guess it's right what I've heard about you; you don't care if I live or die."

Totally inappropriate, untrue and a really, really bad idea....to say those things to God.

The next day I went to work at a summer job I had taken on with my friend Clarence Richardson. He ran a company that resurfaced bowling alleys, and I signed on as his general flunky. The job that week was at a 24-lane place in Denver. For several days, we had sanded the lanes, first with rotary sanders, then with a huge belt sander that could be adjusted right down to hair-breadth dimensions. Finally after a good buffing, we were ready to apply the acetone-based varnish. It was incredibly tough but also incredibly flammable.

Before starting, we locked all the doors so no one would come in with a cigarette, then went through the kitchen to make sure there were no open flames. The fumes were intoxicating, so Clarence hung a big sheet of plastic across half the bowling alley to try and keep them from the other half while we worked. Later it was suggested that this actually concentrated the fumes, making them more susceptible to ignition, but I think it also saved our lives.

During a break, I went to the payphone to try and call Marsha. I was feeling a little guilty about my harsh words to God the night before, and was thinking that maybe He just needed to work on the situation overnight before giving me an answer.

There was no answer, neither from God nor from Marsha, and I took my change from the phone and turned to go back to work.

Just then, a contract electrician opened the back door of the bowling alley with his key, went to the big breaker box and threw the light switch on. The electric spark created by this action made the perfect scenario and the fumes ignited, blew the back door open and tossed him out into the street, burned and bruised but otherwise okay. Clarence and I were thrown to the floor from the first shock wave. I looked up, and from the other side of the plastic sheeting, I saw a huge ball of flame, extending from wall to wall and floor to ceiling, slowly rolling toward me. Clarence had given me plenty of warning that morning about safety, concluding with the comforting words,

"But if anything sets this off, you're dead, so don't worry about it."

I looked at the ball of flame, thought briefly about the locked doors 100 feet to my right and decided, "I'm dead".

With my face on the floor and my arms over my head, I waited for the light at the end of the tunnel.

"That's funny," I thought, "if I'm dead, why is my leg hurting?"

Raising slightly, I looked back to see an apocalyptic gargoyle in the form of Clarence who was beating on my leg and shouting,

"Get the hell out of here!"

At that moment, his face was exponentially more frightening that the approaching wall of flame. I jumped to my feet, not bothering to mention to Clarence the issue of the locked door. I glanced to my left just as the flames reached the plastic sheeting. For about a second, there was a beautiful image of a clear gelatinous waterfall as the plastic melted then vanished in a fiery maelstrom. A second shock wave soon followed, the locked doors were blown open, and Clarence and I were shot through separate openings, hitting the parking lot like two bouncing Messerschmitts, our feet churning the whole way. I kept running around the building to get to my car, which was already beginning to feel the heat from the broken windows of the bowling alley wall. I passed the electrician, who was standing in the middle of the street, face and hands blackened by the smoke and mumbling,

"I did it. I did it."

Taking a quick glance through what was left of the back door, I saw another image from Dante's Inferno, *The Remake*. The flash fire had fused all the electrical wiring in the bowling machines, causing them to turn on and go into a constant reset mode. I watched in fascination as a set of flaming pins were swept off the deck, then replaced by 10 more equaling flaming pins. This went on for about three more cycles, then the fire took over, completely gutting the building in a matter of minutes.

Coming home that night, I tried again to call Marsha. When she answered, I choked out,

"I'm okay!" to which she replied,

"So?" She had not watched the evening news, and the conversation went downhill from there. Getting ready for bed, I sat down to take my work boots off, and discovered that the plastic coating on the laces had melted. Remembering my tantrum before God the night before, I prayed,

"I'm really sorry You had to burn down a bowling alley to make a point. I'm glad no one was hurt bad.... I'm sorry."

The rest of the summer was spent mostly in depositions, as fire investigators tried to piece the story together. Everyone agreed that the electrician's actions had resulted in the fire, but could never determine if the plastic sheeting had contributed to the combustion or had in fact saved our lives.

The biggest mystery they struggled with was the question of where we were when the first explosion occurred. Laying out a floor plan of the building, they had us mark the spot where we were. When they saw my mark, they said,

"No, that's impossible. The shock wave would have blown you back to the other side of the building, not at a 90 degree angle toward the doors."

I insisted, and we finally all went to the building so I could show them exactly where I thought I was. Searching around, I finally found a ball of black plastic that had been the phone I had just used. Turning around, I sifted through the ashes, and came up with some scorched coins that I had been holding when the blast knocked us down. That settled the issue, but not the mystery. Which for me, was no mystery at all. Whether God had actually torched the place or not, I couldn't say, but there was no doubt that it was His Hand that brought me out.

As the summer of 1968 came to an end, I headed back to Fort Collins to start my 3rd year at CSU while Marsha moved to Omaha, Nebraska to attend Grace Bible Institute. I still had hopes that I might have a chance with her, and there had been a tender moment or two, in fact I'm pretty sure we were falling in love, at least I knew I was, but she had made it pretty clear that I was "lacking something." There was actually a good reason for her stand, and in retrospect, I admire and love her all the more for it. But it still hurt to think that I might lose out this time.

Marsha here: This story gets complicated but let me add my two bits here. If this were a movie, we could jump back and forth through the scenes, but just imagine that this following section was all happening pretty much in about four months.

Except for this part that happened a couple of years before.

When I was 17 years old, I was sitting in a very boring Wednesday night Bible study and the thought popped into my mind, Why don't I go into full time Christian service?" I shared with the little group my thoughts.

 My boyfriend was there and actually he might have even influenced me by saying, a few days earlier, to my protests that I had nothing to offer as a missionary, "Don't be silly, you like to sew and you could make dresses for all those little natives in Africa!"

In retrospect it was a rather naive observation, but it got me to thinking......

At the end of the study I shared with the group that I was feeling a call to ministry and they all prayed with me. My boyfriend was there, but I made a mental note that if there was ever another boyfriend, he would not know of this decision until he had the same one. I realized that this was a serious life changer and I wouldn't feel right wondering if a guy made a 'decision' based on what I felt and not what HE felt.

I wanted a guy who'd had his own life changing call.

But back now to the relationship with Tony:

Our church youth group went camping in southern Colorado's Sand Dunes National Park towards the end of that fateful summer. My boyfriend and Tony were both there. Everybody was getting along fine, until one afternoon when a spontaneous hike was organized. Writing this now I can't imagine having the energy to hike in the heat of the day, but at the time it seemed like a good idea! Boyfriend wanted to stay "cool" in the sweltering tent, so he opted not to go.

His mistake. Again Tony and I found ourselves having the time of our lives. We were truly beginning to meld into one mind about so many things.

When we got back, we found boyfriend pretty grumpy, but life went on, at least for a few more weeks. Then it began to be time to say goodbye for the summer.

I'll never forget the evening of July 31st. We'd been to a movie with friends and Tony drove me home as usual. Imagine my surprise when he said, "Well, at the risk of spoiling a perfectly good evening......" whereupon he leaned across the seat and kissed me. It was mutual, believe me.

Talk about your 'game changer'! Now we had to sort out a lot of stuff. I was off to Omaha, Nebraska in a couple of weeks, I still had a 'boyfriend' or at least the boyfriend thought we were still an item..... but more than that, there was this CALL to full-time service issue. Tony, when questioned, would say that he was committed to being a GREAT Christian forest ranger, or else a GREAT Christian

English teacher! ....and so we parted.

My roommate Patti and I settled into our dorm room, although I think it was the hottest place I'd ever been! Who would guess that Omaha, so far north of Colorado, could be so hot? We were pretty miserable. Grace Bible Institute had a rule that freshmen couldn't date for six weeks so that was a much relieved gap for me to get my head together about the 'boyfriend' and Tony.

When we had parted, Tony pulled his "cool college guy" routine and said, "Now don't expect too many letters from me because I'll be really busy".

Who were we kidding, we'd fallen into such a close friendship, we BOTH were writing one and two letters a day. It was like we were trying to fill a void left by a lifetime of not-yet-knowing each other. However, I was still trying to identify what this Christian service 'thing' was supposed to look like, and now how Tony would fit into that scheme.

Living at Grace drove home to me the idea that you can look pretty on the outside and be rotten on the inside. Let me explain. I had been in a Christian high school for four years and now I was in an even more rigid Bible School. I knew the rules. I also knew how to manipulate the rules and act pious when maybe I wasn't.

Tony had only experienced public school and yet, as I thought about it, he was one of the most honest and devoted to God guys I'd ever come across. Many of my friends memorized Bible verses to impress or because they were forced, but Tony did it because he loved the Lord and wanted more tools to work with. That sort of thing. I began to see the hypocrisy of some of the people I was with in the

Bible school, and it left me wondering. I'm not saying everyone was this way......some great Christian leaders have come from Bible schools, but it's not the doing, it's the being!

Six weeks came and went, boyfriend went, (he later married a girl from our high school class and together they raised a wonderful Christian family before her untimely death to cancer.) and Tony and I somehow got more serious. All the while I was saying, "There's just ONE thing I have to have for this to work," but not telling him what that one thing was.

Finally we were so desperate my roommate and I sat down in our room and PRAYED that Tony would 'get it'. It was Saturday night when most of the girls were out dating and there we sat, two 18-year-olds, praying for a boy who didn't have a clue, 500 miles away. I remember thinking we must seem pretty lame, praying away like two old maids!

A week later something amazing happened.

Let's jump back to Tony to hear his side of the story:

Then came that fateful night. It was a Saturday night, November 23rd, 1968. I was studying for a chemistry test. I had my textbook laid out on the desk and was thumbing through the material, trying to anticipate what questions might come up.

"What are the properties of a filtrate?" Check. "What's the formula for hydrogen peroxide?" Check. "Why not go into full time Christian ministry?" .....

What? I looked closer at the page I had been staring at. Nope, nothing there. I flipped back a few pages. Nope. I started to ignore the distraction, but the question came back, clear as a bell and almost audible.

"Why not go into full time Christian ministry?"

The question itself blindsided me. I had never considered ministry as a career. Not that I was opposed to it, but, well, it had just never come up. Now it had come up, and I knew I couldn't ignore it. Feeling a slight tingle at the back of my neck, I began thinking about the question. Where had it come from? This was no ordinary moment, I realized, and for the first time in my 20 years, I slid off my chair and got on my knees by the desk. At first I just knelt there, seeing if there were any more messages coming. Then I said quietly,

"God? Is that You?"

The sense of peace and joy that swept over me at that moment is something I can't begin to explain, but I knew in my heart of hearts that God had called me. I didn't know yet what the ramifications might be. Just what do we mean by "Christian ministry"? Do I become a pastor? A youth worker? A missionary? And when does all this begin? I still had quite a way to go before finishing college, and I felt pretty sure that I needed to get that degree, no matter what career path I went down.

The next day was Sunday. I pondered the event, but didn't talk to anyone about it right away. I was still pretty confused. Then during the invitation time at the end of the service, I went forward and stood before the church to share what was going on.

"I really don't know what this means," I said. "I just need you to pray for me." They did, and the peace continued.

The next day, Monday, I did something that to this day still mystifies me. I wrote Marsha a letter telling her about my call. Remember these were the days before email and texting. But I do remember what I said.

"Guess what? I'm going into ministry! Whaddyathink?"

Ten days later, her reply came, and it was smoking! I wish I had saved it, but it said something to the effect of, "Ministry, huh? Well, I would NEVER marry a minister. What on earth were you thinking?"

Now I was really confused! I expected her to say something, but why the venom? She was off at a Christian school, no less. Surely she would appreciate the idea of full time service. I wrote her back, and said, "I don't know why you answered the way you did, and I don't know why this decision would immediately close the door on the one person I love. But I guess that's that. Goodbye."

A week later, when the letter arrived at her place, she called. Without even a hello or how are you, she started in on me. "Did Patti tell you?"

"Tell me what?"

"That I made a decision a long time ago to go into full time Christian ministry."

"No....."

"We need to talk."

She hung up soon after that, but we agreed to discuss this when we met during the Thanksgiving holidays.

And here's Marsha's spin on the same story:

I got a letter from Tony, just like I did most days. This time it said, "You'll never believe it, but last Saturday night I was studying for a chemistry exam and a thought came into my mind......why not be a minister? I kept looking at my book for whatever brought that on, and it came again and again. Finally I closed the book, got on my knees and gave my life to the Lord, for whatever He wanted to do with it. I told the church on Sunday and they rejoiced with me, and now I hope you'll be happy with this decision too."

Did I mention that somehow over the years I had become a cynic?

I was furious! HOW had Patti gotten the news to him for him to 'fake' this decision? Even though Patti denied any such action, I was so sure there'd been some subterfuge that I immediately sat down and wrote, "I would NEVER marry a minister, what on earth were you thinking!" and mailed it.

Ten days later, the mail returned a short note.

"I have no idea why God would honor my decision by taking the thing I love the most, but goodbye. Love always, Tony".

As long as I live I will never forget putting the many quarters in the hall payphone. The sound of his voice made me think he'd been crying as I yelled, "That's the one thing! That's the one thing! I'm sorry I couldn't tell you but I had to know your call was real!"

Well, as you can imagine, things moved quickly after that. By Thanksgiving break I could run into his arms at the airport with true freedom.

We told Tony's folks and they rejoiced with us by telling him that they'd dedicated him to the ministry when he was born, but like me, hadn't wanted him to make the decision because of obligation. It was a very happy moment in our lives!

The Proposal

Tony here. This is where it gets complicated. There was this girl back in Fort Collins. She was a nice girl, came to our church, but had been through some tough times. Divorced, with a two year old, and barely making ends meet. I admit I was a little thick, but it didn't really occur to me that she had planned for our friendship to move to the next level, sooner rather than later. Well anyway, the holidays were coming up, she had no place to go, and her son was off visiting his dad.

"Uh, would you like to come to my parents' place for Thanksgiving?"

Thinking back now, I should have realized her answer was a bit too eager….. "I'd love to!"

I'm sure you can see the disaster in the making. There we were: her, my parents, myself, and Marsha, all together for Thanksgiving dinner. The tension was so thick, you'd need the carving knife to cut it. Celebrations over, it was time to pack up and head back to Fort Collins. She had settled right in, helping me pack. The last straw fell into place when she purred, "Tony, did you get your socks from the dryer?"

At that, Marsha headed for the front door. I followed her out and found her crying in the driveway. Ever the typical dumb guy, I asked, "What's wrong?"

"Oh nothing's wrong," she spat out. "It's just that she acts like she's your wife!"

"She will never be my wife," I said. A moment's pause, (remember I was a bit slow on the uptake) then, "Do you think *you* could? Be my wife, I mean? Please don't say no. Engagements can always be broken." (I still kick myself for that stupid comment). "Will you marry me?"

She said, "Yes,"

I said, "Great!"

We may have kissed to seal the deal, I can't remember, but we went back inside, quiet as church mice, unsure where to go with this new development. We both agreed that we needed to let this gel awhile before going public. Several issues would need to be resolved, like finishing university, defining what "Christian ministry" means, figuring out where I stood with the Vietnam War, and the most daunting of all, asking Marsha's Dad.

I want to include this episode, because I believe asking the parents for the bride's hand is still a very important part of the whole proposal/engagement/wedding/marriage thing. Some may see it as a rather quaint tradition from generations past, but believe me, as one who has experienced this from both sides of the fence, I can say that it does more for future in-law relationship than just about anything else a young man can do. Maybe these days, what's being sought is more "blessing" than "permission", but let me assure you, in the absence of either, a marriage will be off to a rocky start in the best of times. I'm proud of both my son and my son-in-law for asking for the girl's hands, and I love the relationship that we all have as a result.

Marsha's Dad may not have been the West Texas lawman my grandfather Cannon was, but I saw lots of similarities. He only spoke when he had something important to say, and when he did, people stopped to listen. Marsha tells me that as a young girl, all it took was a raised eyebrow to turn her into a shivering glob of jelly, ready to confess to every wrong thing she had ever done, thought about doing, or saw anyone else doing.

Bob Smith was a scientist. There was mention of several achievements, including some that were patented, but because he was an employee of Coors Porcelain (founded by the brother of the famous brewer as a more scientific enterprise), he could never claim for personal profit.

I do know that he was instrumental in developing rocket nose cones, artificial heart devices, and a set of rubber/porcelain tires that never wore out the whole time he was employed there.

His main job, though, that actually took him to a different company in the Silicon Valley, was to make a tiny set of porcelain insulators that would hold four metal rods. These were the heart of a mass spectrometer, and the more accurate they were held in place, the more accurate the machine worked. Mr. Smith had developed a system for making the insulators that was so innovative, the company he presented this to allowed him to set up a lab in Colorado, and employ about a dozen employees, all for the end result of producing one set a week.

He tried to explain the process to me, but I was so lost, I finally concluded with, "So you basically drill four holes in a piece of porcelain?" I know he loved me, but that must have been hard to hear from his prospective son-in-law. This was the era before computers, and we'll always remember him with a pencil behind his ear and a slide rule in his pocket.

By now, we were home for the holidays and it was a Sunday afternoon, Christmas break. I had been invited to Sunday dinner at the Smith home, and I was determined not to leave before I had asked his permission for Marsha's hand in marriage. Dinner was over, dishes were done, and at any moment I could have been shown the door. I followed him all over the house, looking for the golden opportunity that would never come. To this day, I wonder if he knew my agony, and was prolonging it. Finally, he went down to the workshop to shine his shoes. Chance!

I followed him down, commented on the importance of a good shoeshine, then took a deep breath. "I guess you know by now that Marsha and I are, well…. that we would like to, uh…. we'd like to get married, and I'd like your permission."

Mr. Smith kept polishing his shoes for what seemed like another hour, although I suppose it was no more than a minute or two. Finally he spoke without looking up. "Well, actually, no boy is good enough for my daughter."

My heart went into fibrillation while I searched my mind for a proper response. Fortunately, he rescued me.

"But I've been watching you, and I figure you're as good as they get."

High praise from Bob Smith, and I accepted it as such.

"Marsha has never been a strong girl, physically, and I imagine that she will need a lot of care in the years to come. I have two things to say: I want to see her finish her college degree, married or not. And I think it would be a good idea if you got married as soon as possible. Long engagements are never easy."

So there we were, Thanksgiving 1968. I popped the question, she said yes. Now at Christmas we had our parents' blessings and permission, but we still kept it to ourselves. There were a few issues to work out before we could officially be considered "engaged".

The very basis for her agreement, after all, was the fact that I had been called into ministry. I still felt that, but ... just what does "that" mean? Pastor? Missionary? Baptist Student Union leader? Really great Christian layman? Marsha wasn't all that clear on the topic either, for that matter, and according to the philosophy of the "Tyranny of the Urgent", before any of those questions could be answered, we both had to finish college. Marsha still had three years to go, and I was starting year three of my seven-year experience, but I said I didn't want to talk about that anymore.

Fortunately, just before Christmas, I received a great present from the government: a 1-A exemption from the draft. Because of a shotgun explosion in my youth, I had too much gunpowder in my right eye to deem me fit to fight. We were certainly OK with that!

Mr. Smith had said only that Marsha had to finish school, but that she could do that after we were married. What he didn't say to me, but did say to Marsha was, "No engagement announcement until you have a ring."

Wise advice, but the problem was, rings cost money, and I was just barely making ends meet, paying the rent on my apartment, buying enough groceries to ward off starvation and keeping my '64 Ford Falcon in gas and oil.

Now here's a secret that our parents never found out about until decades after we were married: when I confessed to Marsha that the ring would have to wait until I saved some more, and she told me what her father had said, we came to the first financial arrangement of our soon-to-be married life. She loaned me $70 so I could make a down payment on a ring. I did pay it back the next month, mind you, but I felt terrible about doing such an irresponsible thing. I still do, in fact, but we had to do what we had to do, and by Valentine's day we had mailed out announcements that said, "God works in mysterious ways. For example, Tony and Marsha.... engaged!"

If everyone had only known how *mysterious* that had been to this point...

At Christmas, we had determined that with our new status, our first goal was to get ourselves in closer proximity to each other so we could move seamlessly into married life. I was still at Colorado State University, and Marsha had gone to Grace Bible Institute in Omaha, Nebraska. By January, we had decided that she should transfer to CSU over winter break. I agreed that she and I should drive to Omaha (about eight hours away), pack up her stuff and hustle back to Fort Collins and take her place in one of the CSU dormitories.

Two problems became immediately apparent to Mr. Smith. It was highly unlikely that my '64 Falcon could make the trip, especially in a Nebraska winter, and no daughter of his was going to make an overnight trip with her boyfriend without a chaperone.

To solve problem #1, he loaned me his car, a big Chrysler, not unlike driving a boat down the freeway. But it was reliable, and it had snow tires. The solution to problem #2 came in the form of Sandy Richardson, a 12-year-old church member whose parents agreed to let her be a part of this great adventure. Her father was Clarence Richard, by the way, the man I had worked for during the summer of the Great Bowling Alley Inferno and who had saved my life in the process.

I'll let Marsha take it from here...

I remember I was a little miffed at Daddy for insisting that we take a chaperone. I was all of 18 and pretty committed to behaving myself until marriage. In fact I mentioned to Daddy that he didn't trust me, but he assured me that he trusted me implicitly, but one didn't need to give one's self for a sullied reputation at this point. Taking Sandy with us would keep that gossip from happening.

Years later, I came to understand the importance of "Keeping up Appearances" as the title of one of our favorite British sitcoms suggests.

We traveled to Nebraska with good snow free roads and found ourselves nearing the goal in record time (maybe because the Chrysler ran so much better than Tony's Ford Falcon). We arrived in Lincoln, which is about 50 miles from Omaha, much earlier than we'd anticipated and had a brilliant idea!

"Let's stop and take in a movie, and get to Omaha later since we just have to split up and stay with friends when we get there," we conjured.

So I called my daddy to say, what wasn't technically a LIE, but let's say it was an 'omission'. "We're here!" I shouted into the payphone. Again, because of the lack of technology, he had no idea where 'here' was, which was the plan.

We went to the movie and came out to finish off the trip. Sandy was sitting between us, which seemed to be her favorite place in the front seat. Before we could turn around, four or five policemen bore down on us in their cruisers, red lights and sirens blazing. "Stay in the car," the bullhorn blasted out.

"Whaa?" we looked at each other as an officer banged on the window. I rolled it down and he stuck his head in the car past me to Sandy. "Are you OK?" he shouted, meanwhile opening the door and tugging at me to get out.

Sandy, of course, burst into tears.

Tony and I were shuffled to separate cars to be interrogated. Apparently a young girl matching Sandy's description hadn't arrived home from school, and here we were, in the gathering dusk, out of state license plates and all. We lost track of where they tookSandy.

Finally, after several minutes of intense questioning, cross referencing, calls to the Colorado Motor registration (Bob Smith......right, as if that isn't an alias!), a call came to them that the actual missing 12-year-old girl had been found.......

We wobbled back to the car, reunited with Sandy and left town vowing never to lie to our parents again!

Chapter 3

Marriage, Early Days, Ministry Begins

Into a New Chapter: August 1, 1969

With our engagement finally out in the open and Marsha living just a few minutes away in the CSU dorm, we could begin wedding preparations in earnest. The Smiths gave her $500, which was to cover everything from invitations to reception. That probably doesn't sound like very much, but take into account, first, a dollar went a lot farther back then than it does now. Our apartment, for example, rented for $60 a month and my first full time job as a school teacher paid just under $6000 a year.

But besides that, expectations for a once-in-a-lifetime event like this were different than they are now. The venue for the ceremony would be our church, the reception in the fellowship hall downstairs. The food would be provided by friends and family; products of their love for us both. Marsha made her own wedding dress, and it's still a precious work of art. Never once have we looked back and wished that we had been able to afford something more lavish, because we felt that we had all the money in the world. Add to that, we felt that what we had was priceless (and we still do!).

The date was set for August 1st, 1969, eight months away. As it turned out, Mr. Smith's advice turned out to be prophetic; long engagements are never easy. Once the decision was made, plans devised and put into place, waiting became the toughest challenge of all, and I think you know what I mean.

But I want to put this in writing for all to know and understand: Marsha and I honored our commitment to enter into marriage as virgins, and I can't tell you what a difference that has made in the foundations that were set. I know this is a concept that seems to have fallen out of vogue these days, and to even bring it up probably causes some to laugh at such a Victorian attitude. But let me tell you this: what we learned as man and wife, we learned together, by trial and error, by bold discovery and by mutual consent. There was never a moment of comparison to some previous experience, and in the years since, there has never been the shadow of a doubt regarding faithfulness on either part. This may sound rather prudish, but in a marriage commitment where everything rests on absolute trust in one another, it goes a heck of a lot farther than any other philosophy I've come across. Add to that the shared faith and trust we had for God and His Plan for us and we had the makings of a rock solid relationship that has endured (at the time of this writing) 50 years of everything the world could throw at us. My heart breaks for young folks today who don't have that, and pray that God will make up for the loss in ways that only He can.

***

Marsha here:

August 1, 1969.

Exactly one year and a day from Tony saying, "At the risk of spoiling a completely wonderful evening" and then kissing me, here we were about to get married. To say I had the jitters would have been an understatement. The friends and relatives were gathered, all the sewing was done (I made five dresses for the wedding apart from my own wedding dress as well as the elaborate backdrops for the podium, and about everything else I could get my hands on. When I looked at the tiara I had made myself instead of buying a proper one, I had to admit I may have gone a bit overboard.

Everything was falling into place the morning before the wedding when Daddy came downstairs, knocked gently and coming into my room. He had done that every morning for as long as I could remember, sitting on the edge of my bed and rubbing my back. I can still smell his coffee breath as he would say "Good morning Sunshine". I stirred and rolled over, smiling up at him. He interrupted me by saying, "I have some bad news. Grandmother Woods died peacefully in her sleep last night."

I rolled back onto my stomach as the wracking sobs started coming. I'd only met her once before she arrived yesterday (we lived in the Colorado mountains at 8000 feet and she'd come on the bus from Texas). I liked her as much as any 19-year old could like someone 'old'. I think she was about 63.

I was crying, not completely for her or the family, but for my perfect wedding. Now we'd have to cancel, all my dreams were crushed, just because a lady with a bad heart couldn't take the altitude. Tony was still up in Fort Collins at college, due to return that day and hadn't even seen her. I cried and cried until my Daddy, still sitting there, suggested getting up and facing the day might be the right thing to do.

The rest of the day was a blur. I remember Tony coming to pick me up and take me to his house, where the bulk of the Texas relatives had gathered. I was still crying, but had managed to get dressed and comb my hair.

Within a few hours, the decision was made to continue with the wedding even though the rehearsal dinner would have to be outsourced as Buddy and Jody wouldn't be able to host. The relatives all agreed that she'd loved her grandson so much and had come to his wedding so we had best be getting on with it. To this day we treasure the beautiful star quilt that she had made for our wedding and shown me the night before. Most of the time it's hanging on our living room wall.

Tony says he remembered waking up that morning in his apartment with a start and sitting up in bed, wondering, "What was that?" Then he thought, "Oh, I'm getting married tomorrow!" And as he was lying back down, he glanced at the clock. It was 3:30 AM. A few minutes later the phone rang, and his Dad told him that Grandmother had just passed away.

You can try and "theologize" it all you want, but I think the simple fact is that she asked for and was granted the chance for one last hug for the boy she'd half raised and loved so much. This became clearer as Tony recalled that night. Earlier in the evening before bedtime, his folks called and put Grandmother , who was perfectly fine and had enjoyed a wonderful evening with the rest of the family, on the phone. Tony said he was looking forward to coming home the next day, and her only comment was,

"I just wish I could have seen you one more time."

He hung up the phone confused, but as we look back now, it makes sense.

So.......here I stood, in line outside the doors to the sanctuary. My bridesmaids all in front, and my little niece Rhonda wiggling and adjusting the flowers in her basket. To say that I was nervous was an understatement. My only sister Sherry, who had herself been married in the same church six years earlier, had shared with me numerous times that before they walked down the aisle, Daddy had taken her hands and prayed a beautiful prayer for her and the marriage.

I had been 'dreading' that moment for years. Daddy was my Daddy and I loved him dearly, but he and I had sort of a pact of "no emotions" and I knew that praying would not only break my resolute will to never cry, but probably smear my face up as well.

As we turned the corner and the final doors opened, I shrugged my shoulders euphemistically and thought,

"I guess I don't get prayed for" and relaxed.

Years later when asked for an explanation, he laughed and said, "Oh, I guess I didn't think you needed praying for." Privately, I think he just forgot.

Seeing all the beaming faces in the candlelight, as we strolled in, was an unforgettable memory. I distinctly remember saying to myself,

"Enjoy this Marsha, because you're never doing this again!"

The wedding proceeded even better than we'd hoped, followed by a fun and tasty reception, marked with the surprise of seeing both of our uninvited last boyfriend and girlfriend in peripheries of the crowd! Tony's old girlfriend even managed to get herself into one of our candid wedding pictures.

Then we headed for a quick change after a good cry when my sister called to wish us well from far away Guam where she and her husband and family were stationed as teachers. She had desperately wanted to come, but in 1969 flying half way around the world for something as trivial as the wedding of your only sibling was unheard of. Besides, they were in the throes of adopting a beautiful little girl, Jinja, to add to their first child Lyle, and needed to be home.

When we stopped saying, "Are you married?" "Yes, I am" and then repeating ourselves several time and crying, I hastened to the back room to change for the dramatic send off.

I had carefully sewn my going away dress out of ecru pineapple cloth that Sherry had sent me. I'd added a green floppy hat and shoes. I thought I looked pretty good. As I was closing my suitcase my bridesmaid who herself was a newlywed, looked down at my rather sad bathrobe and grabbed it out saying, "Oh, I guarantee you won't need that!"

Again, the jitters.

Off we spun out of the gravel parking lot, in Tony's 1964 Ford Falcon convertible, to cheers and rice flying. Our friends had attached the obligatory tin cans to the back bumper, and Tony let them enjoy the racket until we got just out sight. Then he opened the glove compartment and pulled out a set of wire cutters he'd placed in there for just such an occasion.

We had a 45-minute drive down to an unknown (to me) destination. It was already 10:30 and our hearts were filled with love and colored by trepidation. A friend had offered this unforgettable wisdom earlier,

"So, you *don't dare* for the whole of the engagement and then on your wedding night, *you better!*"

Sure, I'd glanced at some books, even visited a doctor, but seriously, I had no idea. And neither, as it turned out, did Tony. And we loved each other all the more for it.

As we drove into the city of Denver, Tony told me that his dad had taken him aside during the reception and said this to him, "Whatever you do, don't be silly like us. We didn't stop till about three in the morning and by then it was impossible." I'm sure in the dark my face turned white.

"They didn't STOP?!? I'm not sure how to even START and here I am married into a family of sex fiends!"

Tony, looking over in surprise at my expression, burst out laughing as he realized what I was thinking. "Oh not THAT! They didn't stop DRIVING till three and then they were too tired!" We both had a good laugh and then Tony added, "But… would you mind if we stopped at the A&W and I got something to eat? With all the stress I don't think I've had a bite in two days."

Later he would admit to stalling, but after eating hamburgers in our wedding clothes, car all decorated and festooned with tattered crepe paper, we made our way on to the Holiday Inn. In 1969 this was a first class hotel, maybe 15 or 20 stories high and beautiful. He'd picked well and I was impressed.

Again, a long wait in the car as we gathered our courage to go in. Our marriage certificate, with the ink still drying, was in the hands of the pastor for registration and we had no 'proof' that we were married. I was scared we'd be turned back as silly teenagers. Obviously I didn't understand much about business then. As Tony came around to open my door, I looked up at him, my beloved hat still firmly in place, and said, "Shall I wear my hat?"

Without hesitation he said, "Nah." Years later my "Thirty Minute Wonder Hat", at least to me, got the cut in some move we made. I hope it made someone else as happy as I had been.

Just six hours later, Tony was standing by the bed tugging on my arm. "Let's get up! I want to get us to Yellowstone by dark." I can still remember the feelings rushing into my conscience numbness.

"I've made a mistake!" I mumbled, a "morning after" comment he's never let me forget. Who knows when you don't live together that you've married an early riser?

And then I managed, "Wow, what a guy! We're going all the way to Yellowstone National Park? In another state? What a great adventure we're about to have!"

And so we did.

Honeymoon and Early Days

(Tony here; I'll take this one as I'm the one who planned it)

I hadn't given much thought to a honeymoon, but did understand that we had to go *somewhere*. The problem was time and money. I could spare just a few days away from work, and as always, money was so tight it squeaked.

At the reception, Dad had surreptitiously handed me some wadded up bills amounting to $60. I didn't have the heart to tell him that was about all we had, so I took it gratefully and decided that we should turn the car north and go as far as we could, hopefully as far as Yellowstone National Park in Wyoming. Neither one of us had been there before, and it seemed like the end of the world.

There was no way we could afford a week's worth of hotel rooms, so I threw in the camping gear. I had seen Marsha at church camps, and knew she could be a real trooper.

The first night we stopped in Denver at a Holiday Inn I'd booked, which was a beautiful, romantic and an all around good idea. Years later, it was nice to come back to "where it all started" and re-live the memories.

The second night, on the other hand, was at a cheap motel called the "Purple Sage". Our plan called for us to be well and truly settled into Yellowstone camping but a blown out retread just across the Wyoming border had cost us not only a lot of our honeymoon money, but time as well. When we arrived in Rawlins, still 4 or 6 hours from Yellowstone and already 9:00PM, the only hotel we could find that had a vacancy.

It was truly a dump, but they said for $6, if we could wait an hour, they'd clean up the room after some truckers left. They asked us, as they eyeballed our still decorated car, if we wanted to pay the extra dollar for a TV. We shook our weary heads an emphatic "no". Only because it was our honeymoon, we were delighted with the room.

We took off the next morning, buoyed up with some rest and a car wash and began the next leg of the trip. Not much chance of the motel being around very long, it had seen better days. When we did finally get up that away about forty years later, we found that the Purple Sage had become the Rawlins Asphalt Company before finally allowed to crumble into the plains. Obviously the place didn't fare as well as our marriage!

We arrived at Yellowstone on the third day, and now we come to the part in the journey we shared back in the first chapter about "the Bear in the tent". Thumb back and read it again if you need reminding.

⚜

The rest of 1969 and 1970 were some of the busiest we would ever know, trying to finish college and pay the bills. There was an interesting dynamic at work with our parents. My folks had always struggled with money, so the fact that Marsha and I were living on a shoestring didn't seem all that unusual to them. They couldn't have helped us much financially anyway, since they were pretty much strapped as well. Marsha's folks were comfortable financially, and very careful with what they had. It wasn't that they were unwilling to help us, but Mr. Smith wanted to demonstrate his trust in me as a provider, and so very seldom offered anything in the way of help. He even gave us the 'opportunity' to pay for Marsha's college tuition, something that he had faithfully done till she married me. Remember he'd made me promise that she'd finish, and now that too was my responsibility!

I need to digress here and unpack what I mentioned earlier about my stuttering issue. I believe it started as simply an age-appropriate pre-school thing. Back then, though, people didn't know how to deal with it, and tended to overreact when I stumbled on words. As I said before, my Grandfather Cannon took the toughest approach, but really, he was just verbalizing what most other adults were feeling: "Why can't he just slow down and stop stuttering?"

In fact, I was thinking the same thing, but lately I remember some wise words from my good friend and ex-kamikaze pilot Naoki Noguchi. As a boy, he tried to learn to ride a bike. Thinking back to that time, he told me, "You can tell yourself all day long, 'Don't hit that pole don't hit that pole' and no matter what else may happen, one thing is certain: you're going to hit that pole."

As late as my second year in college, I was struggling, even going so far as seeing a speech therapist. They tried something new, having me put on headphones and talk into a microphone. My words would come back slightly delayed, so that it would make a normal person stutter. For me, though, I was able to speak a lot better, but decided it wouldn't be too practical to carry around a set of headphones and tape recorder.

Now jump ahead to early 1969. I was in my third year in college, engaged to Marsha, and committed to full time Christian service. My church's pastor, Dr. Autry Brown, knew of my commitment and set out to help me identify what exactly that ministry would look like. I found myself leading the youth, leading the choir and sitting in church business meetings. The result of all the added responsibilities was to eventually drive Marsha and I to another church, but that's another story. One thing Dr. Brown did do, though, was to get me an invite to go to a little church north of town and preach. My first reaction was, "N-N-N-N-No way! With my stuttering, a 15 minute sermon would take an hour!"

But Dr. Brown was right: I needed to get my feet wet in all different kinds of ministry, to see where God might be leading me. Marsha went with me on Sunday to hear my very first sermon ever, from Psalms 37: 3-5, "Trust in the Lord, delight in Him, commit your ways to him." Marsha said I just about rubbed the wooden pulpit down to the floor, I was so nervous; but get this: I didn't stutter, not a word. From that day, I learned a great mystery. Whenever I preached, I didn't stutter, and as time went by, the problem diminished little by little until it was gone completely. Does God have a sense of humor or what?

For the next year or so Marsha and I put our backs into the challenge of finishing school. I had a job as a stockroom clerk at J.C. Penney, working in the morning then heading for class in the afternoon. As it turned out, Marsha found a job as a sales clerk at the "Classic" department store, working afternoons and most evenings, with her classes scheduled for the mornings. We saw each other at breakfast, a quick lunchtime if we were lucky, then dragged ourselves home late each night. Of course we only had the mostly running Ford Falcon so we had transportation issues as well. It was a tough schedule, but it made us tough, and we quietly disdained our friends who waited until after graduation and securing a job before getting married. We always felt that the struggle together better prepared us for the struggles ahead. Looking at the dismal track record of many of our friends, I might affirm that today.

By the summer of 1972, we were in the home stretch. Marsha had one more year of class work to go, and I had one more CLASS. As I was thinking about which elective to sign up for in the fall, I got a letter from Pawnee High School, about 50 miles east in the town of Grover. They were asking me to come for a teaching job interview! People were selling their souls for teaching jobs, and I hadn't even applied. This seemed too good to be true, so I set up a time to go see them. I DID call them before I drove out there to tell them I hadn't graduated yet, to which they replied, Oh, that's no problem, we'll work something out!" (and they did get me an 'emergency teaching certificate').

Grover couldn't really be called a "town", since it's made up of a few houses and a high school. The sign on the highway listed the population as '53'. The nearest community in any direction was 50 miles away. Pawnee was a "consolidated school", which meant that kids were bused in from as far as two hours away. Even then they could only manage to consolidate about 400 students from grades 1 through 12. Not surprisingly, no young teacher hopefuls had found Grover and so no one had applied. The school was desperate, so they got a list of CSU graduating seniors and sent letters out. I was the only one who had responded. To keep their certification, they needed a high school English teacher, but what they REALLY needed was a football coach. There were not enough boys for a proper team, but Eastern Colorado had devised a special division of "Eight Man Football", and had a regular season, playing other consolidated schools across the state.

I have to say with a mixture of pride and shame, after a season of my brilliant coaching, we tied ONE game, and it was like winning Olympic Gold. But let me explain: I had one young man who was my hope for salvation. He could pass, he could run, and he had a *brain*. I made him the quarterback, and on the first play of the first game of the season, he was tackled low, his right knee was shattered, and he spent the rest of the year watching the games from the sideline.

The season would have been a total annihilation except for Gerry, a sophomore who stood 6'2", at least on the rare occasions when he was on his feet. He was going through a growth spurt, and was so clumsy, he couldn't take a step without tripping. I placed Gerry in the center position, told him to simply hike the ball and stand there. He provided an impenetrable wall that gave my backfield a chance to carry out whatever plan they had for moving the ball down the field. It wasn't the best of times, but it did allow us to hold our heads up by the end of the season.

After football season was over, the basketballs came out, and the junior varsity team surprised us all. They were small but quick, and somehow we managed to go all the way to State. I was actually beginning to enjoy the job, but by spring was reminded that my contract was only for one year. I did manage to finish my CSU coursework by mail, but the school really needed to find someone with more experience, and especially someone who could produce a win in football next season.

Here's Marsha's eye view of that year:

Being born and raised in the mountains west of Denver, our family had colloquial joking attitudes about what we called 'flatlanders'....

anyone who didn't live and enjoy the mountain life. Mind you, my parents worked down in the flatness of Denver and commuted every day as well as our once a month much-anticipated trip to Denver for groceries. Still we all loved the mountains (and still do) maintaining that it is "God's Country"

When Tony accepted the teaching job, we were too delighted about being employed to realize that we'd be VERY much flatlanders now, at least 50 miles out into the great plains, separated from civilization in all directions. Grover was on the far edge of the Great Plains, where they stop 50 miles west where finally the Rocky Mountains soar up above. Towns like Kiowa, only 20 miles or so from Grover had prospered thru the 1800's and then when the gold rushes were over, the great Dust Bowl of the early 1900s, trundled through and the town just dried up and blew away. There were a few old pictures of Kiowa for anyone who was old enough to remember, in the gas station in Grover.

But trusting God and wanting a paycheck, we decided to BE flatlanders and moved out to a tiny one bedroom house, built by an old bachelor farmer years before. The most significant thing about this house was the built-in gun case, completely lined with rattlesnake skins. A bit macabre, but talking to the locals and the landlord, we realized that rattlesnakes were a main 'feature' of this town, culminating with the annual hunt where one guy would find a den in the cool of predawn and pitchfork the slumbering snakes out into the open where others would happily blast them away with shotguns. Fortunately we never were invited to participate.

I think we learned a couple of things out there in the flat land. I had never seen either stars or sunsets to the magnitude you do on the Prairie. How great is our God and what a beautiful world He has created even without trees. We enjoyed hiking around discovering Indian artifacts and one time even using ancient Indian toe-holds to climb one of the two towering "Pawnee Buttes" that are 300+ feet high. I'll never forget the terror of turning to climb back down, wishing our arms were longer and our knees hinged the other direction as we searched with our dangling feet to find the indentations that, out of sight, were not as obvious now. The experience left such an indelible impression that Tony wrote about it in his one-year devotional book, *The Road Rising*. In that story, the protagonist has to climb down a sheer rock wall reminiscent of the Pawnee Buttes ordeal. He says he still can't read that part without feeling the same old gut-wrenching fear.

The other thing we learned was about finances. In our euphoria about the new job and promised salary of a whopping $6000 a year, we took Tony's company issued J C Penney credit card and bought several large appliances at a healthy discount. You can imagine how thrilled we were with our shiny new range, fridge *and* freezer........at least until the first credit installment was due. I remember struggling to keep up with the bills. Of course, I'm not proud to say this, our tithe was the first thing to go out the window. Who could think about giving God any money when we were stretched to the limit? I remember one month having $4 after we paid our debts, even though we'd ditched the tithe.

As for church, I think we were exercising our "now we're all grown up, we don't have to live like our parents" phase in life. Sure, we had no problem with God, it's just a long 50-mile drive back into church and since we're doing that every day (as I was commuting into CSU to finish my degree), who wants to make another trip. Better to lay in bed and watch Bugs Bunny all day on the weekends.

Then one night, as we were headed for the folks and a weekend of free food and laundry (sure, we're all grown up, right?), we heard an ominous clunk and the engine stopped.

Tony flagged a trucker going back in the direction we had just come from and he was able to ride to where there was a pay phone. He called his dad, walked the mile or so back to me and we snuggled into some sleeping bags and opened a coffee can full of treats that our parents had given us to carry in case of emergency. I think they had in mind the peril of me driving by myself in a land prone to blinding blizzards, but we deemed the three-hour wait an appropriate emergency.

We towed the car to the garage and three days later when it was fixed it was EXACTLY the amount of money we'd stiffed God by not tithing. The irony was obvious. As if God were shouting at us, "Trust In ME!!"

And while we're talking about trust, there was one particular weekend trip home I have to share. We'd taken our cat Oliver, as we always did, as well as my very heavy old cast iron Singer sewing machine. I guess Jody and I had some project going, I can't remember. Everyone had a good time, and then we started home late Sunday night.

From Evergreen to Denver, it's all downhill. First a two lane winding road over to Interstate 70, the highway that transverses Colorado, and down into Denver. We would then turn north on I-25 for another hour or hour and a half as far as Fort Collins, then turn east on a set of farm roads all the way out to Grover. By now, I had given up driving in and back from Ft. Collins every day and had taken to living with our pastor's family in town during the week. I remember paying $25 a month for 20 days of food and lodging. It was a gift, I'm sure. Anyway, on Monday morning, I would kiss Tony goodbye and take the same car and head back west to Fort Collins to spend the week studying before coming home late Friday night. It was a schedule for young people.

That Sunday night we were cruising along the highway headed for Denver. From Mt. Vernon to Golden, there is a deep canyon about 10 miles long. The lanes were divided, two lanes going up and 2 more going down, separated by several vertical feet, so that the going up ones were high above you and almost out of sight, and Denver bound ones still towering above the river at the bottom, but nearest the cliff edge. Of course there were guard rails but they rarely did any good as the cars and trucks occasionally flew over them to land hundreds of feet below.

We even knew of an elderly widower from church who had accidently launched himself over the edge just months before. No one knew what happened, maybe a stroke, we all hoped, but he was found dead the next day when someone noticed an anomaly in the guard rail, most likely killed on impact at the bottom.

As we drove along with the cat and the heavy sewing machine nestled but unsecured in the back, I suddenly had the strangest feeling. It was sort of like in the movies when the space ship goes into a black hole, complete with the 'whoosh' and everything.....it was if we were careening. It was not a feeling I could put into words, but the message came through loud and clear from the farthest reaches of my heart, that cold chill in your soul: "the Bear is back".

I said to Tony, in quite a normal voice, but inwardly feeling very eerie. "Do you feel like you're in control of the car?"

He looked at me and said, "Yes" with a question in his voice as he eased over into the middle lane, away from the cliff on our right. It was a long straight part of the highway, and the speedometer was pushing up to 80 MPH, a combined result of gravity and the open road. Then in less than a heartbeat, there it was: a dead horse in the lane we'd just left. We sailed by, missing him by inches. Tony hit the brakes and pulled over to the shoulder, trying to think of a way to warn the cars coming from behind. By the time we got stopped, two, then three cars had come into view, hitting their flashers. We continued on down, shaking, but knowing the people would be alerted and that things would be okay from that point.

I don't think we'll ever even be able to fully articulate the horror and wonder we still feel when we recall that night and the obvious evidence of God's Hand at work. It still gives me goose bumps, as I'm reminded that yes, God was and continues to be at work among us His children. But the Bear is never far away either, a predator of opportunity seeking whom he may devour (I Peter 5:8).

❦

With our year's contract in Grover finishing up, we started thinking about a place to live back in Fort Collins. Marsha still had a year to go before she finished her degree, and although we never forgot the commitment to pursue full time Christian ministry, this was a time for getting foundations laid, finishing what we had started and gearing up for the ""Next Big Thing. Being gainfully employed was a given, and I set out on a litany of jobs that began to read like a genealogy in the Old Testament. I think my jumping around was mostly based in the fact that in most cases I was being hired as a 'temporary employee'; but I'll have to admit there were a few that I couldn't wait to get away from!

But there was one job, and it turned out to be one of the fulfilling times of my life, even leading a few years further down the track to a career crisis. I came across an opening in the local ambulance company, applied and was accepted on the condition that I complete Emergency Medical Technician certification in the process. I could start right away as a trainee, working night shifts and still keep my day jobs until I got my EMT card.

I had never thought of myself as a medical practitioner. In fact, I had almost fainted while studying for my first aid certificate that summer working for the Forest Service. But there was something about the EMT training that was different. Instead of being cooped up in a smoky bunkhouse watching old first aid training films, now I was dressed in the red and white uniform of an ambulance attendant, resting on the equipment I might find myself using before the day was out. One morning I was learning how to operate the "Jaws of Life" hydraulic metal spreader, that evening I was applying it to the dashboard of a Volkswagen that had come down on the legs of a young woman looking to me for rescue. This wasn't just textbook stuff; this was the real thing, and I was loving it. At the end of each shift, I could look back over the traffic accidents, heart attacks and overdoses I had responded to and honestly say, "I've made a difference in someone's life today."

Ministry Beginnings

By 1973, Marsha and I had both finished our degrees at Colorado State University and were ready to get on to "full time Christian ministry", whatever that was. We were committed to going to seminary, but frankly, we were tired of studies for the time being.

As we were struggling for direction, we came across a brochure at the Baptist Student Union in Fort Collins. It talked about something called the "Journeyman Program."

Simply stated, it was a two-year commitment to go to a foreign country and work alongside Southern Baptist missionaries. This seemed like just what we needed: a chance to get our feet wet while we thought and prayed about God's will for our lives. We filled out the application forms, and after a lot of interviews were accepted and were asked to go to Zambia, Africa.

Actually, we had put down Switzerland and Indonesia (thinking of "Sound of Music" and "Bali Hi", in that order) as our preferences, and had to run for the atlas to see where in world Zambia was. I remember thinking "Oh No! How can this be? Africa?? Do they even have music? I think they beat on sticks".

Why indeed Africa? We might have said no, but all of our friends and family were confident that we were going, and in fact, we realized, we were committed to trusting what the leaders decided, so off we went. (We were told years later that we had been chosen for Africa because of our 'maturity' if you believe that).

What Zambia turned out to be was a life changing, life *taking* adventure of a lifetime, and I can't begin to imagine how things might have developed if we had gone some place else. Zambia taught us independence, patience and a whole new way of looking at things like disease, poverty and guerrilla warfare. The experience also gave us a real appreciation for the life we'd been given, and for the joys of family and friends.

Personal computers hadn't been invented in those days, and the internet was not even a part of our imagination yet. We communicated with folks back home by making cassette tapes and sending them by post. It was always a big deal when a tape came in the mail. For that matter, it was a big deal when ANYTHING came in the mail. The Zambian postal service was still in the development stage, since Britain had granted them freedom from colony status in 1964, and much of the nation's infrastructure suffered breakdowns from time to time. We went 6 months without sugar, another 6 months without soap, and one day when I took a letter to the post office to mail it, the clerk took a look in his directory and said, "Oh sorry sir, we don't have mail service to America (we should have suggested that he look under "United States"). When I assured him that I had both sent and received mail from America on several occasions, he assured me that I had not. Then just as I was about to lose my temper, he looked again and said excitedly, "Oh, I see we have mail service to SOUTH America. Perhaps you have a friend there who can forward your letter!" Marsha had to usher me out the door.

But aside from all the adventures, Zambia succeeded in giving us a heart for missions. We loved the people, and we loved the chance to tell them about Jesus. On more than one occasion one or both of

us would remark, "Can you believe we're getting PAID to do this?"
Actually the term "pay" was a bit of a misnomer, since Journeymen
are for the most part considered to be mission volunteers. But until
that time in our married lives, we had never experienced a way of life
where the basic necessities were provided along with $50 a month
for extras! It was a situation that we worked under for the next 40
years or so, and it definitely spoiled us. I still marvel today that I
was allowed to devote full time to things like teaching, preaching
and baptizing, while many of our contemporaries did these things in
their spare time while holding down "real" jobs.

Life on the mission field was not always so glamorous, though. We
still had to contend with homesickness, physical shortages and a
lack of Christian community. We were able to weather these things
mostly because we had each other, and our hearts went out to the
single young men and women who had to go it alone. I think this is
another factor in the strong marriage Marsha and I have had. We've
worked together, played and cried together for most of our lives, and
this has bonded us like nothing else could have.

Marsha doing what she does best: teaching children about Jesus

Zambia was also the place where "the Bear" reared his ugly head, not once but twice, although we wouldn't fully recognize his path of destruction for fifteen more years. First, Marsha developed a malignant melanoma. It was surgically removed in Zambia, and we didn't consider it an issue anymore, not realizing that it was far from finished with us yet. Then, it appears that our unborn child developed a genetic defect that would remain hidden until he became a teenager. In retrospect, Zambia was for us the time both of our greatest joy and our deepest sorrow, and I doubt seriously I could have survived without Marsha's love and support.

I'll come back to this later, but briefly said, our first child, Trevor, was conceived in Zambia. Fifteen years later, when he contracted Burketts Lymphoma, a type of leukemia, we went through an eight-month ordeal that culminated in our holding him tightly as he breathed his last.

And then another fifteen years after his death, in a casual conversation about Trevor's life and death with an Australian doctor friend, we learned that Burketts was first identified by a doctor of that name just a few miles northeast of the place where we had lived and worked in Zambia. They still don't know much about the disease, except that it's viral in nature, targeting boys in Central Africa, who, when they are in their mid teens, manifest the Cancer. That points ominously to the possibility that it could have infected Trevor in the womb, setting up a chromosomal time bomb that would not be discovered until he was a teenager.

Whether that's true or not, we won't know this side of Heaven, but you can be sure that the Bear was quick to claim the credit. Just slightly short of an audible voice, the message was received loud and clear: "I killed your son because you were involved in things that were none of your business. Now back off, or who will be next?"

I told Marsha about it, and said, "If Satan could make good on that, I'll have to think long and hard before I open my mouth for Christ again." Fortunately after a few days of prayerful "heart to heart" with God, I finally had one of those "Aha!" moments. "Wait a minute!" I thought, "Satan's not the final word on life and death. He's just a liar who wants to cash in on our misery." After reminding him of this truth, I was finally able to recommit my life to the calling God had given us. At the end of the day, we live in a world broken by sin, and in this world people suffer and precious children get sick and die. But that doesn't mean God is any less powerful; what it DOES mean is that God is all the more awesome because of His willingness to sacrifice His only Son so that people like me could get out from under that burden of sin. I know I'll see Trevor again someday, and together we'll look back on those times and praise God for all He's done. Until then, I just want to walk the path set before me, one day at a time.

By July, 1975, we had finished our Journeyman commitment, and in the process had experienced a fundamental change in our lives. At first, Marsha and I would precede discussions with things like, "*IF* we do go into career missions, we'll …." Now as we were packing to head home (which as it turned out would never really be "home" again), we caught ourselves saying, "Oh be sure to save this! We'll need it *when* we become real missionaries."

Of course the other 'fundamental change' was that we were pregnant!

Chapter 4

Next Steps

Marsha here. We left Africa four months pregnant. We hadn't told any of our relatives, mostly because we planned on touring Europe for two months with our good friends from our Journeyman group, Ray and Bev Hicks. Ray and Bev had just completed two years in Israel, so we said our goodbyes to Zambia, clutched our acceptance letter to Golden Gate Baptist Seminary to begin in the fall (I wasn't due till October, so we felt confident about the timing) and headed to Israel to meet up. I discovered something interesting about people and perspective in that week as we went around with Ray and Bev.

"Oh look at that? We have similar ones in Zambia" or, "Oh, this is so much cheaper/tastier/more lovely in Zambia." On and on this conversation went until about the 5th day I caught Bev rolling her eyes at her husband when I made another observation comparing something to Zambia. I didn't really understand what was happening until we left Israel and landed in Amsterdam. Then the conversations took a turn.

"Oh, I remember these in Israel, they were so much cheaper there"......

Yes, we all realized, we were grieving. We had given two years of our lives and walked away, possibly never to return and all we could do was remember. Sad but comforting to realize we both needed to talk through this sadness and move on.

And move on we did! We rented a two door tiny Fiat to carry the four of us. Each of us had a small carry on bag and as soon as we landed, we bought two tents and 4 sleeping bags. We were on our way. What a fun filled 'Grand Tour' of Europe. We had a 'kitty' that we each contributed to from time to time, out of which we bought food and petrol.

We were often fond of sharing around the four of us a 2-litre bottle of something called "Applesaft" as we meandered along the lanes and byways. Later we found out quite humorously when someone took the time to read the label, that we four complete tee-totallers were guzzling 4% alcohol. Who knew.......but it was good!

In order to maintain our commitment to follow Arthur Frommers "Europe on $10 a day" mantra, we committed to only one restaurant meal a day, preferably ethnic to the country we were in, with fruit, snacks and yoghurt for the other two. Our rule was for us each to order something different so that if disaster struck, we could bail each other out.

This plan went smoothly until it didn't. It backfired once in Belgium when we were so hungry we ALL ordered "Fillet American". We rationalized that we'd been on the road for some weeks now and we could do with a good steak.

Of course now we know that "Fillet American" is RAW hamburger mixed with onions and spices. That took a lot of effort to eat, but we were on a budget and this was our meal for the day......

Another time Tony leaned over and said to me, "Make sure you let them see you're pregnant" as the waiter approached the table with a heaping dish of whipped cream. It was called 'Chantilly' and the price was right but we had to bust the budget and order a round of strawberries to finish it off.

Another cardinal rule we made up was that we never wanted to be known as Americans, as they still had a pretty bad reputation for their manners in Europe at that time. We were trying and succeeding on staying on budget with Arthur's book, and so we, by default, missed most of the places where rude, arrogant Americans haunted, but still. If we were around anyone we thought might find us out, we reverted to Arabic, which Ray and Bev spoke, having worked two years with the Palestinians, and us and our pathetic stab at Chibemba. The only problem with this great subterfuge was that we had no hope of understanding each other but it did manage to send the hawkers scurrying to more fruitful targets.

In a blink of time the summer past. Tony was beginning to dig a hole under the tent to accommodate my growing bump, as I like to sleep on my stomach, but other than that we were all healthy and happy. In Oslo, I bought a dress to wear back into civilization. Europe had been swept by a long skirt fashion, superseding the era of the mini skirt. I was somewhat relieved since I was 7 months pregnant by now and really showing. In Boston we changed planes for Denver, and looking around I noticed that skirts were still appreciably short. Running into the restroom, I hiked up my dress and with a pocket sewing kit, put about an eight inch 'tuck' in the hem, raising it well above my knees, making me look a bit like a teetering cake top, but stylish.

When we landed in Denver and came out of the gangway to about 30 friends and relatives, the only comment I remember was my friend saying, "What's with the dress, you look like a MISSIONARY!" Everyone, after the initial shock of my 'long' dress, realized I was carrying a pretty big bump and exploded into hilarity! What a fun surprise that was.

Back to Tony:

By the time we left Zambia, we were in regular communication with the Southern Baptist Foreign Mission Board. They were ready and willing to talk to us, but made it clear that before we could get too serious, we would need to go back to school. Career missionaries then were all required to have a seminary education, and wives were no exception. I would need a Masters of Divinity degree and Marsha would need at least 20 hours of seminary credit under her belt.

Looking at the five Southern Baptist Seminaries, Golden Gate in San Francisco seemed the most promising. They presented themselves as a missions-minded school, which grabbed our attention. Then the clincher came when we noticed that San Francisco was situated right at the bottom edge of America's "Northwest". If for some reason, overseas missions did not pan out, our next idea was to consider pioneer missions in someplace like Washington State, or Idaho. It wasn't until we actually worked one summer on a mission project in Potlatch, Idaho that we learned that Southern Baptists rarely sent Golden Gate graduates into the Northwest. Apparently it was deemed that California Baptists are too "on the edge" theologically already and therefore not reproducible.

We were told. "The Northwest needs good solid preachers from places like Southwestern Baptist Theological Seminary." Thinking back now, they may not have been too far wrong. The older I get the more I see what a liberal education I got at Golden Gate. But God was there to help me process the teaching and keep me (I believe) on the straight and narrow and I've never regretted the experience.

(Marsha) And so we moved to San Francisco, Tony got a job with the ambulance, and we began to gather ourselves for the baby to be born.

We bought our first new car, a Ford Pinto station wagon. It was the stripped model and cost most of our accumulated money, $3000, but we were so tired of junk cars that we figured with a new baby, we'd like to make it down the road without a break down.

Also we'd found out that by subjecting myself to the scrutiny of the entire student force of the University of California Medical School, I could have the baby from beginning to whatever end for $400. Of course we hadn't qualified for insurance yet, so this was a Godsend.

❦

(An observation from Tony) For one thing, life in California helped cement my call to full time Christian ministry. I mentioned earlier that I had really enjoyed ambulance work in Fort Collins. The thrills and excitement of blasting around town with red lights and sirens was enough in itself, but more than that, I had the daily affirmation that I was making a difference in people's lives. It seemed natural then, that the first place I would apply for a job near the seminary was the local ambulance service. To my surprise, they hired me right away, based on my EMT certification and my experience in Fort Collins. The hours would be 7:00pm til 7:00 am. I thought about that, then decided, Perfect! Driving night shifts in Fort Collins was good, because I could study or sleep in between calls. I should be able to manage nights with the ambulance and days in seminary.

The first night was a bit of a shock. To begin with, technology had developed a bit since my days in Colorado. We now had direct access to the emergency room from the back of the ambulance, so that even before we arrived at the hospital, the doctor was looking at the reports coming in and having me start IVs and set up for procedures. It was exciting, but to be honest, a little scary.

Then those "breaks" between calls that I had used as study time in Fort Collins? Never happened. As soon as we finished one call, changed the sheets and cleaned up the blood, we contacted the dispatcher and were given the next address to go to. Twelve hours, non-stop. After the first week, I was beginning to have second thoughts, but still came back to the "making a difference" thing. I was still saving lives, comforting the hurting and being Christ to the hopeless. I still entertained the possibility that ambulance work was in fact my "full time Christian ministry." One night as I prayed, I found myself saying to God, "I'm going to move ahead on the assumption that this is the career You have for me. Just let me know if it's not."

Remember the "very bad idea" prayer I made the night before the bowling alley fire? History does repeat itself. You see, I *knew* in my heart of hearts that this was not God's will for my life. He had other plans in ministry for me, plans that I was committed to, and I was here at seminary to prepare for them. What I was doing was testing God, to see if I could change His will for my life, knowing all along it was a mistake. A week later, I understood the gravity of what I'd done.

In the next seven days, God showed me a side to ambulance work I had never seen, and hope to never see again. Dead children, strung out drug addicts, disgusting drunks and senseless tragedies. Then on the last night we were called to the home of an accountant who was having chest pains. We got him in the ambulance, I hooked up the EKG to his chest, and to try and calm him down a bit, we talked. I asked him about his family, his job, life in Marin Country. He was a nice guy, and easy to talk to. Then I looked over at the EKG and saw things going south. He was about to have a major heart attack. He came to the same conclusion, and his last conscious moment was a "help me" expression of pain and fear.

I started CPR, trying to get the attention of the driver, who was talking to the man's wife in the front seat and keeping her from looking at the drama going on in the back. Years later, I would learn that these things happen frequently, but for me it was a first: I felt one of his ribs break and what had been a firm chest compression was now soft and spongy. I'm not sure if he was still conscious by now, but I could have sworn his eyes bore in on me with an accusatory look that quickly became a "hundred yard stare of death." The whole experience haunted me beyond my capacity to comprehend.

We left him in the emergency room and went on to the next call, but something had died in me. I left the job after that, not even returning for my last paycheck. What had been for me an exciting and fulfilling career possibility was now something so revolting I knew I could never go back. I won't say I contemplated suicide, but I did find it interesting to realize I was calculating the height of a small bridge I had to walk over to get to school the next day. I came to the conclusion that the leap would probably not kill me but in all likelihood would leave me an invalid.

Marsha was my solid rock during those terrible days. She thinks she wasn't sensitive enough to my suffering, but what she provided was worth far more than a "poor baby" and a pat on the shoulder. She brought me back to reality.

"Do you remember that our first child is due to be born in a matter of days?" she scowled at me as I was crying into my tuna sandwich. "Have you thought about what we're going to do for money? What about your studies?"

I didn't want to hear those things at the time. I wanted someone to tell me that my life was not over, and that we would get through this. I wanted Marsha to tell me that she loved me no matter what I had done, or would be doing in the days ahead. In fact, she did tell me those things, but in words that I hadn't expected. Through her probing questions, she was actually telling me, "Man up! Life is not all about you, it's about your wife, your child and the commitment we've made to God. Get those things straight, and the rest will fall into place." Looking back now, those were the best, the most appropriate things she could have told me, and in fact she was the only person alive who could have told me and gotten away with it.

Life *did* go on, and things did fall into place. I don't know what prompted me (aside from the Holy Spirit, of course), but within a couple of days after leaving the ambulance, I found myself in the office of Stanton Nash, the seminary's "go to" man for everything from housing to on campus parking. I shared with him my ambulance debacle, and the first question out of his mouth was, "Why didn't get a job in church when you first came?"

"Are you kidding?" I asked. "At the first day's orientation, *you* told all of us not to even think about church work in the Bay Area. There's way too many hungry seminary students around here already, you said."

Stanton sat there in silence for a moment, then picked up the phone and dialed a number from memory. "T.L.?" he said. "I think I have one for you. I'll send him over tomorrow." He hung up, then wrote, *T.L, Epton, Clinton Avenue Baptist Church* on a piece of paper and handed it to me. "Ex-army sergeant. Wounded in the Korean War. Runs his church like a platoon. He'll make a man out of you if he doesn't kill you first," he said.

Marsha again:

Things rocked along for a month. After setting up our apartment I was so huge and so bored that I enrolled in a class at the seminary. I was only 4 weeks long and kept me busy. It also gave me a start on my education there, which would be required when we went into missions.

Of course on a routine pre-natal check when I casually mentioned that I'd had a Melanoma removed in Africa, everyone went into panic mode. However, since I was about to give birth, apparently to a child I would have been ill advised to conceive if anyone would have told me, they told me to come back in a few months after the birth.

About four days before I was due, Tony had his 'event' with the ambulance where he quit and I was not kind. I still regret that I could not fathom his deep despair and could only think, "What on earth are you thinking about, just HOW are we going to live? I think I'll blame the hormones and the voracious appetite.

The next week was pivotal as Tony was put in contact with T L Epton and the Clinton Avenue church. I was two days overdue as we waddled into church to hear Tony preach.

Apparently he did a good job because two days later the call came that they would be hiring us immediately. They would give us the amount of salary that we had provided them as our "needs"; $400 a month. We were all set and God saw fit to put me into labor that night around midnight.

Tony was composed and ready for this now overdue birth. We had the dollar bill ready to cross the Golden Gate bridge and we were both well schooled on the breathing we would be doing, as the Lamaze method was in vogue in 1975.

Everything went better than the text books. My only complaint was the preparation (seriously, nothing they did to get me ready for birth is even thought of these days) and the fact that Tony was just a bit too enthusiastic as my 'coach' At one point, being careful not to offend him, as we'd been taught in pre-natal classes, I had to reach up and gently push his face away so I could breathe the way *I* wanted to.

At 11:36 AM Trevor Johann Woods literally burst into the room. The enthusiasm was so great with all the student cheerleaders; I bear the scars to prove it. It might have been better if someone would have told me to take it a bit slower, but then Trevor was that kind of guy, rushing everywhere. I walked out of the delivery room, buoyed up on so much hype from the whole thing. Fortunately when the nurse's voices began to fade, there was a wheelchair to scoop me up and a nice nap waiting for me in the ward before they brought him to me. He was everything we'd ever dreamed of, demurely sleeping the day away.

In fact, he was quite dopey, even though I had had no medicine whatsoever (Lamaze). Perhaps with all the breathing, he had become as hyperventilated as me, I don't know, but late in the night the nurse brought him in saying, "Well, he just peed in his face and I think he's awake now"

And he was. He was my child that fought sleep like it was a weakness, always busy and on the go. We were exhausted as a result. After all, we'd been married for 6 years by now and pretty well used to having our own way…….that was all gone now.

By now we were finding our rhythm of life, Tony and I working at the church about three or four times a week, Tony taking a heavy load of classes that would enable him to graduate in 2 ½ years instead of three. We wanted to get back into missions, so we put our backs into it.

That was until my doctor's visit…….about the Melanoma.

Now that I live in Australia, I realize how terribly dangerous a Melanoma can be. It's the real killer of skin cancer, the only one that will 'jump' from the skin to metastasize in other parts of the body creating other kinds of cancer. It has a 'lifespan' and depending on the level, can appear to be under control only to be lurking, for as many as 30 years, waiting to pop up somewhere else.

"WHY were you allowed to get pregnant so soon after having a melanoma?" The doctor queried me with a accusatory frown. I had several answers about personal liberty in my mind, but I answered meekly, "No one ever said anything, and besides, the results said 'completely excised'."

"Oh, that doesn't matter, we have no idea how deep it was or how involved. We grade by 1-5, 5 being certain death and 1 being almost nothing. We have NO information about that, but will be checking with the doctor in Zambia. Meanwhile we'd like you to come for the routine tests, including x-rays, and wait for the reports from South Africa". He glanced at my postnatal stomach with disgust.

So NOW the time had come to face the music. Trevor was a healthy two-month old, so I made an appointment for further tests. First on the agenda was to take a full history as well as an exam with an x-ray of my chest. Almost immediately after the chest x-ray a young intern came out holding the film with a very somber face. "Mr. and Mrs. Woods," he practically moaned, "Please sit down, we have some very bad news". As we practically fell into nearby chairs, he held up the x-ray and pointed to several large circles. "These appear to be tumors. That would mean that the cancer jumped past the lymph nodes and is now in your lungs. I think we can be optimistic in saying you have about two years to live. But come back next Tuesday (five days away) and let us take some more tests to confirm."

Without a doubt, the Bear had shown up at our tent yet again.

The ride home was silent. Each of us was lost in a world of 'whys' and 'hows' surrounded by fear and despair. This time we DID reach out to friends. Within hours our friends, who were normally just fun loving young adults, came and sat on our couch and offered to pray. We were 25 and 27 and somehow them offering to PRAY made it not comforting, but even more scary! But pray we did, and as the days drug on, we struggled with all the things you do when you hear this kind of news. I think I was OK about the Sovereign Will of God thing, I could see that God was in charge, but I worried that Tony would be the young handsome widower with a young gorgeous son and a trail of husband hunting seminary women slobbering after him wanting to "help"......it wasn't something I wanted to think about, leaving them behind.

Finally on Monday night, Tony and I got some real peace through......you guessed it, prayer! We were learning to trust God. Tuesday morning dawned bright and early with us at the doctor's office. When the intern walked in, I thought to myself, "Wow, what's wrong with him, he looks so sad!" and then I remembered, it was ME that was making him sad. I was again ushered away, this time to a relatively new instrument called the "CT scan". When it was done, I returned to Tony.

But only briefly before the intern danced into the room wearing the biggest smile I'd ever seen (and perhaps the only one). "We were WRONG!" he fairly shouted as he shook Tony's hand, "We must have been looking at some bronchial tubes that were uncharacteristically facing the camera! Your wife is healthy!!"

Wow, that was a day to remember. We walked out of the hospital shaking our heads, how in the world can you get it so wrong in a TEACHING hospital.........or did they? Did God just heal me? I'll never know till Heaven, but as you can see that I'm writing this forty plus years later without another day of serious illness, we have to thank Him either way.

⚒

The next two years passed without a hitch and in December of 1977, Tony was graduating with his Masters of Divinity degree.............

six months early! Apparently his job with the church gave him the free time to pick up extra classes and accelerate his course load.

We were ready to go to the mission field permanently, but the mission board 'suggested' that we needed to wait a year to have everyone feel better about my Melanoma. By now they'd finally tracked it to that South Africa Lab and been able to label it as a "Stage 3" and were happy that it most likely wouldn't be a threat, but still, the board had rules and wait we must. We began to wonder what to do with ourselves for the next year or so.

Back to Tony: I won't say that T.L. Epton nearly killed me, but I will confess to some "Come to Jesus" moments when his brand of leadership left me emotionally drained and bleeding out on his office floor. Clinton Avenue Baptist Church was his battlefield, and the parishioners his foot soldiers. His was the only church I ever came across that never had business meetings. Instead, there were regular "briefings" when he would announce decisions he had made concerning budgets, worship themes and staff shuffles. I watched these meetings spell-bound and speechless, but looking around at the church members, I saw nothing but smiles and nods. I soon realized that these folks had come to accept T.L.'s no-nonsense style of leadership and even preferred it over endless discussions from everyone in the room with an opinion. Things ran smoothly, and that was the way folks wanted it.

Of course even in a place like the area where Clinton Avenue Baptist was, things could never stay the same. The kids grew up, the professionals retired, and a subtle change began showing itself along the streets surrounding Clinton Avenue. Houses were still neat and tidy, but had lost a bit of their former luster. Property values declined as newer subdivisions opened up to the north. That fact, coupled with new expectations associated with the turmoil of the late 60s and 70s meant that the area was no longer a typical "White Anglo Saxon Protestant" community. Minority families, mostly Black and Latino, began taking advantage of better prices and more tolerant attitudes. Slowly at first, then gaining momentum, the community experienced a transition unlike anything the older generation there had ever experienced.

Most folks took the changes in stride, but within the walls of Clinton Avenue Baptist, there was felt a growing need to redefine themselves. Most of the professionals had moved on to newer suburbs, leaving behind a strong and steady blue collar membership. An oil refinery nearby provided jobs for many of the church members, as well as a naval base. It was a unique blend of working class Christians with a twist of military discipline, and former Sergeant and Korean War platoon leader T.L. Epton was just the man to take the reins.

And to Pastor T.L.'s credit, he did allow me a certain degree of freedom in our youth ministry and choir programs. When I would ask him about the theme for the next Sunday's service, he would usually respond with something like, "You talk to God about it. I'll do the same, and we'll see how well everything matches." And, with all the credit going to God, most Sundays were an inspired mix of music and message. I did learn one thing, though: whenever I would bring a brilliant new innovative idea to Pastor T.L. and he would reply with, "Let's hold off on that awhile," I know now that what he was actually saying was, "This is never going to happen on my watch."

All in all, though, Clinton Avenue Baptist was one of the best things to happen to us during those seminary days. Friendships were established back then that have carried us through forty years and more. As a church body, the people were invariably generous to a fault. During our interview, Marsha and I were asked what kind of salary we expected. This was a totally new concept for us, and we didn't know how to answer. "What are your living needs?" they asked. Taking a piece of paper and listing all the monthly expenses we could think of, including the tithe, we said, "Here is what we need; we're happy with whatever the church decides to pay us, and we can supplement that income with part time work elsewhere."

Rev. T.L. thought a moment then said, "As a church, we see a major part of our ministry as helping to facilitate the next generation of pastors and missionaries. We'd rather see your energies directed to the work here and your studies at seminary, without a lot of other distractions. We'll provide for all the needs you've listed here so you don't have to get another job. And by the way, as soon as you get settled, the church is planning a pounding for you."

That first part was music to our ears; the last part left us scratching our heads. What on earth was a "pounding"? A couple of weeks later, we learned the answer, and were left speechless. It was a Saturday night, before we would officially began our employment the next day. Arriving at the church, we were greeted by just about everyone, along with well wishes for upcoming studies and for our newborn Trevor. The fellowship hall had been set up for a covered dish dinner, which judging from the way each dish was presented, looked more like a serious competition. At the front of the hall, however, was the focus of the room: a mountain of food, the size of which was rarely seen outside a grocery store warehouse. True to the name given the event, each church member had brought at least one pound of something: coffee, flour, sugar, beans, bread, bacon, baby food, diapers and canned goods beyond counting. When we got ready to go home that night, it took several attempts before we managed to fit everything into the car. The next challenge was trying to fit everything into our tiny seminary apartment!

For the next two and a half years, Tuesday through Saturday was filled with seminary work, while Sunday and Monday (along with Wednesday night prayer meeting and choir practice) was occupied with church duties. Clinton Avenue helped define us as ministry people, encouraging us to look at every aspect of life as a part of what we do for the Kingdom. How often was Tony heard to remark over something someone said or did, "You know? There's a sermon in there!" Relationships took on new meaning for both of us, with all of our acquaintances falling under one of two categories: friends, or people to whom we ministered. Once in awhile, those in the "friends" category moved into the "ministered to" column, and in many cases those to whom we ministered became fast friends.

Sometimes the lines were blurred, as in those times when casual meetings produced both a chance to reach out with the Gospel as well as the chance for new friendships. Tony still recalls a particular Monday when he was doing visitation, calling on church members who had found themselves in need. Going to the local hospital to see a lady who had undergone surgery, Tony noticed a young black girl in the same room and struck up a conversation with her. She was being prepped for surgery, and Tony tried to offer her a measure of comfort, telling her he was the youth minister of Clinton Avenue Baptist Church.

She thought a moment, then asked, "Is that church white?"

Ever mindful of past racial tensions in the area, Tony explained that, while the church at present was comprised of Caucasians, with the exception of one young black college student, they were open to anyone and everyone who would like to come worship. She would be more than welcome, he insisted.

The girl's reaction was somewhere between disgust and pity as she interrupted, "I meant the *building*!"

And that, in a nutshell, describes our time at Clinton Avenue Baptist: filled with opportunity for ministry, potential for life-long friends, and more than one occasion when we missed the point entirely. Among the many happy memories we cherish from those days, we've also picked up some useful phrases that can be applied to any number of situations. For example, when one of us makes a suggestion that is something less than acceptable to the other, someone will make the comment, "Let's hold off on that awhile," and we will both know that any further discussion is pointless. And, when one of us completely misunderstands the other (as frequently happens), rather than falling back on ridicule, a simple, "is it *white?*" will often put the conversation back on course with a minimum of hard feelings.

And, one shining beam of sunlight at a time, God weaves His tapestry.....

Back to Africa (Tony):

By late 1977, we were getting close to graduation from Golden Gate, and Marsha and I began to think more seriously about what "full-time ministry" we might pursue when our time at seminary was finished. By now, my parents, Buddy and Jody Woods, had been appointed as Southern Baptist missionaries to Rhodesia (later to become Zimbabwe) and were finding their niche as dorm parents for the MKs (missionary kids) who had come into Gwelo to attend the international school while their parents served in bush stations around the country. It was a match made in Heaven; Mom and Dad were "naturals" when it came to working with young people, and it wasn't long before they were doing a lot of direct evangelism as well. By the time they retired, they had served in Zimbabwe, Liberia and Taiwan, and collected enough stories to keep folks both entertained and inspired for a lifetime. One of the most dramatic stories involved us.

As Marsha and I were finishing up at Golden Gate and exploring opportunities for ministry, Mom and Dad arranged an invitation from the Baptist Mission there in Rhodesia. Would we be willing to buy a used VW van, fix it up and ship it over? Marsha and I would then come over, outfit the van as an ambulance and become a driver for Sanyati Baptist Hospital, way out in the country's west. This was too good to be true. While I had put the notion of ambulance work as a career behind me, I still missed some of the experiences, and felt that my training was being wasted. On top of that, we had just learned that Marsha had become pregnant with our second child, making us think that we might have to delay any overseas missions. But hey! This would be going to work at a hospital, with constant access to doctors and nurses.

Looking back on that time, and our decision, I'm left awestruck at Marsha's faith and fearlessness. Experience and subsequent events have taught us that having a baby can be fraught with danger, both to mother and child; and yet Marsha saw no problem in going to one of the most inaccessible places on earth, putting her life on the line for the sake of ministry. It makes me love her all the more, and even more as we endured what was coming our way.

Back in San Francisco, we announced our decision to the church, and they were behind us all the way. They helped us find a VW van, get it painted, do some brake work and general tune up, and never stopped praying for us. In addition, we spent every waking hour fixing up the interior, with new seat cushions, curtains and the like, to make it a 'proper ambulance'.

So it came as a shock when a phone call came just a couple of weeks before we were to ship the van. It was the Foreign Mission Board's representative in Richmond, Virginia.

"Hey Tony, I'm afraid I have some bad news. For reasons we can't really understand, your visas for Rhodesia have been denied."

"No way!" I exclaimed. "The Ian Smith government there is looking for all the white faces they can find. Why would they refuse us?"

We wouldn't learn the answer to that question for ten more years, but I'll save that for later. The phone conversation continued. "I don't know what's going on over there, but bottom line is, you can't go to Rhodesia."

"We've fixed up a van and bought our tickets. What can we do?"

"Well, now that you ask, we have a request for dorm parents in

Liberia. Would you be interested in that?"

It was really pretty much of a no-brainer. *Of course* we'd be interested. This would get us back to Africa. The capital city of Monrovia *must* have decent hospitals, and by the way, where was Liberia?

Over the next few days, we changed our airplane tickets, repacked and managed to sell the van to some seminary friends who had been watching us fix it up. I remember they paid us exactly the asking price, which was exactly what we had put into it. The next day, after driving it around they appeared at our door and handed us a hundred dollar bill. "It's just so wonderful, you need some profit for your work!" What sweet friends.

My folks in Rhodesia were naturally disappointed to hear we weren't coming their way, but my Dad said something that in hindsight proved to be Divinely inspired. "Well," he said, "I've been praying that if there was any reason you two shouldn't come to Rhodesia, that God would close the door."

We did manage to talk about our future on the way to Liberia, and the parting words we'd been given by the Foreign Mission Board representative just before we left. "When you get back in a year, be prepared to tell us where you want to serve. Provided you're still healthy, we can make it happen." They even told us what date to be in Richmond in order to be commissioned.

"You're kidding!" I exclaimed. "I thought you told us where we would go."

"No, that's just for the short-termers. Career folks work with us;

between you, the Lord and the Board."

Marsha here: Ever since we'd been planning to go to Africa for a year, we had been preparing to sell our car and fund ourselves to fly over, first, we thought we'd be going to Rhodesia but now it was to Liberia to volunteer as dorm parents. This was back in the day when we had to use the Board appointed travel agent, even though it was our own money, they liked to keep a close watch on their personnel, no matter in what capacity they were in. I came to really appreciate that in later years, but at the moment it irritated me.

In all fairness, we need to remember that in 1977 there was no internet, no online shopping, and unless you'd trained somewhere and got a license, you were at the mercy of a professional travel agent for airline tickets and travel suggestions.

By this time, I'd travelled enough to know there were always options, so I rang up the agent and asked, "We're leaving from Dallas and I've heard of people dropping down into South America and then over to Africa, thus avoiding Europe. Could we do that?"

"Absolute Rubbish," he shouted into the phone. "I'll book you through New York, London, Nairobi, Johannesburg and Cape Town. Then I'll put you up the continent through Rhodesia, (where we wanted to visit Tony's folks), and then through Zaire and on to Monrovia." He finished brusquely.

And so off we went. There was a bomb scare in New York, delaying us on the plane for a couple of hours, then fog in London, where we languished for four more hours. In Nairobi I was so tired I thought I could lie down on the floor as we waited for a different plane since we'd so effectively missed our connection. To this point Trevor had failed to sleep even a moment, and we were all starting to go totally nuts.

Then just an hour or so out of Johannesburg, the lady in the seat in front of us, having taken in the screaming and all for as long as she could, turned and said in a thick British accent, perhaps tinged with just a little distain,

"Would you *ca-eh* for something for the baby?"

I had been gritting my teeth in a jealous rage that her little one was out cold for the entire flight, so I shouted an affirmative, "Yes!"

And she ladled a teaspoon of something into Trevor's screaming mouth. I caught the words "Baby Calm" on the front of the bottle as Trevor collapsed into my arms. All my life I will bless this woman, even though she quite possibly gave him some unknown drug I would have never allowed in a more sane environment.

We arrived almost 12 hours late, dragging our luggage and a sagging, tongue rolling child. Soon we discovered that, yes, they would be helping us continue on to Cape Town, but since it was Christmas, we were at the bottom of a 'standby' list that would take two or three days to get on a plane. I worried and wondered while Tony, in a seldom seen "Hero" mode, possibly fueled by insanity, pointed out the window and said, "Do you see that Holiday Inn (in Johannesburg!) over there? We're going over there and checking in."

"Oh" I whined, "it might be expensive, and what about your folks in Cape Town?" We were scheduled to meet them and drive back along the coast of South Africa taking it all in with smiling bliss. This wasn't playing out as I had planned.

"I'll call them from the hotel but we ARE going to the hotel no matter how expensive it is!"

For once I was too tired to protest, perhaps because I was pregnant as well. We'd 'planned' this child like the other one, sort of on the spur of the moment, but I was about three months along, so according to all the reports, it would be fine for me to travel. I wondered if this was what the authorities meant by 'travel' as we made our way to the Holiday Inn.

It was reasonably priced, but they could only let us stay three nights as there was a full house from Christmas day. We agreed and checked in, falling into bed to get some sleep until Trevor's drug haze wore off. We called the elder Woods and suggested we rent a car and after a rest, head down to Cape Town but they said the drive was boring and they'd just come back up. Being who they were, they threw the Christmas tree in the car, still fully decorated, and drove non-stop for the three days it took them to come up to Johannesburg. I'll never forget late Christmas Eve hearing the tapping on the door that woke us up. We opened it to see a full sized tree concealing two very happy people.

We gave up our bed to the more tired road warriors, after all we'd had three days to rest and recuperate. Then at breakfast I gave them their Christmas present, the face that we were expecting. Very happy memories.

As soon as we went upstairs from breakfast, I was very ill. Must be the pregnancy, I thought, but I couldn't seem to recover. It was Christmas day and we needed to be out by noon.

We decided that I would rattle around the room with Trevor and the three still standing adults would go to the nearby church and fish for an invite for dinner, thereby fueling us for the fact that we had to find shelter before nightfall. We never did that normally, but we had no other plan and so off they went. Hours later they arrived back, just in time to prop me up and shove ourselves out the door. They brought home with them not an invite for dinner but better yet, the keys to an apartment of someone who was back in England for the holidays.

We arrived at the apartment, no Christmas lunch, and me a pale shade of green. Going in we noticed the cupboards were bare, but there were two cartons of milk in the fridge with a note "help yourself". Obviously these folks had been gone awhile because the milk was solid and beyond sour.

Tony and his Dad decided to 'suss out the neighborhood' for something to eat while Jody watched Trevor (now more or less returned to normalcy) and I reclined on the couch. Our dashing heros returned in an hour or so laughing and carrying bags of groceries. They had finally found something open, a Sikh Indian grocer. They had cans of tomato soup and crackers.......a perfect 'feast' for me. I began to think I could live again. This remains in our memory as one of the best Christmas's we've ever had.

We had a lovely few days in the apartment, enjoying the sights of Johanesburg until it was finally decided it was time to head north into Rhodesia. This would by necessity take us through some of the most dangerous part of the country, in terms of terrorist activity, but Tony's Dad insisted, "No problem! A military convey leaves every morning at 7:00. We join them and travel in safety."

As was always the case when we traveled with the folks, we arrived at the meeting place the next morning just a little late at 7:05 and were told by the soldier at the roadblock that the convoy had already left.

"Do you have any guns in the car?" he asked. When we answered no, we did not, the soldier pointed at a Citroen just pulling away ahead of us. "They have guns. I suggest you get on their bumper and stay there."

It sounded like a plan, but as soon as we got out of town and started onto the bush road, the Citroen tromped on the gas pedal and left our poor VW van behind like we were sitting still. I suddenly got very sleepy and decided to take a nap in the floor of the back seat. To this day I'm teased about my cowardice.

About half way up to Rhodesia, we naturally needed petrol, but because of blockades and whatever, there was no gas in the small village. We were assured that there would be some the next day so we had no choice but to go into a game park (where there were the least amount of curious villagers to peer in on us, and hopefully even fewer terrorists) and spend the night in the van. I can't say any of us slept too well, cramped in every position imaginable.

During the night we were literally terrified to hear scratching and thumping sounds literally in stereo coming mostly from the top of the van. Dad got his flashlight out and nervously peered around. We were prepared to start the engine and tear off if there were terrorists involved, but to our relief, we soon discovered it was a troop of curious baboons, dangerous enough if we'd been on the outside but we were safe and secure inside. We had a good laugh and went back to sleep.

We did make it safely to Salisbury, and after a nice visit with Tony's folks, we said goodbye, boarded a bus for another town to the north and showed up to the airline ticket agent. Showing them our prepaid tickets for Liberia, she did a double take, then started yelling at us.

"Dis airline she stop da flying Africa, 'bout two years ago!"

Our Pan-Am tickets had been somehow booked on a defunct airline, making them completely void. Remember how much I disliked the board's travel agent?

She pointed with her chin to a couple of folding chairs and we gathered what luggage we still had and went to sit down. We had no way to contact anyone. We'd already lost two suitcase somewhere between Dallas and Johannesburg so we figured now we'd be 'lost' as well, languishing somewhere in some back room. Maybe with luck we'd end up wherever our bags were. But fortunately within an hour, the agent returned, this time smiling and announced that the German airline, Lufthansa had agreed to take responsibility for us and our defunct tickets, and we could board the next plane for Kinshasa and on to Monrovia soon.

Indeed that was a trip we'll never forget and definitely never want to repeat. In Zaire we were 'trapped' in a waiting room for eight hours (with no A/C and a two-year-old). Tony, at one point, stepped out of the room to ask a question and a soldier confiscated all of our passports. He came back, question unanswered and now passport-less. We had to only wonder if we'd ever see them again. I visited the restroom and as worldly wise as I was by now, at least when it came to travelling, I was shocked and reviled to see that the restroom was just an empty room with just a very large 'pile' on the floor (some things can't be unseen). I spun on my heel, grabbing my nose and made a hasty exit, vowing to never even consider it, but as soon as they saw me leave, they rushed over and quickly locked it up anyway, so my only option was to wait. Maybe that particular facility wasn't supposed to be for passengers, I'll never know. I do know that by early evening I teared up with relief when a lovely plane landed on the tarmac and the door opened. We were on our way again.

Back to Tony: We did eventually figure out where Liberia was: on the west coast of Africa, east of Sierra Leone, west of Cote d'Iviore, with an ocean of water to the south and an ocean of sand to the north. The name, "Liberia" was given to it in 1847 on the occasion of it becoming a bona fide country, populated primarily by freed slaves from all over the world. Following America's Civil War, the country got a huge influx of new citizens, along with no small measure of support from the American government.

So this was to be their place of "Liberty"; a chance for a fresh start at least on the same continent howbeit nowhere near the place from where their families had been captured and taken in chains into slavery generations before.

Then there were the indigenous Africans who were occupying Liberia when the first ships from America started arriving and unloading thousands of former slaves, encouraging them to "Be free!" They weren't exactly welcomed with open arms, and in fact in many respects they had been transported from one war zone to the next, except in the case of Liberia the freed slaves were not the victims of the hostilities but were now the targets.

America didn't leave them totally helpless though. Undoubtedly seeing this as an opportunity for a new market, they provided the freed slaves with enough support to survive and even thrive. Until the revolt and take over by Samuel Doe in the early 1980's the country was run largely by these freed slaves.

In my office, I've hung an old muzzle-loading flintlock rifle, acquired from a man in Liberia who said he used it to hunt elephants. A little research tells me that it was manufactured in London in the early 1860s. It doesn't take much imagination to see that gun making its way from England to America where it was put to use during the Civil War, then finding a place on a ship bound for Liberia where a freed slave used it to stake his claim to a new life there. And then we can wonder how the Elephant hunter got it from the freed slave. Oh, if that weapon could only speak!

So we finally did arrive in Monrovia after a series of adventures. My Dad's last words to us as we left their place still made its way to the surface occasionally, though. He said, "You know, I still wish you were coming here instead of going on to Liberia. But you know, I prayed that if there were any reason at all you shouldn't be coming here, that God would shut the door on you." How those words would chill us to the bone just a few short months later.

⚶

Besides the life-changing incidents that lay ahead, I should also point out here that by the time we left Rhodesia, Marsha and I both were struggling with the question of where God might send us the next year when hopefully we'd be starting our next big chapter as career missionaries. We had been told to pray about where God might be calling us, and to have at least a broad idea in place by the time we left Liberia. A big part of me was "defaulting" back to Africa, having spent two years in Zambia already. But returning to the area brought back a lot of the issues we had come up against and since then had pushed to the backs of our minds.

For one thing, we could never get used to the fact that we were the "rich foreigners". We tried to convince the people we worked with that we were not rich; in fact this assignment was considered a "volunteer" job. But it was soon pointed out that we did receive a monthly food allowance that exceeded most of their annual incomes. We had a house to live in, a car to drive, enough insurance to cover just about everything, and if things got too tough, America would send in a few Marines to extract us and all her citizens from any unpleasantries. The door to Africa, in my mind, was closed once and for all one morning as I stood in the front yard of our house in Liberia, enjoying a cup of coffee and watching as the ladies from a village across the road came and filled their water buckets from our garden hose. I smiled and said "Good morning!" but a part of me felt like the plantation owner surveying his vast estate. I didn't like that feeling, and I said so to Marsha.

"What about Japan?" she asked, reminding me of a conversation we had had back in South Africa, on the way here. "You wouldn't be the rich guy there."

True, but then there was the fact that I was a "country boy". Cities had no appeal for me, and in fact I had to admit to a certain fear of any place with more than a few thousand in residence. The Japanese language, as near as I could tell, was unlearnable, as confirmed by my French teacher in college who, after two years of struggling, suggested that I try Spanish. And what's with the raw fish? If God intended for us to eat sushi, why did He give us fire?

Well, I agreed to pray with her about it, but I confess that my prayers were a little "tight". "Lord, you know this topic of Japan has come up, and you know how I feel about it. But... I'll keep an open mind."

And with that prayer, the door opened a crack. We prayed together. We talked together. We visited Tucker and Liz Callaway, our missionary neighbors, who it turned out had spent many years in Japan and he was considered by many to be *the* expert on Buddhism, at least from a Christian perspective. He had done his doctoral thesis on the topic and even published one of the best books I've come across, *Zen Way, Jesus Way*. When I mentioned our interest in Japan, he was quick to tell us, "I would never convince you to go to Japan; that's God's responsibility. I will however answer your questions."

After several months of sitting at his feet, we were both convinced that this was indeed God's will for us.

That conviction was underscored the day we got news from Rhodesia. Sanyati Mission Hospital, (where we had been headed until our visas were denied), had been attacked by terrorists, and one missionary, Archie Dunaway, had been killed. That was enough in itself to recall Dad's words about praying for the "door to close", but in light of what was going on here in Liberia during that time, the incident was elevated to an obvious God-directed series of events that would erase forever any doubts about His Presence and Power.

As mentioned already, Marsha was pregnant with our second child when we arrived in Liberia. The journey there had been grueling, and probably contributed to the fact that she began having problems. We went to a local hospital in Monrovia and were not comforted by what we heard. Everything was ambiguous, English being sparse and hard to understand. To top it off, they'd given her some unknown medicine in the form of a shot, against her will and we were concerned at the least of how this would play out. True she'd had a perfect labor and delivery the first time, but could she do this next one pretty much on her own, with only the 'help' for an incoherent doctor who didn't mind giving drugs without her consent?

While we were pondering all that, I was driving alone one day when I saw a white man walking along the road, looking confused. This was something you *never* saw in the area, so I pulled over and asked if I could help. "Thank you," he said, relieved to find someone who spoke English. "I just arrived in the country and I'm supposed to go the ELWA Hospital where I'll be working as a doctor."

I had never been to ELWA, but I had heard of it, a huge base for the Sudan Interior Mission out in the country somewhere. I had some time, so we drove out the main road and past the airport, occasionally stopping to as a person walking or herding, saying "ELWA"? We would always receive a big smile and an enthusiastic chin nod to continue.

Finally after about 20 miles, we found it. I was pleased to see that it was a typical thatch-roofed mission station with a clinic attached. It looked clean, though, and I noticed there were screens on the windows. Later we heard that people would travel for days, often on foot, to be treated there. I said goodbye to my new friend and headed for home.

"Marsha," I said, "I don't feel this strongly very often, but you *must* go see this doctor. Please!" She was hesitant, but finally, possibly reviewing in her mind the last visit to the Liberian doctor, agreed to look into it when she had a chance.

The chance came a few days later, and she came home very pleased to have been assigned a British doctor. She was confirmed to be three months pregnant and was scheduled to go in the next month for a checkup.

The next time she went however, they ascertained that somewhere in the process, the baby had died. She was told that her body would possibly reabsorb the fetus. Recalling the visit, she told me that somehow the doctor seemed more upset that she did, because of the strange things that had happened with the local doctor. We hugged each other and agreed that we both saw this as a 'relief' that God had taken our baby to be pure and healed in Heaven. We'd had no problems getting pregnant and we'd have other children, so we weren't too sad.

Then after about six weeks of nothing, the expected miscarriage happened, in the form of a big gush and then nothing. No pain, no nothing. Everything seemed okay, and she was not excited about seeing another doctor. But Liz Callaway, Tucker's wife, who lived next door, heard about it and insisted that she go to ELWA. I had rearranged my schedule that day to go to the airport and pick up some guests instead of preach, so I was at home when she came back.

"They've told me they'll do a D&C tomorrow to see what happened, and that I'm supposed to take it easy the rest of the day." She didn't seem happy for the bother of going back to ELWA, but Liz said she'd drive her again. The next day, I took Trevor to his day care center for the day and went to the media center. Liz and Marsha had left for a 7AM appointment earlier.

About 8:30, I was surprised to see Liz at the door of my office, her face ashen. "Tony, you need to get out to ELWA now! Something's happened to Marsha, and it doesn't look good. You hurry, I'll pick up Trevor."

The Divine sequence of events played out, which in retrospect would look all the more interwoven. When Marsha got to the hospital, she met the doctor, who suggested they get right into the surgery as there were countless others waiting as well. She no sooner got comfortable and asleep on the operating table than the hemorrhaging began. It was an episode of epic proportions. Later, the doctor would say that, had they not been in the surgery with all the necessary facilities available at their fingertips, she would have bled out in about two minutes.

Unbelievably, in my race to be at her side, I was held up by road works and there was no convincing anyone to let me through. All I could do was pound the steering wheel and pray.

By the time she was partially stabilized, I arrived. The doctor took me to an adjoining room and said, "This is very serious. We've stemmed most of the blood flow, but she's still bleeding inside. We don't know what's wrong and we need to operate, but we can't do anything until that's under control. I think we should pray."

The rest of the afternoon, I waited outside her door and prayed, joined by missionary friends, Brian and Ruth Clarke, who had come by.

Finally by 7:00pm, the doctor came out again. "Frankly, as a doctor, I don't know why she started hemorrhaging when she did and not before. Even now, I don't know why the internal bleeding seems to have stopped about an hour ago. But it's given us an opportunity to open her up. I'll come see you as soon as I know anything."

The surgery lasted a couple of hours. What the doctor discovered was something called "Placenta Accreta", a rare condition where during pregnancy the placenta adheres to the uterine wall. From that moment on, the life of both mother and child is in dire straits.

There are so many "ifs" here, we can't begin to list them all. What if she'd have stayed at the local hospital? What if she had hemorrhaged on the way to ELWA, or even at home, fixing a meal for guests while I had made the airport run, Trevor toddling around at her feet? What if I had not stopped and given the doctor a ride and so had never known about the facility and the Christian staff available right down the road?

But the biggest "if" became clear a few days later when we got word of a terrorist attack back at Sanyati, where we were headed until our visas were denied. Counting backwards, we realized that it occurred at the same time as Marsha was having her medical crisis. She would have been in the hospital, unable to move, with no care available.

I have to add one more thread to this tapestry before I move on. Archie Dunaway, the one missionary who was killed, had stumbled upon the terrorists while they were telling the African staff that they were about to kill every white person on the station as a message to the Ian Smith government. Archie turned to run, yelled out a warning and was bayoneted to death. Meanwhile, the rest of the missionaries ran into the bush and hid until government soldiers arrived the next day.

But the fact that Archie was even there at Sanyati was a miracle in itself. Just a few months previously, his wife Margaret had been diagnosed with a brain tumor. Unable to be treated there, she and Archie returned to the States and checked into a specialist hospital in Nashville. After hours of examination, studying the x-rays she had brought with her and making calls to the doctors back at Sanyati, they concluded, "We can't explain this, but today you have no brain tumor, and no evidence that there ever was one. You're free to go back to Africa."

She and Archie returned, and a short time later the terrorists came. Margaret had been at a ladies meeting that evening, and was driving back home. Turning into the driveway, the car's headlights passed across who she thought was Archie standing by the road, his right hand up as if to say hello … or goodbye. Going into her house, the phone rang and a friend said simply, "Terrorists are here; run and hide." She did, and the next day heard of Archie's death and the warning he had given that saved them all.

A short time later, Margaret's headaches returned. She went back to the States and within a few weeks had died, victim of the brain tumor that had so successfully hidden itself until Archie's work was done.

Back in Liberia, Marsha was making a recovery, although progress was slow. The first challenge had been to replace the huge amount of blood she had lost. When we assured the doctor that we had no problems with African blood as long as it matched, he replied, "But African blood would have a big problem with you." It seems that by the time a Liberian was old enough to give blood, he or she had survived the whole gamut of local maladies, the remnants of which still flowed through their veins. Introducing that into Marsha's system would be not unlike drinking river water from the Ganges. She would not likely survive.

A call to the US Embassy in Monrovia led to a query being made to the Navy's Seventh Fleet that happened to be passing by a few miles off shore. A helicopter was organized, and seven sailors made their way to ELWA to donate blood. We were so shocked and distracted; we never got enough information from them to follow up. How we would love to find those men today and tell them what a beautiful thread they added to God's tapestry!

The next drama came when she contracted Malaria on the second day. This is a potential killer in any situation, but was expected because of the blood transfusion. As she began spiking a fever that reached at least 106 degrees, she experienced fear for the first time since the event had started. Until now, she had merely been a spectator in everything. Now she was alert enough to realize what was happening. Her friend Ruth, who was an Elwa nurse, and who'd been there thru all of this wrote the verse from Joshua 10:25 in giant letters and taped it to the wall where she could see it, "Do *not* be *afraid*; do *not* be discouraged. Be strong and courageous".

During that time of slow recovery, God sent us another word of encouragement in the form of a huge black lady, adorned from head to foot with bright "lapa" cloth and jewelry, and accompanied with an entourage of people clutching notebooks. Coming directly to Marsha's bedside, she swept her up into her arms and planted a huge wet kiss right on her lips. When Marsha could catch her breath, she smiled and asked, "And who would you be?"

"Now don't you mind that, Child. I'm just here to pray with you and give you a word or two from the Lord. My husband, by the way, is president."

"President of what?" Marsha asked, a little more comforted. The lady, whose name was Victoria Tolbert, just laughed out loud and said,

"The country, of course!"

And indeed it was so. Her husband. William Tolbert, was president of Liberia, head of the country's Baptist Convention, a committed Christian and grandson of a freed slave from South Carolina who had emigrated to Liberia in 1878. The Tolberts own daughter, Victoria Yancey Tolbert, had died of the exact same malady in 1971, and hearing of Marsha's ordeal brought Mrs. Tolbert running.

It was a unique relationship that we missionaries were admonished to *never* take advantage of, although I have to say there were a couple of times when we were confronted with corrupt policemen looking for a bribe, that the news of our personal association with the President swept us from the position of potential victim to honored guest in a heartbeat. The concern of course, was that, if we relied too much upon our status, we might find ourselves in a much different situation if anything were to happen to Tolbert. That turned out to be a self-fulfilling prophecy when, a few years later, Samuel

Doe, a young firebrand from the country swept into Monrovia and took over control of the government overnight. Killing Tolbert, he threw Victoria dressed only in her thin nightgown, into a bare jail cell where she languished on a concrete floor for several months before American pressure resulted in her being allowed to come to Minneapolis and join her children who were living there.

Doe continued as dictator over a country that immediately lost most of is infrastructure, all of its public support … and those Marines I mentioned earlier came in and extracted the last of the Americans. Doe himself was eventually overthrown and executed, but the poor nation of Liberia has never fully recovered. But all this drama with the president hadn't happened yet, and we were coming to the end of our time there, happily well and starting to prepare for our return to the States and career appointment. One of our biggest concerns of course, was what to do about the MK dormitory we had cared for. The parents of the children living there all lived and worked in Liberia's rural areas, so if they wanted their children to continue attending the international school in Monrovia, someone would have to step in and take over the dorm.

The tapestry Weaver had no such concerns, however, and in a stroke of Divine timing, Buddy and Jody were invited to move in and continue as dorm parents. After the attack on Sanyati, most of Rhodesia's MKs had been moved out of the country to other schools considered safer, leaving my folks with no job, at least in Rhodesia. They were thrilled to take on the Monrovia dorm, though, and were soon "Uncle Buddy and Aunt Jody" to a whole new set of kids.

That turned out to be a Divine move as well, since a few months after their arrival, Tolbert was assassinated, the country was thrown into turmoil, and the lives of foreigners everywhere was in immediate jeopardy. For several days, gunfire was heard all around the mission compound while the MKs huddled together with Buddy and Jody, comforted by her chocolate chip cookies and Uncle Buddy's famous stories.

On the worst night of rioting, a huge storm swept over the dormitory, enveloping them in an inky black cloud that resulted in zero visibility. The wind was so strong the screens were nearly pulled off the windows. Blankets and towels were spread in front of the doors to turn back a flood of water that poured in. The next morning dawned clear, and Buddy ventured outside to assess the damage. Across the road, he saw the headman of the village, Ba Nyuma. Going over to greet him, they talked about the violence all around the city, with people being killed indiscriminately and homes ransacked. Buddy said, "Well, I guess that storm last night kept the rioters away, at least."

Ba Nyuma looked confused and asked, "What storm?"

Buddy replied, "That HUGE storm we had last night. It went on all night long. Our house was nearly blown away!"

"Baba (honored elder)," the headman said, "there was no storm last night. Only the rioters and soldiers running up and down the road shooting at each other."

I suppose this side of Heaven we won't know for sure what happened that night. Something God-inspired, to be sure. I have no doubt that the Bear was on the prowl that night, seeking whom he might devour, He never found the MK dorm, however. But to what end? Now that's a thread of the tapestry I'm looking forward to seeing one day.

Chapter 5

Hello Japan

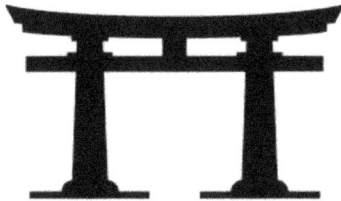

By November, 1978, we were ready to pack up and leave Liberia. We had only been there less than a year, but what a year it had been! Trevor by now was three, and starting to talk in full sentences, howbeit with a trace of Liberian accent. He had nothing but good memories, especially of the daycare center where he spent a few mornings each week. For months afterward, he talked about the "blue ladies", which we mistakenly thought was a reference to their ebony black skin until we looked back over pictures and noticed that all the staff wore crisp blue uniforms.

It had been a time of spiritual growth, having to deal with the loss of our second child, followed by severe medical complications Marsha often describes as "coming to the edge and looking over". But those experiences had to be tempered with the obvious intervention on God's part that led us away from near certain death at Sanyati Hospital while leading us to ELWA Hospital In Liberia, to just the right place, the right time and the right people whom He would use to accomplish His purposes. And that part of the tapestry was still coming into focus, with further revelations in the months and years to follow related to why our visas to Rhodesia had been denied in the first place. And there's more: one of the doctors responsible for saving Marsha's life was also used by God to open the door to adoption and the blessed event we named Nathan … Gift of God.

It was also a time that would invoke countless hours of introspection. Saying goodbye to new friends, we had no idea that within a year the country would be in shambles, its president dead, his wife imprisoned, and virtually all infrastructure including the country's one power generating plant totally destroyed. What had once grown into an oasis paradise civilization in a country where in the late 1800s the average *life* expectancy of a newly-arrived missionary was less than six months, the nation was to find itself thrust back into the chaos it had once been.

But the next stop in the journey was Richmond, Virginia, where we would be officially accepted for appointment as career missionaries to Japan. Bob Shoemake picked us up at the airport, tired and disheveled with our just three year old in tow and took us to a mission house. There on the kitchen table was a box of donuts with the slogan "It's worth the trip" (and it was), the keys to a loan car and the admonition to be ready to be taken to church in three days. We thought we'd arrived in Heaven.

Baker James Cauthen, president of the Foreign Mission Board, urged all of us to think long and hard about our decision. Missionary life was *hard*, he insisted; and he was an experienced missionary from China who knew what he was talking about. "If you can do anything else in this world, do it," he said. "The missionary role is not for the uncalled. But on the other hand," he chuckled, "If God is leading you, then I know that nothing else will ever make sense until you surrender to His Great Commission."

After appointment, we got the official invitation to come to Pine Mountain, Georgia and 14 weeks of orientation. Having survived the "boot camp" experience of Missionary Journeyman training prior to going to Zambia, we both felt cold chills coming up our backs. That ordeal was only seven weeks long. How could we make it through *fourteen* weeks? However, this time we were told by a soft spoken mission representative in Richmond, "Oh no! This time we're not trying to kill you."

And it was true, in a sense. Journeymen are fresh out of college, not yet settled into their careers but willing to invest two years of hands-on ministry with real live missionaries. They all have good hearts, to be sure, but not all are ready emotionally or spiritually for the rigors of the Journeyman program. For seven weeks, trainees are given the opportunity to test their limits in all areas before packing their bags and heading overseas. Mercifully, a few come to the conclusion before departure that the time is not right, saving the mission a lot of dramas.

Appointed career missionaries, on the other hand, have already packed and have one foot on the platform. By definition, they have already served in ministries long enough to establish references, they've sold their homes and said goodbye to family and friends. What is now needed is a transition period between the life they're leaving behind and the new life to which they're headed.

For us, this was not much of an issue, having already left home and spent three years overseas. We were chomping at the bit to move on to the next chapter in our lives, and didn't need to take a lot of time reminiscing over the last chapter. For several folks, however, "MOC" (Missionary Orientation Center) was not unlike a Protestant's image of Purgatory. The established preachers, for example, couldn't imagine fourteen straight weeks without a chance to preach. In deference to their needs, we did have a daily chapel service where opportunity was given for them to use their gifts. We were left a little confused when every sermon ended in an altar call for salvation, but remembered that this was what those men had been commissioned to do, and do it they would.

There were a few folks appointed to serve as missionary doctors and nurses, and for them, orientation was a time of perceived profound guilt as day after day offered no chance to use their healing talents. I won't say that there was a certain level of rejoicing whenever someone in the group would suffer minor injuries needing medical attention, and it was interesting to see how those men and women were transformed through the process of being doctors and nurses again.

To try and help all of us through the transition time, Callaway Gardens at Pine Mountain, Georgia was a champion. During most of the year, the place is humming with vacationers and golfers coming to relax as well as to compete on a world class golf course. During the winter, though, things slowed down to a crawl, a fact that didn't go unnoticed by a few insightful folks at our Foreign Mission Board's headquarters in Richmond. After a bit of negotiation, a permanent lease was established with Callaway Gardens, where most of the facilities would be available from September to May, ample time to conduct two fourteen-week orientation sessions. When not in classes or other organized activities, missionaries were invited to make use of all that Callaway had to offer, from PGA approved golf courses, to hiking and jogging trails, bicycle paths and exercise gyms. This was by intention, part of the stated goal of helping the missionaries put their past lives behind them while preparing for what was to come.

Every part of the daily schedule pointed in the same direction. Each day we were exposed to veteran missionaries, theologians and seminary teachers who made sure that we had a firm foundation of faith under our feet. Carpenters and mechanics came to give us lessons in "shade tree repairs". Did you know that ladies' nylon stockings can be used as a temporary fan belt? In the absence of compressed air, grass can be stuffed into a flat tire, giving it enough support to carry you back to civilization. Have you considered that a childs hair, if long enough can be braided over a scalp wound instead of getting stitches? Much to the delight of our medical personnel, they were given an opportunity to share some wisdom about what to do in situations where no doctor was present. By the time we were done, we felt like we could do minor heart surgery with little more than a rubber hose and a Swiss Army knife.

We were also taught that, under absolutely no circumstances were we to get involved in our host country's political situations. As missionaries, we were to be "Switzerland", with no stated opinion about anything other than Jesus Christ and Him crucified. And speaking of that, this might be a good place to finish the story I started above:

We had been missionaries about ten years, and were at a conference in America. Stepping onto an elevator, we were joined by a tall man a few years older than us, who kept gazing intently at our name tags. Finally his face brightened, and he spoke up. "Tony and Marsha Woods! I know you, at least by name."

He introduced himself as Norman Wood, Rhodesian by birth, now naturalized American citizen, Southern Baptist and fellow missionary serving in Mauritius, and then much later in Japan. He explained, "Back in Rhodesia, I was a chaplain for the army led by Ian Smith. Walking through the immigration office one day, I thought I heard my name and turned to see who it was. No, they said, it wasn't me; they were referring to a couple, Tony and Marsha Woods, with an "s". Their application for a visa had come across the desk and had been denied because of the Woods' missionary status."

Just prior to that time, a couple of Catholic nuns had made some disparaging remarks about Smith's government and the result was that from then on, no religious worker visas would be granted. Norman looked at the application and said, "Oh don't worry about these guys; they're Southern Baptist and as such they're under strict rules to avoid any political involvement whatsoever. They'd be okay, I guarantee it."

The visa was reconsidered and eventually granted, but by then we had sold the van we were going to ship and made new travel plans to go to Liberia, a fact that would later save our lives. Sharing "the rest of the story" with Norman was a huge encouragement for all of us, and we had to stop right there and pray, thanking God for His watch care, and for allowing a glimpse of it at work.

But back to MOC, our time there was magical, a constant buffet of amazing people and unique opportunities to prepare. There was also the buffet offered three times a day at the lunchroom, and it proved to be the biggest challenge for all of us. I think the average weight gain was about ten pounds on the average.

With so many countries being represented by the missionaries, it wouldn't have been practical to start language study at MOC. In fact we were urged to wait until we found ourselves immersed in the people to whom we would be ministering before taking any serious lessons. Instead, we were visited by a team of well-known linguists who taught us the basics of how to learn a language.

When not attending lectures, we spent hours in the language lab, where we would break down sound patterns and tones, trying to reproduce aspects found in many languages outside English. Then for a hands-on experience, we were blessed to have a young man spend some time with us. He was an MK, raised in Papua New Guinea, and the whole time he was with us, he never wore shoes and spoke only Papua New Guinea "Tok Pisin" or pigin English. If we wanted any social interaction with him at all, we would need to adapt, (being a form of English, it is barely understandable, but we got by) and the only place he seemed interested in communicating was on the soccer field. It was an exhausting, frustrating time, but I think of all the facets in orientation, the time with him was perhaps the most useful for all of us, regardless of what countries we were going to.

Cultural issues were presented, along with an overview of body language and how it could torpedo the best intentions if used incorrectly. In many cultures for example, the sole of the foot is considered the most reprehensible part of the body, and to sit legs crossed, with the bottom of your foot pointed at someone would in some cases be grounds for violence. While in many third world situations, ladies going topless would attract no attention whatsoever, but a glimpse of the upper thigh or in some Asian settings the back of the neck would elicit cat calls of the rudest kind. Using your left hand (and Marsha is left handed) is rude because it's considered 'unclean' in most of Africa and other parts of the world.

Another "hands-on" experience for Marsha at MOC was learning to ride a bicycle. Many others were tasked at learning to drive manual transmission cars, as those were the most prevalent on most of the fields they were going to. However, Marsha, having been raised on a mountain in Colorado, never had much opportunity to move around on anything less than a four-wheel drive Jeep. She had the manual shifting, complete with 'double clutching' on hills mastered so as Callaway Gardens had an unlimited supply of bicycles and miles of beautiful trails to explore, she decided to get to know bicycling.

By now Trevor was holding his own with a bike just his size, outfitted with training wheels. As the three of us headed out one cold winter morning, we thought of picnics by the pond, glimpses of local wildlife, and family bonding like never before.

Well, one out of three is not bad, I suppose. The picnic was scattered along the trail by countless collisions with trees, rocks and each other. Any local wildlife wisely chose to avoid the area. But there was a certain amount of family bonding, which was so aptly expressed by Trevor, who was getting better at one-sentence expressions. After one particularly impressive pile up occasioned by Marsha's failure to negotiate a slight bend in the trail, Trevor pulled his bike upright, dusted off his pants and said, "Mommy, I feel sorry for you."

Here's Marsha:

Fourteen weeks, a time that seemed so eternally consuming while standing before it, passed in an instant. It was time to pack up and head for our assigned countries. We left Georgia for a quick stop in Idaho where we had built a crate to be shipped to Japan. After a few more last minute items, the box was filled and the lid nailed on. During that busy afternoon, Trevor managed to have a bad fall off the top of some open stairs, so I took him for a walk (carrying him) on the assumption he shouldn't sleep in case of concussion (is that even a thing nowadays?). Anyway, my nephew Lyle, the family dog and me carrying Trevor managed to spook a rather large bear who had his head down in the bushes. Farah barked, I tried to back up but was trapped from behind by bushes. We all looked at each other for must a moment, and then the bear, fortunately, was as scared as we were and shot off, unfortunately in the direction of the house, but we were all glad to be safe. We chose to take the long circuitous route home as not to spook him again.

My brother-in-law had a friend with a bobcat used to pick up logs drop by, and somehow, with our hearts in our throats as we watched all our earthly possessions teetering high in the jaws of this bobcat, we got our large crate onto the flat bed and on it's way to Japan.

On Our Way

I had mentioned this *African trip to the other side on a plane that didn't exist* so many times in our orientation sessions that as we graduated from our training and read out the class prophecy, my prediction was that I would become a travel agent and send this particular man on a one way ticket around the world with no visa! How funny, but again he was able to make us crazy just one more time.

In early May, 1979, we left the USA to well wishers and naysayers. My beloved "Mother Gay", who I've mentioned before, told me over the phone in her kindly, now wavering voice, "You go tell those Japs about Jesus". I was taken aback until I remembered she'd singlehandedly raised four boys after their father died at 36. The boys all served in WWII one way or the other and "Japs" would have been the only nomenclature she had ever heard. Fortunately, the "Japs" were wonderful and welcomed us with open arms.

As we came into immigration after a long flight, exhausted, laying our passports up on the counter, the agent immediately seemed agitated. He didn't yell though, but pointed to our fidgeting son Trevor, aged 3, and pointed to the passport.

"NO beesa", he growled

You guessed it. Our travel agent had overlooked a visa for Trevor.

We were given three days to sort it out and allowed to continue on out the door. When we exited customs it was to the waiting arms of our longtime friends, Bob and Gail Gierhart.

From our experience in Africa, where every missionary arrival, no matter how insignificant, was usually met with a pink tea party including everyone coming from far and wide to eyeball the new arrivals. But I soon found out that this wasn't Africa.

The Japanese mission had sent us a letter saying something about being very busyand it was a long way away, etc. Enclosed in the envelope were directions to catch the train into Tokyo. Somehow Bob and Gail must have sensed our surprise and came out there to meet us, thus bonded us for life, and in retrospect, I believe it was a good revelation about the Japanese mission and the independence that they fostered in us. After all, it was and still is a first world country and we are adults, we should be able to manage.

But first let me tell you about our 'ride' into town.

Bob and Gail had been on the field for 6 months, making them veterans. Bob had served two years before seminary in the military town of Misawa hundreds of miles to the north, and now, after marrying Gail, they were career missionaries in language school. Gail had been raised in Hawaii as a 'sansei' or third generation Japanese, so she had some inroads initially.

We couldn't have been happier to see them. At that time, Narita airport was only brand new and was about 50 miles out of Tokyo. It was built in spite of some heated opposition for it taking up rice growing farmland, and there were still armed guards everywhere, awaiting any anticipated riots.

The old airport was practically down town and was being overgrown by the city, so this was the only option.

We chuckled to ourselves as we left for the last time almost 40 years later that the guards were finally but only recently gone, I guess they gave up on a possible riot.

We travelled thru beautiful growing fields of rice, verdant greenery everywhere. "I can get used to this" I thought, as we rolled down windows and basked in the fresh springtime sunshine.

Then Bob and Gail said, "Do you feel like taking a short stop to see our house?" Of course we were game, and as we exited the freeway and ground to a stop, the glitter began to fade. Within 15 or 20 minutes Bob braked and pulled at a 45-degree angle over the curb and stopped abruptly in front of a wall.

Remember we'd just left the vast expanses of Idaho, so my first thought wasn't 'home' but rather 'wall'. We opened our doors and stepped out, being careful not to miss the tiny sidewalk and we wiggled around the building. There it was, their pride and joy. An old mission house, supposedly large and rambling, but to us, very small. I still remember my shock at their 'yard', which was about 3 feet wide on one side of the house.

Without giving ourselves away, we oohed and awed and said how lovely it was, trying to see what they saw in it. Then we climbed into the van again and continued onto the Mission headquarters in Shibuya, Tokyo, where literally HOURS later we arrived. We had sat stock still in gridlock traffic for long periods at a time, only inching forward here and there. Bob was a confidant driver but the tolerances were something we'd never seen in our entire lives. The smog began to sting our eyes, but when we mentioned it, they said they hadn't noticed it, shrugging their shoulders and rolling up the windows just ever so slightly.

After what seemed like an eternity, we arrived and found the missionaries were there to joyfully greet us. Now we were going to get the pink tea party! That was a great relief, that they actually DID want to meet us, and after our ride, we now understood why they were so hesitant to come to the airport!

We had dinner, smiling wanly and hoping it would end soon since we were so exhausted.

Bob and Gail left to start back home and we were shown to the mission apartment where we would live till our crate arrived, hopefully only two or three weeks later.

We opened the door and it hit one of the twin beds. We pushed hard and saddling in sideways, we could see another twin bed and a line of drawers. There was a shelf kitchen of sorts and a tiny toilet and shower. We put Trevor in the bed that wasn't attached to the door for everyone's safety, and because he was exhausted, he fell asleep immediately.

Keep in mind, now, that by the time we touched down at Japan's Narita airport in the spring of 1979, we had already served two years as missionary Journeymen in Zambia, one year as mission volunteers in Liberia, West Africa, and perhaps most challenging of all, two and a half years as seminary students in California's Marin County. We'd been able to do some traveling thru Europe as well as other parts of Africa and the Middle East. So considering that, it might have seemed surprising to see my comment that night as I jotted off a postcard to my folks. I said, "I think we've FINALLY found a foreign country."

As I put the card in my purse to mail the next day I looked up at Tony and almost burst into tears. I'll never forget what he did. He took me in his arms and said wisely, "We'll talk about it in the morning". What a wonderful man.

⨎

Remember what I said in the last chapter about mission family? It was never more beautifully illustrated than by the sight of fellow missionary Harriet Parker standing at our front door the next morning. Before she even spoke to us, she crouched down in front of our 3-year-old Trevor and said, "Hi there! I'm your Aunt Harriet and I'm SO GLAD you're here!"

A few minutes later, we'd managed to eat some cereal that was thoughtfully placed in the cupboard for us, and just about had Trevor's shoes tied when there was another knock on the door.

Opening the door, we were pleased to see another one of the older missionary ladies from next door (it was a compound) Her name is Eloise Lovelace and at the writing of this book both she and Harriet are still alive, so they mustn't have been that old, but you know how it is to someone who isn't even 30 yet!

She smiled at us and I noticed that she had THREE umbrellas hanging from her arm.

"Sorry to arrive unannounced, but there's no phone in here". She stepped in a step and looked around approvingly. She noticed the pallet we'd made in the corner and winced slightly. Maybe she didn't have kids or had forgotten, but neither of us wanted to be kicked all night by Trevor.

"I thought if you have time, I could take you to 'the village' to get some basics".

"The VILLAGE?" I screamed to myself. I wanted to leave and never see Tokyo again last night and now she tells me there's a VILLAGE?

With lightening speed we bolted out the door when she stopped us and said,

"Do any of you need to use the restroom before we go?"

OK, we're adults but I guess I appreciated her taking special care with us. Three umbrellas, bathroom stops...... She must have visited some of the 'benjos' that were available to the public, usually consisting of just a trough with a modicum of privacy and shelter.

We walked about two blocks along a narrow cobbled street and it opened up into a block long line of little open shops. A scene right out of a Japanese wood block print.

The first stop (we stood outside and the proprietor stood inside) was a drink store. After she had made a fuss about how cute Trevor was, we bought two cokes. (Remember we were just 30, so Coke was a food group). I carefully selected the money with the missionary helping me. Then she handed me the cokes and two glass drinking glasses.

I looked surprised and she beamed,

"Sabisu".

The missionary translated, "She's saying they're 'service' or complementary. Must be a campaign Coke is having at the moment".

And that was the moment I decided I could live the rest of my life in Japan.

We carried on down the street, greeting people, letting them pat Trevor's blond hair and generally having a good time. We saw little noodle shops with wax models of food out in front so you could point at what you wanted to order. At the meat and vegetable shop we noticed that everything was very, very fresh; the fish still wiggling, straight from the predawn market. After buying Trevor a pair of slip on shoes to avoid more shoe tying hold ups, we headed back to the apartment.

Yup........I could make it in a village. I could get to know people and they could know me, they could relate us and to Trevor and with some effort we could someday communicate beyond "Yasuii" (cheap) and "Kawaii" (cute).

Before we knew it, we were launched into what the mission liked to call "Survival Japanese". A tutor, a young man called "Harada San" came and escorted us to the mission office to begin our lessons. We were still in the tiny apartment but were daily filling it with food and odds and ends that we'd need when we made our move. A Japanese young lady was called in and watched after Trevor and of course he was thrilled. I'll never forget Harada "Sensei's" (as we were told to call him since he was our teacher) first word to us. Not, "hello", not, "How are you", just, "Ka".

We looked at each other and at him, clearly befuddled, and he continued, "Ki" and nodded his head to the large alphabet hanging on the wall. The next syllable out of all three of our mouths in unison was, "Ku".

We had begun learning Japanese. This process would move into full time study in the fall and two years later, if no one blinked, we would be deemed to be 'ready' to begin our life ministry in Japan.

Back at the twin bedded tiny guest room, we tried to learn some basic Japanese and entertain Trevor until finally after about three weeks word came that our crate had arrived in the Yokohama port and would be delivered in several days.

We had a brand new Toyota Corolla that the mission had awarded us, along with the admonition that it was ours for 10 years so we should take good care of it. We'd been driving around the suburb of Shibuya, trying to learn left hand driving again after our times in Africa, as well as a learning few painful lessons about Tokyo streets; none of them remain straight or the same name (supposing we could even read the name) for very long. We got lost many times and had to resort to good will and gestures to untangle ourselves, but we were confidant that our new home would be better because it was about 90 minutes south in the city of Yokohama.

Never mind that you were never out of sight of deep full city for that entire ride. In 1979 there were about 20 million people in the Tokyo-Yokohama corridor and now at the time of our leaving in 2015 there were close to 40 million.

Our crate arrived and we began to unpack. Back in the States we had been given a limited amount of space, so we packed very carefully, working hard to leave no empty spaces. Imagine our surprise when I slid open a file cabinet drawer and was greeted by about six little mice sitting in a hollow they'd created by chewing down into my much prized brand new towels! They had somehow entered from Sherry's garage as the crate sat there thru the winter in Idaho, and had thoughtfully filled it with enough dog food (again from the garage) to make the trip and have some left over.

In unison they all looked at me and in the time it took me to scream, they'd bolted and were out the front door, which was thankfully open. After the initial good laugh, we apologized to the environment for 'introducing' a foreign species to Japan. I'm sure they thrived. I told myself that I was glad to have a nice supply of fluffy soft rags to start my life in Japan.

Years later, after even a move to Sendai, I happened to lift the cook top of my range to clean, and there found a mother load of Kool-Aid, unscathed by years of heat from the burners. It's a wonder the kitchen didn't burn down.

The next thing to tick off was Summer. While we were with the tutor those first few weeks before we started formal language study, (the course was set up to be two years long), we avoided all talk about where we might go after graduation. But the door opened a crack when we found ourselves at our very first mission meeting. What an experience!

At that time, there were a little over a hundred missionaries, along with enough MKs to keep things at a constant hum. It was there that we saw the mission as a family. The kids referred to all the missionaries, even us, as "Aunt" and "Uncle". Looking back, we realized that in fact we represented the most consistent and supporting family they knew. Aunts and uncles back in the States were wonderful, but only seen about once every four years. We on the other hand were just a phone call away. And during mission meeting, it was a reunion like something out of a Norman Rockwell painting.

It was a real eye-opener to see the spectrum across the mission family, from young firebrands determined to win Japan in their lifetime, to the old patriarchs and matriarchs … not discouraged by any means, but perhaps a little more "road worn" than the younger folks. One night at Amagi, the Christian camp where we had our meetings, we hosted representatives from the Japan Baptist Convention. They brought reports of the work going on in their local areas and spoke about Convention-wide plans for evangelism. Then as we closed the time together, we sang the familiar hymn, "What a Friend We Have in Jesus" in Japanese. We all had hymnbooks, but they were in Japanese, so our ability to sing was limited by what we had learned to read. Marsha and I were quite proud of the fact that we had mastered *hiragana,* the phonetic alphabet, so we sang our best when we came to those characters. Then there were the *kanji* taken from the Chinese system of writing, where a single character can communicate whole concepts. The way they are pronounced depends on the context. By now, we knew maybe half of the kanji in the hymnbook and belted out the notes when those came up. As for the others, we hummed.

Looking around the circle, we had to snicker to ourselves as we watched the newcomers struggling to figure out which way the hymnbook was to be held. Then there were the "hummers" like us, singing out and then holding back. Then I noticed Bob Boatwright, standing across from us. He and his wife, Betty Faith were from Atlanta, Georgia, but had been in Japan for close to forty years by now. His hymnbook was down by his side, unopened, his eyes closed as he sang with tears in his eyes, "Itsukushimi fukaki, tomo naru Iesu wa…" What a Friend we have in Jesus… all our sins and grief to bear.

After the service, Marsha and I sought out the Boatwrights. There was something in them that drew us like a moth to a flame. Looking back, I know now it was a fire set by the Holy Spirit. We started talking, then we just listened as these two saints shared a bit of their lives. It soon became apparent that Bob was the dreamer: always ready to try something new if it would help the Japanese come to know Jesus. Betty Faith was the velvet brick: pure southern genteel wrapped around a way of looking at life that was as solid as they come. The more we came to know them, the more we saw ourselves in them. They were a great team, and a couple we would do well to emulate.

We had been praying too, about where we would possibly go when and if we ever graduated from Language school (that we hadn't even formally started yet). This casual acquaintance with the Boatwrights resonated with us and we continued to source them out in the crowd as mission meeting continued, until one day Betty Faith leaned over quietly and handed me a note.

It said, "Some of our friends, all who think you're fabulous and want you on their team, are beginning to insinuate that we're trying to proselytize you to come work with us, so we'll be ignoring you the rest of the week. Here's our phone number, after this meeting we're going to 'the lake' and you'd be more than welcome to drive up and stay in our house while we're gone. Help yourself to anything and stay as long as you like while you have a look around!"

Bob and Gail were also going up to Misawa, where he'd been a short term missionary years before, so we agreed to meet up. After all, it was weeks before we'd be starting language school and with all the 'big missionaries' at the 'lake', whatever that was, and with no language skills, we'd have nothing of any real import to do anyway.

When the meeting was over and many people headed out for 'the lake', we caught the Boatwrights at their car and using low tones, made arrangements to get the key from a neighbor. They told us the words to use to communicate, information of which we were thankful.

The proposal sounded good on all counts, and the next week found us on our first Japanese "road trip". Sendai was about eight hours north. Fortunately it's much more accessible now at the writing of this book 40 years later, thanks to the opening of a divided highway running straight as an arrow.

So we drove to Sendai. I remember we left at dusk so Trevor would sleep, thinking we'd get in about 2 or 3AM and also get some sleep before he woke up.

However, because of our inability to speak the language or read signs and maps written in Kanji (Japanese pictographs) further hampered by just the hugeness of the challenge, we were still driving in circles thru Tokyo hours and hours later. Finally we stopped at a 24 hour noodle shop and said, "Tohoku Ko Soku Doru", (Northeast

Expressway) a carefully rehearsed phrase that we'd already used to no avail several times. This time, at nearly 1AM, a man, standing behind the counter, took his apron off, motioned us to come with him and jumped on his moped.

We took the hint and followed carefully behind, turning and twisting for about 30 minutes until we arrived at the entrance to the freeway. As we honked and waved, we saw him in the rear view mirror, off his bike and bowing very respectfully. Japanese.

Five hours later the sun was up as well as Trevor, and we had arrived in Sendai. It was love at first sight. When we rolled into town, the place was jammed. We didn't know it at the time, but we arrived at the peak of the "Obon" festival, a time every summer when Japanese return to their hometowns. It's a time of great family reunions and a chance to honor the ancestors. All over the city, Shinto shrines, some as small as a steamer trunk and others as large as a bus, are hoisted on the shoulders men dressed in colorful kimonos called "Happi", yelling "Yoi sho! Yoi sho!" as they take the local gods for a stroll. It was a party of epic proportions, but compared to Tokyo, not so much different from what we were used to. We loved the place.

Then we learned that Sendai is a college town. At least thirteen universities, in fact have campuses there, including one of the Big Five government schools: Tohoku Daigaku. (Northeast Imperial University) By now Marsha and I were thinking that some kind of student ministry might be where God was leading us. What better place than Sendai?

Now we had a goal to pursue, but first we needed to get through language school.

We drove, after a few days, up to Misawa for another few days with Bob and Gail and were able to experience his world that he'd had for the two years we were in Africa. I remember taking our first "Ofuro-style bath in the famous Komaki Onsen, complete with a gym sized dome, waist high fence separating men and women.

 Bob, having lived there for two years previously, knew what to do, but Tony, Gail and I (and Trevor) knowing very little what we should do. Tony went in with Bob but that left Gail and I with Trevor on our own. I remember carrying our large bath towels and placing them here and there on the rock, trying vainly to keep them dry, and then me getting into the almost boiling (it seemed) water and then Gail sticking her toe in the water and screaming. Everyone looked at me because I was the White Body. You'll remember that Gail is the Hawaiian girl who looks Japanese! So unfair. We topped it off with accidently ordering a horsemeat dinner. This is the stuff of legends! Ha

After an uneventful run down the freeway to Tokyo, about eight hours, we arrived back home rested and refreshed with a goal to work towards.

Language School

We have a rule in our family. I think, if I remember right, it made its debut in September of 1979. All three of us were scared. We were going to start language school at "Saint Joseph's Japanese Language School in that part of Tokyo known as "Roppongi". We knew the address but didn't know how to say that big name in Japanese. We just hoped we could navigate the bus and train and get there.

By now we'd learned the two alphabets that Japanese use when they write in characters they borrowed from the Chinese. Chinese is a great language with at least 40,000 characters, but because they have no grammar to speak of, the Japanese had to invent an alphabet called "hiragana" to make it readable. Because it's phonetic, they come in handy for enabling small children (and foreigners) to be able to read until they've memorized the Chinese-based characters called "kanji".

The other alphabet is called "katakana" and is much more stylized with almost boxy letters. This was invented to be used along with hiragana, but is dedicated to Japan's "foreign words", those not part of their original language. You know by looking at it that it's an imported foreign word. For example, there is no word in Japanese for "ice cream", or "table", or "Tony Woods". Therefore when you read out a katakana word, it's "Ai-su ku-ri-mu"(ice cream) or "Te-bu-lu" (table) or "Toe-nee Ud-dzu" (Tony Woods). Those are as close as they can get to the actual spoken sound and you get used to it after awhile. We became accustomed to being called "Ud-dzu" because there is no "W" sound in their language.

So back to the rule. We were ready for school.

We'd been next door to the Catholic Kindergarten and Trevor was enrolled for three days a week. He was almost four, so he would be in the youngest class of three consecutive years. I spent the rest of my summer sewing all the different bags he needed for lunch, shoes, chopsticks, earthquake head protection complete with the requisite information of the wearer; name, date of birth, emergency contact numbers, blood type, you know, the usual stuff needed in Japan.

I say we were ready to go to school. There was one bump however. One day I got a phone call from another young missionary. She'd been there about a year longer than me and called me to give me some "advice".

"Marsha," she cooed in a big sisterly way, "I just want to tell you that if you go to language school, your kid will go nuts without you and your husband will die of neglect. By all means you need to stay home and take care of them". Then as an afterthought she added "After all, no missionary wife has had formal language training for years, they just make do"

Wow, that was a shock. We had been told all through training that wives would be working alongside their husbands, being treated equally.

But on top of that, and possibly a bigger issue, was that with only weeks to go before school started, I still didn't have a babysitter for Trevor.

I was explaining my plight in English to our pastor's wife one day at church. She spoke a modicum of English and seemed to be understating my predicament. We would have to leave by no later than 6AM to get into Tokyo by the 9:00 start. Then we wouldn't be home till 5 or 6PM. That was every day of the week and kindergarten would only cover a fraction of that... if Trevor could even get himself there.

From the corner of the room and old lady slowly got up out of her chair and wandered over and sat down. After a few moments there began an animated conversation between Tochimoto san and the pastors wife, of which I had no clue.

Finally the pastor's wife turned to me and said, "This is Tochimoto san. She's 78 and says she gets up at 3AM every morning. She'd like you to consider having her as a babysitter for Trevor so that you can get the language. She would consider it her gift to God."

I was humbled and a little bit wary. Could she even see? Could she walk? What would Trevor think? I had a few days to think and pray and then the answer came as clear as a bell.

God must have reminded me of who I am, because just like that I thought, "Wait a minute. I've given myself to lifetime ministry! God did that for me!! If I can't speak, my children will suffer because I'll be locked in the house moping. My husband will be neglected because again, I'll be locked in the house peeping out the window wishing I knew what was going on!" I called the kind big sister back and told her what I'd decided. I think the next decision that day was that we wouldn't be friends.

In talking to the administration as we finalized our plans for school it was pointed out that recently word came down from the Mission that beginning immediately all women missionaries, married or not, would be taking full time language study. Gail and I were the first two to graduate in a generation. My big sister "non friend" resigned and left soon after. There were murmurings about 'failing to thrive'. Sad.

We invited Tochimoto san over for a visit and to see how we got along without a translator, and she immediately stole our hearts. Trusting our only child to a complete (and a little bit weird) stranger was hard, but those two fell in love and became an inseparable team.

Tochimoto san would become Trevor's Japanese Grandmother, guiding him through those first difficult days of adjustment, laughing and talking endlessly with each other in a Japanese dialect that I could never fathom. One day I queried her about a bandage on her hand and Trevor piped in, "Oh she fell over me when we were skipping to school!"

And so day one came. And went. Everybody survived. That day we invented the 'Three-Month Rule'.

It's really very simple. "We'll hang in for three months and then decide." On the same first day, all three of us toddled off to 'school', Trevor in Tochimoto san's arms and us on the bus.

The three months lasted two years with Tochimoto san, first as babysitter, and another 24 years as a friend. I still treasure the notes in hiragana (Japanese phonetic alphabet) that she took meticulously every day about Trevor. I kept them initially until I could read them and then realized it was pretty routine, "Pooped real good at 7:00, ate a lot at noon, slept for 2 hours" etc. Every day, every day. We would call at noon and say "Dai Jou Bu?" (OK?) to which she would replay "Ehhh" (Yup).

Of course I had to learn a few things with her. For example, don't walk in looking tired because she would grab you and start massaging, never mind that Trevor was jumping on your stomach wanting attention. Come to find out she was a master Shiatsu practitioner and was well known around the city. Also, never say you're hungry because something, usually weird, would come out of her bag and she would stand there making sure you ate all of it.

One morning at 6:00 AM as we were leaving, she came running out of the kitchen with two steaming mugs of the most disgusting white slurry I'd ever seen. I found out later in describing it that it's called "amazake" and it's the collected dregs from making the alcoholic mainstay of Japanese drinking culture, Sake. Yummm .We smiled and bowed as she did the same, and when we got a few blocks away, Tony stopped the car and we both opened our doors and poured it out. As we drove away the pavement was steaming and Tony laughed and said, "Someday we'll appreciate that woman". And we did.

Interestingly Tochimoto san was active and worked in the church till she died at her ageing daughter's house at 104. She outlived her darling Trevor by many years. I'm glad they're in Heaven together now, probably skipping around eating dried fish.

As part of our 'language study" requirement, we were told in no uncertain terms that for the next two years, we would be given no work assignment except that we learn to speak Japanese. To help facilitate that, we were "encouraged" to attend the Japanese church next door and cautioned not give in to the temptation to become a part of the international church that met upstairs. We abided by that encouragement – for the most part – although we did make some good friends who attended the international church, and enjoyed their connections to Yokosuka Naval Base.

Tony's turn to talk:

Our first day at Japanese church, which went by the name "Taki No Ueh" (meaning "above the waterfall"), was a real adventure. No one spoke English, although we found out much later that several were actually quite proficient, but for the sake of our language acquisition chose to keep that a secret. Sometimes allowances did need to be made, however. The first man who met us at the door kept pointing to his nose and saying "hitsuji!". In the first place, we didn't realize that Japanese point to themselves by pointing to their nose. So my first thought was, "Ah! A language lesson! *Hitsujii* means nose." Pointing to my ear, I asked, "What is this?"

"Ie! Ie!" (no no) he said, once again pointing to his nose and repeating, "Hitsuji!"

"Oh! You're sneezing! God bless you!"

Finally, he moved closer and said in a whisper, "Deacon. I am a deacon."

So he spoke English, eh? Good to remember. At the end of the worship service, as the final hymn was being sung, Marsha and I came forward to join the church, as we thought might be expected. But when the pastor gave us a horrified expression, I turned to the deacon and whispered, "Help me?"

He came up and I explained what we were wanting to do. At that, he kindly explained that this was not done. Instead, we would need to attend for some months while the church got to know us, after which *they* would decide if we were membership material. "In the meantime," the Deacon went on, "please give us a history of your face."

"My…..face?" I stammered. "Well, I do have some scars. This one was from a particularly bad case of chickenpox when I was 16. And over here, I had a shotgun blow up in my face, and…"

By now Marsha had put it together, remembering that the Japanese don't do well with "L" "R" and "Th" sounds. "Faith!" she whispered a little too loudly. "He's asking for a history of your *faith*!"

And so, while my wife stood there snickering, I shared our personal testimony with the church, kindly translated by the Deacon. And that, for the most part, was the last English spoken with these new brothers and sisters in Christ.

"Language acquisition," as our teachers at missionary orientation had impressed upon us, does not come naturally, but only after long, hard hours of effort that would prove as exhausting as moving coal with a short-handled shovel. No matter how "proficient" we may have imagined ourselves, any attempt to try new skills on a "real live Japanese person" resulted only in a painful 3-D color reminder of the depth and breadth of our ignorance. Most times, our efforts to communicate were met with either a blank stare, a terrified response that sounded something like "Solly! Solly! No speekie Engrish!" or an equally discouraging (but actually slightly affirming) reply in non-stop, lightning speed Japanese vocabulary that never found its way into our textbooks.

There is of course a universal exception to this rule of language acquisition, and it applies to every language on the planet. Set a missionary in the middle of a world where nothing spoken makes sense and it won't be long before he or she is reduced to a blubbering heap of dismal dismay. However (and here's the exception to the rule), place a *child* in that same situation and in the time it takes to make a set of vocabulary flash cards, that child is playing with new friends in a new language. It makes you wonder how the God-ordained fiasco at the Tower of Babel might have gone if children had been working there.

Our son, Trevor, was living proof of the Great Mystery. At three years of age, his brain was a newly-formatted zillion terabyte hard drive just waiting for data. Nothing escaped his eye nor his ear, and the synapses were working overtime looking for applications to plug into what he was learning.

His grasp of the language was disconcertingly spot-on, like the day I went to the service station, had the gas tank filled, then realized that I had left my wallet at home. I was trying desperately to explain my dilemma to the poor station attendant when he gently but firmly pushed me aside in order to speak to my 3-year old son in the back seat of the car. Before I could explain that, no, he was American too and unable to …, Trevor kept on playing with his Hot Wheels car and said rather absent-mindedly, "Daddy, he says you can bring your wallet back later."

I do want to give credit to our mission, who at the time of our arrival in Japan were undergoing a transition in language study methodology. Until then, our missionaries were sent to a school that focused on rote memorization and repetition. The idea was, if you looked at something long enough, eventually you'd get it. The sad truth in Japan, however, was that more and more missionaries were getting new interpretations of their call to Japan. Many were concluding that God must have been mistaken in sending them to this land, described by many over the years as a "missionary graveyard". Indeed, there were a few "amens" heard around the room when one of our folks found and repeated a quote by 17th century missionary to Japan Francis Xavier who declared, "Surely, Japanese is the devil's language."

There must be a better way, it was thought. Over the years, that "better way" has been developed and modified into what seems to be a fairly successful approach to language acquisition these days. It involves a lot of time spent on the street, trying and failing much as a child would. There is also less emphasis on grammar and more attention paid to the goal of successful communication.

In our case, arriving at a time when everyone was looking for answers, it was decided that we should be sent to a language school where none of our people had gone before, but that seemed to embody all of those positive aspects of learning. It was called Saint Joseph's Japanese Language School, and you guessed it, was Roman Catholic owned and operated. Until our arrival, they had existed for the sole purpose of training priests and nuns from all over the world. For a couple of Southern Baptist kids from America, this was a big deal for us. They were the enemy camp, after all! The prayer heard frequently was, "Lord protect us from the intents of the Mormons, the Jehovah's Witnesses and the Roman Catholics." But one of the first things we learned upon arrival at Saint Joe's was that the failure to communicate is a great field-leveler. Yeah, we would need to talk to these guys about Sacramentalism, Transubstantiation, and the authority of the Pope, but first we'd have to figure out how to say, "Is this the train that goes to Ginza?"

First contact with these strange apparitions whom we had never met but about which we had only heard stories was pleasantly delightful. Most of the new arrivals had come from all over Europe, and there was every extreme, from the Polish nuns in full habits to the British priests bedecked in paisley shirts and "hippie styled" crosses who laughed at the nuns because they "have no legs".

And in keeping with the "field leveler" I mentioned above, with only a few exceptions, the only common language we shared was the pitifully lacking Japanese we were trying to acquire. Break time in the courtyard was spent in desperate attempts to establish some kind of camaraderie in our brand new language. "Me Tony. You? This is a pen!"

There were several "Holy Orders" represented in the groups, from Dominican to Franciscan to Jesuit, and it soon became obvious that they were very similar to our own Protestant denominations, complete with suspicion and begrudging acceptance of each other. The firebrands seemed to come mostly from the Jesuits, and when I was finally able to raise the conversation beyond pens and pencils, I asked one Jesuit priest, "How do you manage to condone things like abortion and birth control when your fellow priests here and the Pope himself opposes them?"

"Oh it's simple," he answered. "We all agree that the Pope is infallible, but our various Orders differ in the degree to which we *obey* him. These issues you speak of are important, but in the parishes where we work, we do what must be done."

Social gospel programs and education systems that took precedence over everything including evangelism were common among the priests and nuns, just as they are among many of our Protestant brothers and sisters, and Marsha and I often had to bite our tongues rather than turn class time into an escalating debate that would leave no one the victor. We did find a few surprises among our fellow classmates, however. One early attempt at communicating involved the obvious difference in the crucifixes worn by the "legless" Polish nuns. While most featured the Suffering Savior, hanging dead on the cross, theirs were empty. One day Marsha pointed to the crucifix, then to the huge cross on the wall, and asked simply, "Jesus?"

The nun broke into a huge smile, pointed to the sky and practically yelled, "Ee not here! Ees alive!!" At that moment, we knew we had found a soul mate, the first of many we would discover over the next many years. Some really true believers aren't just Southern Baptist!

The weeks stretched into months, and before we knew it, the time had come to graduate from Saint Joseph's Japanese Language School. Quietly, I thought to myself, if I'm now considered level 5 on the scale of language proficiency, why can't I put a sentence together that the man at the fruit market can understand? Why do I still call Trevor when a salesman comes to the door? But I kept these thoughts mostly to myself and prayed that I wouldn't be asked to read my diploma out loud.

Chapter 6

Nathan

Something is becoming obvious as we trace the threads of the Master Weaver and the picture of our lives begins to take shape. It actually came to me during one of Tony's Bible studies, where he was unpacking the Book Of Genesis to a class of eager participants. He pointed out that the well-known Creation Story actually comes to us in two ways: chronologically and thematically. Genesis chapter one shows us the chronological account of those first six days when everything was called into being. Then in chapter two, we're shown the same story but with a view to the theme of the whole event: that is, God, and His relationship to Man. The style of writing is called "Toledoth" and you can find all kinds of examples throughout the Bible.

Why did we bring this up? Because chronologically, something happened between language school and our beginnings of ministry in Japan, but thematically it's so significant that we can't just give it a passing notice. So with your permission, I'm we're going to put our "Toledoth" hats on, and regress a bit.

Marsha here:

As mentioned above, while we were in Liberia in 1978, I suffered a severe miscarriage, hemorrhage and almost death. I won't go over that again, but as I lay recovering in the hospital, a man came into the room and introduced himself.

"Hello" he said as he crept up to the bedside. "I'm a doctor from the US, specifically Arkansas. I take my vacation every year and come here to help out with surgeries. A few days ago I heard of your dilemma", he continued, "and I'd like to give you my card. One of my service ministries is pairing missionaries with adoptable babies."

He must have seen the shocked look on my face, so he went on. I held my hand out a moment for him to stop. I needed to process this information, because honestly, I'd been trying just to stay alive the last several days, first with the surgery itself, then the bout of extreme malaria that they expected me to contract from the blood transfusions, and then just the shock of everything. Adoption, at this point, had never entered our minds.

After a minute, he could see that I'd settled, and he stepped closer, perhaps slowing to a more gentle tone and took my hand. "You see", he said kindly, "adoption is very difficult for people who don't have a permanent residence in the USA." I must have given him the, "you may continue" look, because he did.

"I run a ob-gyn clinic in Mena, Arkansas, and here's my card. Because of Arkansas laws, at least for a few more years, it is possible to get a baby and leave immediately. We would be honored to have you consider us." With that he left, and I would never see him again. I lost the card, but he'd planted the seed. Maybe someday we should add to our family.

To that end, we enquired about adoption at several maternity homes in the States. We were always met with different answers but the same meaning: "NO". One dumped us because we said we'd have to *think* about adopting a bi-racial baby. We weren't opposed to the idea; it had just never occurred to us before. If we could have collected our thoughts a moment sooner, we'd probably have two or three lovely bi-racial kids like our friends from Israel do, but instead we were shown the door. Another agency had a seven-year residency requirement. In 1980, adoption was practically impossible, even more so today, I'm guessing.

And so we found ourselves in Japan. We had almost finished our first year of language school and were looking forward to summer break. We were beginning to poke around the idea of Japanese adoption when we received a note from the mission office that a doctor from Arkansas was looking for us. Tony went into the office and came home hours later beaming from ear to ear. "I called them and they say they have a baby girl for us, come and get her!"

We were over the moon. Several calls back to the office had us on the track for a ticket for me to return, and I was packing, when another call came. Again Tony returned to the office, 90 minutes away, and made the call (we could only do international calls from the mission office). This time he came home dragging his feet, "The mother changed her mind," he whispered as he held me while I sobbed.

I cried all summer. Nothing could console me. A few matronly missionaries who heard the news either completely ignored me as if I hadn't gotten the ice cream I wanted or said pithy things like, "Oh, you shouldn't have gotten your hopes up," or "God must be teaching you a lesson."

They were right about one thing. God was teaching me that people alone, especially people with platitudes, can seldom comfort the hurting heart, so I just cried till I had no more tears, then gathered Trevor and Tony to me and went on living.

I learned a lot that summer, how casual comments said by friends could hurt like a hot iron. Talking about another little girl, a close playmate of Trevor's, who by then was almost 5, my friend said, "Oh, what would you expect, she's an only child you know." I just looked at them in dumb agony.

I wanted to say so badly, "Do you think her parents necessarily want that? You have no idea why she's an only child and that's no reason to judge her. It's not her fault." But I didn't say things like that. I was young and timid, and as I matured, I came to realize that everyone says things from time to time that they haven't thought through.

The only comfort anyone gave that was actually helpful was from a friend from seminary days. She wrote, "Marsha, this girl will always be yours…in your heart. You can pray for her like you will your own and one day hopefully you can meet her in Heaven. She'll be your 'prayer child'."

That gave me the thing I needed to hope for, and I have prayed for her, whoever and wherever she is, all these years. Ironically, my son married a girl just about exactly my prayer daughter's age and so I always look at Kylie and feel a sweet memory of another gift, one that I didn't get to hold in my arms but I could always hold in my heart.

After that debacle, the doctor was so chagrined that he said, "I promise I'll never call again unless I have a baby in my arms!" We agreed that that would be an excellent idea.

And so he did, almost.

On the morning of November 5th, 1980, we watched and tried to pick out the Japanese news as we waited with anticipation and then horror as our beloved President, Jimmy Carter, lost the election to Ronald Regan. Our language teachers who were Japanese had been saying for weeks, "Reagan…bakudan" (bomb) that's how the world saw him, no more weakness and kindness and Christian-ness… just "bomb".

Then we got the phone call from the mission office to come in and make an overseas call. It was the troublesome doctor in Arkansas who had promised never to call unless he had a baby. We shuffled our schedule around and arrived two hours later, made the call to him and this is what he said, "I've got a girl to be delivered in March and she wants you to have the baby!" he boomed excitedly into the phone. Among all the other reactions running through my mind right then, I thought to myself, what happened to 'having it in your arms before you called?"

"It's a girl!" Tony beamed.

"Uhm," I corrected kindly, "I think the 'girl' is the mother'," all the while jumping for joy anyway.

And so we began the preparations again. Not wanting to 'get my hopes up' as I had been advised, we signed a promissory note that we'd take the baby unconditionally, made deposits in accounts to support the mother, got a plane ticket for mid-February so that I could go and 'get ready' for the baby, etc. From this point we would be doing all correspondence with a lawyer in order to make the adoption legal.

Of my pregnancies, I say that this one was the hardest. I had four long months of waiting, but none of the daily reminders to enjoy like feeling the kicking, etc. Occasional updates were devoured and read and reread. Again the mission seemed not to 'get it'. I was at a baby shower for two missionaries, both due in February as well, when someone turned to me and said in a conspiratorial whisper, "And when can we have a shower for you?"

"Any time now since we're adopting a baby in March," I quipped back.

She offered me a blank stare and turned to talk to someone else. Fortunately when I got back with the baby I was given a localized shower. The missionaries weren't invited and that was OK with me.

Trevor was 5 ½ by now, and he and I began to have a friendly competition about whether it would be a boy or a girl. He was fervently praying for a boy because he said he'd be 'hazukashii' (embarrassed) to have a sister. By now he was comfortably bi-lingual so the Japanese word best expressed how he felt. I of course, was pulling for a girl, possibly just wanting something less of a terror than Trevor.

On February 14th, a month before the baby was due, I set off on the long cross-Pacific flight to Los Angeles where I would change planes for Denver. When I landed, I called my Daddy to tell him I was safely on the continent.

"You have a son," was his greeting.

"WHAT?" I was in shock. Was he OK, a month early and all?

"Seven pounds, fourteen ounces," was his answer.

"Oh! OK, His name is Nathan Robert Woods," I shouted into the receiver (Robert was my daddy's name). Somehow in the excitement of writing down the details, time, weight etc, I'd torn my ticket in half, but the agent accepted it with hearty congratulations when I explained why.

The next morning, after briefly sleeping at my folks, I was on a plane to Fort Smith, Arkansas. The baby and the lawyer with whom we'd been working lived in Mena, a smaller town about two hours from Fort Smith.

When we disembarked the small prop airplane, we entered an old Quonset hut that was posing as an airport. A large group of black people met a large group of passengers with cheers and hugs, and then it was just me and a scraggly looking teenager in a faded t-shirt, slumped against the wall. Looking around for other options, I finally approached the derelict and asked tenuously, "Are you the lawyer?"

He stood to attention and offered his hand and in his big booming courtroom voice said, "Are YOU the missionary?" I smiled and he continued, "Bob Keeter Junior, at your service." And out we went to crawl up into his pick up for the ride to Mena.

We quickly became friends, laughing and talking all the way to his house. He was 24, married with three little kids and wanted to 'make a difference', so he was assisting in this adoption. He'd already been a lawyer for a couple of years. He insisted on stopping for pizza in a run down truck stop. He said I needed to eat so I could approach the next few days with sufficient strength. As we were waiting for our order, a waitress sashayed by wearing pink leotards and a baggy sweatshirt. Her hair was piled on her head in an attempt to look fashionable but it wasn't working. "That's what I was looking for when they said "Missionary", Bob quipped.

I walked into his house to be tackled by three little kids. We laughed as Bob and his wife pulled them off me and explained that they didn't often have company. I looked up across the room to see the oldest, maybe 4 or so, holding Nathan up, out of the bassinet, at full length, by his EARS!

"Now you put that baby down, what'd I tell you?" shouted the mom as she ran to rescue my precious son. And then in an instant I had in my arms the most beautiful sweet baby I'd ever seen. At two days old, he'd plumped out and was just beautiful. They gave us the guest room and we just sat and looked at each other all night. I don't remember sleeping.

The next morning, we said our goodbyes to the family and I went, babe in arms, to the courthouse with Bob to see the judge. In his office I swore to do the best we could as parents, and the judge shook my hand and stamped my papers. He was ours. Then off again we went in the pick up straight to the airplane. We planned to stop and buy some formula on the way since he'd drunk his way thru all but one bottle that came from the hospital. Somehow that didn't happen, and as we gathered our bits to alight at the airport, Bob adopted his 'lawyer voice' and said, "Now you understand that both you and the mother have agreed that this has happened, and we don't expect to ever see you again."

I honestly hadn't ever thought of the mother's privacy, I was more worried about her finding ME. She legally had 6 months to change her mind, but in MY mind, we would never let him go. I boarded the plane with a screaming infant. It was time to eat and all I had was a few ounces of a bottle left. I dug in my bag, dusted off the bottle and handed it to the stewardess. "Can you run some boiling water over the nipple please".

"Oh, how old is the baby?" she cooed.

"Three days."

"Oh my Lord! And how do YOU feel?"

"Great, thanks," I said, as I turned slowly, ostensibly to put my bag in the overhead, but really to show off my slim figure. One of the only perks of adopting; might as well enjoy it, …… I thought to myself.

And so I flew to Colorado; introduced him around and found

myself on day four of the big adventure sitting in bed at 5 am crying because he just didn't sleep if you let go of him. Everything I'd wanted and now I just wanted some SLEEP!

Later, I called Tony and Trevor and said,

"Trevor, you got your wish, here is your little brother!" In the days long before Skype or even internet, Trevor had to be satisfied to listen to a few happy gurgles. They were buds from the beginning, Nathan calling him "Buba" from the moment he could talk.

As I write this now, 38 years later, I think that Nathan was the 'girl' I wanted. I just didn't know that what I was wanting wasn't frilly dresses and giggly tea parties, (that would come later) but just someone reasonable….. someone who didn't wake up screaming and go to bed screaming. Nathan, as he grew, was my quiet, happy child, usually choosing to hang back instead of barge in. Reserved. What a guy he is!! Definitely true to his name, "Gift of God".

I got back to Japan and Language school when Nathan was three weeks old. It took that long to get a proper passport in his new name as well as a Japanese visa. I'll never forget kneeling down and putting our son in his father's arms in the exit lane of customs at the Narita Airport. I cried, I think for joy........and maybe just a little for relief as I had brought in a 7 lb roast in my luggage. Hey, meat was a delicacy in Japan, seldom affordable.

Straight back into classes (but I did leave Nathan with a young navy wife, not with Trevor and his beloved 80-year-old Tochimoto san) and managed to 'graduate' with the class on time.

Now back to the chronological thing…

Chapter 7

Sendai

Now you remember that we initially felt a 'call' to Sendai the first summer we were in Japan. Nothing had happened in the two ensuing years to change that feeling and we were confidant that we'd be moving there when we graduated.

Unfortunately, the higher ups in the mission had different plans for us. In the southern part of the country, "Friendship House Ministry" had taken hold, and they were looking for people to staff their Kobe one.

Basically, a Friendship House is an all-purpose facility offering everything from English lessons to kendo classes to Bible studies.

It was a socially acceptable way to bring the Gospel into the community, and Jim Watters, the main Friendship House director for the mission had decided that this was a job for the Woods.

We did go down to Kobe at his request and visit the place, but as attractive as it all looked, it had absolutely zero appeal for us. We told him so, and over coffee, and Jim laid down the gauntlet. "I just need to tell you," he said smiling, "unless you have some kind of political "karma" in the mission, you're coming to Kobe."

That was tough to hear, especially after our recent interest in Sendai. But at that stage, we didn't feel we had earned the right to go against the mission's decisions.

Then came another turning point. A couple of months after Jim's "political karma" statement, I found myself in a meeting of mission directors who were beginning to make decisions about our upcoming assignment. When I was asked for any thoughts on the matter, I said rather quietly, "Apparently we're going to Kobe to work in the Friendship House." Later, around the coffee pot, I was approached by Bob Hardy, one of the planners and a man I respected a great deal. Placing his hand on my shoulder, he said, "I sense that you're not completely sold on Kobe."

That opened the floodgates, and I unloaded all of our frustrations, hopes and prayers on the poor man. He promised to follow up, and he did just that. Before Christmas, four months short of graduation from language school, Marsha and I were officially assigned to Sendai, where we were to "research, develop and establish a city-wide ministry to students, making use of any resource available, including the five Baptist churches and the area's thirteen universities."

At last the day had come. In the summer of 1981, we said goodbye to language school and hello to Sendai. I have to admit, it was a little disconcerting that I was still unable to read all the big words on my diploma, but as everyone reminded us, "You'll learn and retain all the words you need to do the work."

At the Boatwright's suggestion, we settled at once in Sendai's downtown Baptist Church, pastored by Rev. Amano. I loved the man, but with my developing abilities in Japanese and the fact that he mumbled in a southern dialect I had never studied, it was almost impossible to understand him. The point was driven home rather painfully several months after our arrival on New Years Day.

Japanese attend church on New Years Day no matter what day it falls on. It's a good custom, I think, to give the first day of the year to the Lord. We came waltzing into the worship service just as the music was beginning. We didn't anticipate anything too long or grueling and were fairly relaxed, kids on our lap. Settling into a pew, I started skimming the bulletin to see how much I could understand. You know I mentioned about the Japanese phonetic alphabet, *hiragana* and the Chinese-based characters, *kanji*? Then there's that third set of characters, another phonetic alphabet called *katakana*, reserved for foreign words, like "Ai su ku ri mu" (ice cream), "Ma ku do na ru do su" (MacDonalds) and "To ni ud zu" (Tony Woods). That last set of katakana leapt off the page of the bulletin, and right beside it were the two kanji that means, "sermon". Now I realized MY name was next to "sekkyo" or sermon. Racing down to the front while everyone sang, I held the bulletin up to Rev. Amano's face. "What is this?" I demanded.

"You're bringing today's sermon," he answered calmly, as if I'd asked about the weather.

"That's impossible!" I almost screamed.

"We spoke about this several weeks ago. You said you would do it."

There's a method of conversation when speaking Japanese. Even if you don't understand something, you keep repeating the word, "Hai, hai." Some people mistakenly think that means, "Yes" but actually it means, "Keep talking; I'll get this eventually." Apparently I had "hai hai'd" while Rev. Amano was inviting me to preach, but unbeknownst to him, I never reached the "got it" stage of the conversation.

The next moment I found myself at the front door of the church. Marsha, sensing something amiss, came and asked me what was wrong. I explained, and she said, "How can I help you?"

"Keep me from running," I whispered.

She did, and I managed to deliver something that morning, but I doubt that anyone knows what I said, including myself. It was a defining moment, however, and it prompted me to take to heart what a fellow missionary had told me during language school. "By the time you get out there," he said, pointing to the door with his chin, "have yourself at least a shallow barrel of sermons, songs, baptism, child's blessing and Lord's Supper notes, and a prayer or two. You never know when you'll be called upon." Since that time, I've never let my barrel go empty, and it's served me well.

Marsha on Education:

In all the hubbub of getting ourselves through language school, adopting and now moving to Sendai to start ministry, we'd somehow given little thought to our children's education. Maybe it was because we trusted God to lead us to safe places, or we were just naive and irresponsible.

At any rate, Trevor was just six and still had a year or so in Japanese kindergarten and Nathan was just a few months old. We'd worry about the future when the future came.

Trevor went every day to Shokei Gakkuin Yochen, a kindergarten run by the educational department of a revered Baptist University. They'd be able to handle the little bundle of energy and we trusted them.

There were other missionaries who had their children in the kindergarten as well, so we were in good company. More than once we mothers misunderstood the notes sent home (because we were all fairly new and couldn't read well) and sent our kids with or without lunch, or not dressed properly for a field trip, etc. We laughed and our kids became familiar with embarrassing parents who were in fact, illiterate immigrants. They bonded as they sat in the office and shared the secretary's lunch since everyone else was on a field trip or such.

Then he 'graduated' and we were faced with the first grade. It seemed natural that he go to the local grade school as he had many friends (and so did I) from the kindergarten who were continuing on to the first grade. Elementary schools are area based and you must go to the one in your area, so Trevor wouldn't be with any other missionary kids, but by now he could hold his own both in the language and in the culture.

Off he went. There was a huge ceremony on the first day as parents dressed up, corsages and all and accompanied their children into the world of school. There is a reason why this day was and still is so significant.

We Westerners have a different idea about education. We feel that while necessary, it does not supersede the role of home life and parental authority. First and foremost we (hopefully) have the family, and then the teacher and education must revolve off the wishes from the former. Of course there are boundaries and these are sometimes stretched to a bad end, but in Japan, at least in 1982, the philosophy of education was diametrically opposed to having a parent in charge. Instead, the school reigned. From first grade thru university, education comes first, parental wishes, plans and personal schedules last. Not to be too harsh, but I believe that both the strength and failure of the Japanese nation is that Japanese are raised to be 'group first, person second".

So of course it was difficult for me to turn him loose out of my front door, just 6 1/2, to walk the mile or so to school. I never sure what time he would be home because that was up to the teacher. Of course he was decked out in his hat (bright yellow) as well as a cover for his Government approved and regulated "Randosel" (leather back pack). The Randosel was black because he was a boy. Girls have red ones. On it in a prominent place was his ID, including blood type. The cover for protection against rain and traffic was again bright yellow, in order to be seen in all weather, at least until the end of the first grade. He would be walking on a 'decided school walking path' thru the neighborhood to the school. It was not direct, but was selected due to the limited traffic. This practice continues in force today. He was never to be off that path unless it was the last few steps to his home.

He would be in a class of 30 to 40 kids, eat a lunch brought in and served by rostered classmates at his desk. He could not leave any food and no one ever did. Then at the end of the school day, he would be dismissed only when the teacher inspected their cleaning of the classroom and halls and said they could go.

Talk about rigid. But the routine seemed to suit Trevor. So much that one day as we had plucked him off the decided walking route in an effort to get him to a dentist appointment, he casually pointed out a house along the way, "Oh, that's where I stop and go 'unchi' (poop) every day" he beamed.

To our shocked interrogation, we realized that she was a complete stranger, no connection to any of his friends and he didn't know her name, but apparently she always opened the door for him and let him come in and use the toilet and then leave. I was too horrified to respond. We told him to stop immediately and I think I baked her some cookies, which she accepted with quiet aplomb as if this thing should be expected by foreigners.

And then just so that there was no mistake understanding 'whos' in charge', one day, in fact it was June 1ˢᵗ, Trevor went AWOL from school.

We were sitting at our fellow missionary's house with a board appointed psychiatrist. This particular psychiatrist made her way thru our missionaries on the field every few years to see that we were in the best mental health to do the job.

In fact, we were struggling in our relationship with this particular missionary family. Most of it was our failure to understand them and their needs, but it seemed to be exacerbated in the behavior of our children. We were proud of Trevor and his accomplishments while they struggled with trusting the Japanese and were trying to educate their kids themselves. These differences in philosophy spilled into our ministries and were beginning to affect our lives. Things weren't getting better as we gritted our teeth at each other. Then the phone rang.

It was our pastor, Noguchi Sensei and all he said was "Trevor's been found and he's OK."

We dashed out of the meeting to the school and there we found a most chagrined little boy. It seemed that on June 1st, every Japanese school in the nation from Hokkaido to Okinawa, open the school's swimming pools and start to swim.

Well, Trevor wasn't having a bar of that. It was most likely only 50 degrees outside and probably windy. As they stood lined up, little scrawny first graders, waiting to jump in, Trevor told his teacher that he had some "Yoji" (business) to attend to. I'm assuming he thought that Trevor needed to use the bathroom so he excused him.

Trevor went back to the classroom, dressed, packed his Randosel and took off for a friend's house. The mother had the sense to call us, but since we weren't home, she called the church and got Noguchi Sensei. Then the mother took Trevor back to school and to his surprise the entire class were scouring the grounds for him.

We arrived, talked with the teacher and Trevor and then walked together with Trevor and the teacher back into the class room where his 30 plus classmates were waiting, even though the bell had rung 10 or 15 minutes before. There, with remarkable maturity, I thought, he bowed low and apologized to the class for putting them out, making them worry and making them late leaving.

Then all was forgiven and nothing was mentioned again. The class was dismissed and as the children scampered home. At that point he was passed back into our care and as we walked toward the car in silence, we figured he'd been punished enough. I think we might have been secretly proud of him for putting common sense in front of blind obedience, but we never told him.

By the time we had a furlough in America for his second grade, we came back with the decision that we would start an American School of some sort for the handful of missionary kids in our area. Japanese school was good, but a Japanese Harvard Graduate professor who knew Trevor well as he was the principal of the preschool Trevor attended, had said to us,

"Japanese school is the best in the world until about the 3rd grade and after that they start putting maniacal pressure on the kids to succeed at all costs of creativity or happiness." And then he continued, "Trevor will not thrive in this environment". Actually after the pool incident, we knew he was right.

And so with a short term missionary from the US, we began a little school in a rented room about 5 blocks from the house. Trevor and four or five students from three other families were 'Miss Sharon's" students. Grades 3-6, I believe.

Two years went by, and our kids seemed happy. The other parents complained about the teacher from time to time, saying that she wasn't working hard enough, that the children had reported that she'd let the children have a 45 minute recess while she was reading a book, etc.

My thought was "What do you expect from a volunteer? We better keep her happy or we'll be in big trouble."

And right on schedule, Miss Sharon completed her two years and went home and we found ourselves in "Big Trouble" when the replacement failed to show up. One mother begged me to take her four children in with me as I was realizing that I would probably have to teach my Trevor. Yes. I'm a teacher by trade but not a masochist, so I declined the extra 4 and we agreed that we'd order up correspondence material and get busy teaching our own children. The other two families were fortunately on furlough in the states!

When Trevor was finished with the 5th grade, we all breathed a sigh of relief as he quipped the line from 'A Tale of Two Cities',

"It was the best of times and the worst of times."

It's possible that the 'best of times' was when a missionary's mother was visiting and taught him for a couple of months. Another section of time my niece Rhonda came out and taught him as well, and even with that much help, it had taken a toll.

I'm not a home school teacher, that's for sure. I think it has to do with patience. I'm fine teaching someone else's progeny, just not mine! I'll never forget the assessment of the year from the mother of four and I still smile when I think about it today.

"I can't believe I EVER criticized Miss Sharon. Believe me, this last year I've heard myself say over and over, "Get your work done and go out play in the street, I need some SPAAACE!" We could both laugh with a new understanding of what angels those who teach are.

By this time Nathan was deeply involved in his kindergarten, a place called Meisen Yochien. It is run by a group of passionate people who believe it is God's will for their group to both 'warn the people' (of Christ's immanent arrival) and educate people for Christ. As 'unusual' as they are, they were a perfect fit for Nathan because the campus had live animals everywhere (his love from an early age) but at the same time was very structured, which we were finding out that Nathan thrived on. My Trevor would have gone nuts in the same environment, but God is faithful to put people where they need to be. Soon he graduated from the three year kindergarten, and was ready for the first grade.

Our plan was to put Nathan into a different public school than Trevor had gone to, mainly because his best friend, another missionary kid, Andy, would be there as well. Nathan wasn't quite as 'aggressive' as Trevor, and we felt that a friend would be nice for him. Of course he had a lot of Japanese friends, but an American friend (and his parents) would be nice for us all.

He did fine in school as he also was bilingual, but actually learning didn't come quite as easy for him. We still laugh about the day he came home with a sentence he'd very carefully written out in the Japanese calligraphy style that's so popular with the more 'cultured' individuals. His style was perfect, but he'd mistaken one vowel so that instead of saying "I want to ride a horse", it said "I want to become a horse"......or maybe that's what he meant as he to this day is quite the animal lover. Anyway, things were going well in the education sector. All we were lacking was a good facility for the American school.

And then one day, for some reason, I decided that I'd like to take on a government agency in the form of the 'Bureau of International Development for the City of Sendai' Although generally I am a shy person, sometimes things just have to be done, so I marched myself into the office downtown and gave them the question,

"What are your plans for an International school if you call yourself so up to date? After all, there are over a million people in this town now, and every year we're seeing more and more foreigners". I was answered with blank stares, but they accepted my card and ushered me to the door.

By now we were holding our American School in a rental house near ours. I seemed to be the only one that was bothered by the fact that it had an "Obenjo" (pit toilet, like an outhouse, but inside) to take care of the needs of 20 people, but that's just me. We had procured, through another mission, not one, but THREE teachers. The house had several rooms so the teachers could live upstairs and the kids could be educated downstairs.

One of the teachers was about a month late because she had no passport......or birth certificate for that matter. I don't remember how old she was, but she was old. The other, a couple, were young and energetic. When school began we had 13 or 14 kids, all missionary kids. We were growing.

I'll never forget the disappointment Trevor felt to be placed in the old lady's class when she finally arrived. It was just him and several younger girls. We were told that Trevor was the only boy they deemed 'controllable' for the older woman. I think it was a good life lesson for him to live with what you didn't want, and he seemed to do fine. The teacher was actually 'old school' as well, and she was good for our kids. They learned a lot under her strict tutelage. Months passed after my visit to the city offices and then, one day the phone rang.

"May we speak to Mr. Tony Woods please," the female voice said in Japanese.

"He's not here at the moment, may I take a message" I replied just as formally.

"This is the office of International Affairs and there is a school here in town that would like to present a proposition to...... Mr. Tony Woods," she continued, equally formally, obviously reading his name off of a memo.

"Oh!" I almost shouted into the phone, dropping the politeness and reverting to my broken and improper Japanese. "He knows nothing about this, it's ME that they want to talk to. When shall we meet up?"

There was a pause.

Then timidly, she said, continuing to be secretarially formal "Uhm. Just a minute please." After some time she returned and said, "I guess you can come along as well if you'll bring Mr. Woods." Then she proceeded to give me the name and address of a very expensive restaurant and we decided on a time to meet.

When I hung up the phone it dawned on me. Wives NEVER conduct business, at least not with the Office of International

Concerns! Wives NEVER go out to eat with grown ups, what had I done!

I called our pastor Noguchi Sensei, hoping he could rescue me somehow. I was thinking maybe he could call and say something about me being left untied for an unguarded moment and mistakenly answering the phone, and of course, this recalcitrant wife wouldn't be capable of coming. Something like that. Instead, I heard him laugh heartedly into the phone.

"Oh! When will you learn?" He said lovingly as laughed some more. Then he collected himself and said, "They're interested in working with foreigners, you might as well go along and let em' see what they're getting into!

And so Tony and I, dressed to the nines and shaking in our boots, arrived at the chic restaurant. We were met by four or five men in suits.

The evening started a bit tense, with a lot of bowing and the like, but almost immediately they dropped the formalities as well as their language level and I think all in all they rather enjoyed the candidness of the evening. Maybe they were surprised that they'd achieved all this without alcohol. And a bond was formed. We began to hatch a plan. Our missionary friends circled away from us and sucked their teeth, whispering things like 'Selling to the devil' and such, but we proceeded because it seemed to us anyway, that if we strictly maintained intellectual control, they could build their million dollar building (they did) pay our selected and vetted teachers imported from America (they did) and leave us to be who we are, which they also did.

The only concession was that we changed the name from 'Sendai Christian Academy' which we'd given ourselves to being called lately, to The Sendai American School. That suited us anyway because the original "Christian Academy" in Tokyo was beginning to suggest we pay franchise rights, etc.

We were confident that we missionaries, as the exclusive members of the board, would still determine *who* went to our school, *who* taught at our school and *what* they studied, and we did......at least for the next several years.

By Nathan's third grade, he had begun attending the American school two days a week, continuing in Japanese school the other three. It was (at least in our eyes) the best of both worlds. Trevor graduated from the 8th grade there. Our plan was that when we got back from furlough in a year, Trevor would be going to Tokyo for high school, but sadly, life would change so that that didn't happen.

As an epilogue, my brother-in-law, who was by then a single and much loved ex-brother-in-law, (but that's another book in itself) came out from the States to be principal. We were on furlough but the story goes that when he sat down with our missionaries, several who were by then become quite liberal, he said, "Do you want an international school or a Christian school, I can do either." They chose International, much to the delight of our hosts, the Japanese.

Within a few years we were gone, through the twists and turns of our life, and SAS had been doing fine for about 10 years. That's when they hired their first Buddhist teacher. We sometimes thought that this might happen down the track somewhere, but we didn't expect it to be an American!

We haven't kept up. I do know it's still running, and our names may still be listed as founding fathers, but when we were asked a few years ago to contribute an article about the beginnings but leave out any Christian ties, we realized that those first missionaries might have been right, I had been playing with fire.

The people who asked for the article didn't get it from me because I wouldn't comply with the omission of the Christian heritage. Goodness, Harvard and Yale started as Christian Institutions and it didn't hurt them any. What's the big need to totally erase the history?

We need to say a word here about "Nojiri", because it was such an intricate part of our time in Sendai. The term itself was destined to carry more significance than we could have ever imagined, but it began slowly, back during the first days of our time in Japan. It was summer, 1979, and we had just returned from our very first mission meeting, followed by a "Look See" trip up to Sendai. Back home in Yokohama, we made our way to our little Japanese church, which was conveniently next door. As we were taking off our shoes, looking for the bulletin (which he had no hope of reading but it made a nice fan), we noticed that the Japanese looked surprised to see us.

"Hachi gattsu," (which means *August*) one lady said in a mixture of Japanese and English, "No rake?"

We finally concluded that the word was "lake", and the question alluded to the fact that there was a missionary routine here that we had yet to discover. It seems that since the 1800s most foreigners, whether missionaries or diplomats, headed out of Tokyo in August. Because the Japanese have their "Obon" week, where they gather, try to pay their respects to the dead as well as visit with their families, mostly from out in the country, most foreigners had no reason to stick around since their target Japanese were all out doing Buddhist ceremonies. It is also ghastly hot and humid in August, with very few air conditioners, so for generations, Tokyo became a 'ghost city' during the month of Obon.

Originally the sleepy town of Karuizawa attracted the foreigners, as well as the rich and Royal Japanese. It's deeply wooded, nice and cool with waterfalls and beauty everywhere you look. It was hours west of Tokyo, deep in the mountains. In the 1800's it took a full day of travel by steam train or horse and buggy. The 'Season' lasted about 6 weeks and was full of high teas and other impressive social occasions. Because things were cheap, there were and still are a number of magnificent houses built in the turn of the century still standing as they hadn't been bombed during the war. Everyone knew there was no strategic need to wipe out a sleepy hamlet mostly inhabited by foreigners, and then only during 'the season'.

And then in the 50's the prince of Japan, Akihiko, met a young and beautiful commoner named Michiko on the tennis court of the Hoshino Hotel and the rest is history. As fate would have it, in the early 1920's a few more courageous missionaries 'discovered' another wooded mountain on a lake, far from anywhere, but now, because of improved transport, again, only about 8 hours away from Tokyo instead of the mere 4 hours it was now taking to get to Karuizawa. Considered 'renegades' these more plucky missionaries opened up Nojiri Lake Association, where people could dispense with the fancy afternoon teas and climb mountains instead.

After discovering no one seemed to expect us to be in town and checking around, we found that we could rent a cabin for a week, so we decided to try it out. That seemed to be what we were doing in our free time, 'checking things out', but we had to say we couldn't imagine why missionaries would want to vacation together. We found that in compound living in Africa, the last thing you wanted to do was 'hang out' with people you lived and worked with every day.

However, having just experienced the thrill of Mission Meeting, where we had that once a year meeting of like minds and more importantly of like language, we thought maybe we might catch on to this 'rake' thing as well. Also, I was still grieving the 'loss' of the adoption and without knowing it, probably needed some time to relax and reflect.

And catch on we did. We had a better trip this time, maybe because of increased skills or better directions, but we arrived in under 8 hours. We found a very, very dirty cabin but it was right above the lake, just in the hub of all the action.

It was dirty because all cabins, even to this day, are dirty after being closed for the winter, or many winters if the owners had moved back to the states etc. When I say "closed for the winter", we're talking about being sometimes completely buried in snow for 3-5 months. That would take its toll on any wooden building, especially one built in the 20's with no nails.

Our friends from mission meeting all gathered and showed us how to get all the bugs out, the windows unshuttered and open, and clean. Musty sheets were pulled out of ancient trunks, aired and put on beds and we were in business. Trevor was out the door the next day for the time of his life.

In the years to come, "Nojiri" would become our special word for a magical place. So many happy memories there, starting with me on my hands and knees scrubbing out all the hurt of my heart after our missed adoption of a dream fulfilled.

We were able to visit most summers for the next 20 years. Sometimes, after we bought a cabin several years after that first summer, and got it weatherproof and fixed it up somewhat, we were able to even go up in the winter from time to time. My children still call it their 'home town'.

❧

Now that we were settled into Sendai, become members of the downtown church and had enrolled Trevor in preschool, it was time to get to work. That time in our lives was some of the scariest and at the same time the most exhilarating experience we had known so far. Up until now, our work had been pretty well defined by those over us. But now we had been given a huge task to do and not a lot of framework within which to do it. Our job was to "establish student work" in Sendai; that much was clear. But how exactly was one to go about it?

We decided to start at the top and work our way down. Tohoku Daigaku is one of Japan's "Big Five" universities, the Harvard of the Orient. Marsha and I figured, if some Christians could graduate from Tohoku Dai, then the repercussions could be felt all over. We didn't know how to set up an appointment, but thanks to a young student we had met earlier, an appointment was made to meet the head of Tohoku's English department. With some feeling of trepidation, we walked boldly onto the campus of one of the top five universities in the country. Several students even stepped aside and bowed as we went by, assuming naturally that we were some kind of visiting professors.

Following the signs to the English department, we found the main office, asked in our best Japanese to speak to the department head, and sat down to wait. A few minutes later, a man came out, I stood, bowed deeply, offered him my card and then proceeded. "I apologize; we're new in town and weren't sure exactly about protocol." I was relieved to hear him responding in English. That was either because my Japanese was so bad (a very real possibility) or because this was after all the English department and I was obviously a foreigner. He invited us to come into his office, offered us a cup of green tea and then asked how he could help.

"Before becoming Baptist missionaries, we were English teachers in America. Here are our qualifications," I said, handing over a file with our diplomas and certifications. That got his attention, so I pressed on. "We would be very happy to teach a class or two in English conversation here at Tohoku Daigaku. But we have a problem." His face fell and he asked,

"What problem?"

"Because we're missionaries, our salary comes from our mission. As such, we would not be allowed to receive support from any other sources. We would have to teach for free."

Now it was becoming more difficult to read his face. He paused, took a sip of tea, then said, "I believe we could work something out."

In 1982, there were very few foreigners in Japan. Even in a university town like Sendai, the local census indicated there were only about 100 Caucasian foreigners in residence. Finding a native speaker in English was extremely difficult, and so this man sitting in front of us was thinking to himself, "I've just won the lottery!"

Both Marsha and I were given two classes each immediately, required English for freshmen. Later we 'graduated' to upper classmen elective English which was much more fun for us to teach, as the students really wanted to learn instead of the exhausted freshmen that were still reeling from the fact that they'd even got in and weren't all that interested in studying.

Soon, I suggested a course in British novels, using C.S. Lewis' *Lion, Witch and Wardrobe* as a text book. The class was conducted mostly in English with a few asides now and then for explanation of specific points. The class loved it, and as we drew near to the end of the book, I said, "Now let's talk about allegory. This book looks on the surface to be a simple children's story. But underneath lies a complex allegory where nothing is as it seems." Then we started talking about characters, and their comparison to people in the Bible. By the time we got to Aslan and His role as Perfect Sacrifice, the students were hammering me with questions. I said, "Well, I'm thinking of making a class down at Sendai Baptist Church where we could talk more in depth about the subject, without worrying about an exam, of course." They jumped at it, and overnight we had a student ministry!

The approach was so successful, I visited two more campuses,

Shokei University and Miyagi Gakuin, housing both high school and university campuses. These two schools were already Christian-supported "mission schools", so they were quick to offer me not only English conversation courses but Bible studies as well. As always, I accepted no money for my services, but in return was given absolute freedom on all three campuses. I took advantage of the opportunity by spending all the time I could in campus coffee shops. I had a beard then, probably the only one among all the few foreigners in town, so I was easy to spot.

One day at Miyagi Gakuin, I was sitting at a table drinking coffee and reading my Bible (another broadcasting tool) when a high school girl walked up and started speaking in passable English. "Excuse me, but I saw the beard and I saw the Bible, so I think you must be Woods Sensei." I acknowledged that I was and she continued: "So you're a missionary, is that right?"

"Yes," I said.

"So when and where is your Bible study being held?"

I had to think quick, so I took a sip of coffee before answering. "Thursday nights, 7:00 at my house, with my wife, Marsha. Here's my card."

I didn't know it at the time, but that was a watershed moment. From that week on, Thursday nights at 7:00 would never be the same. The high school girl not only came faithfully, but sent me students by the droves. We quickly organized into a simple English conversation program, followed by a brief devotion in Japanese along with a simple meal. It soon became apparent that we needed a name, so after a couple of false starts, we settled on "Searchlight Club: a Light for the Mind and a Light for the Heart". Even today, nearly 40 years later, remnants of Searchlight Clubs can be found all over Japan.

One of the products of Searchlight Club was a girl by the name of Yukiko. From the start, she was hungry to know the Gospel. Every chance she had, she would be at our house, asking questions. Part of me thought that she was only coming for the English practice, but I figured no harm was being done. Then one day she came in sat on the floor with Marsha at our *kotatsu* (a low coffee table) and was silent. "So," Marsha asked. "What questions do you have for me today?"

She remained quiet, then took a breath and started talking at light speed. "I am going to speak Japanese now because what I have to say is very important and I want to get it right. Actually I have no questions. I understand what I need to do and I am ready to receive Christ. Can you pray with me please?"

Marsha said a little prayer under her breath, then began to share the simple message of salvation with her. Finally, she thought of Noguchi Sensei, whose church was just a few blocks away. Calling him up, she said, "Uh, Sensei? I have a situation here, and I think we need your help." He came at once, talked some more with Yukiko then we all prayed together. After getting her assurances that it was okay with her parents, after a few months we baptized her at Noguchi's church and she settled right into the church family.

As it turned out, her parents were 'OK with her decision because she had not mentioned it to them, and the day when they accidentally learned of it, they kicked her out of the house and demanded to see me. I went to their home in fear and trepidation, taking backup in the form of Noguchi Sensei. Yukiko's father was a short, stocky man who'd had a rough life. He was also an angry man, to say the least. Eventually though, we convinced him that his daughter becoming a Christian was not the worst thing that could happen, and in fact Christians seemed to do better coping with the rigors of life than others.

He finally relented, although by now Yukiko, having what she considered no viable option for housing, had moved in with her boyfriend, Takakazu, and had no interest in coming home. One day they came to see us, asking if I would marry them. I was happy to hear that Yukiko was under conviction about living with Tak, but still concerned that *he* wasn't a Christian. Of course she was adamant that he was very close and finally, I got a promise from him that he would openly seek to know her faith and respond when Christ spoke to him.

I officiated at their wedding, my first in Japanese, at the beautiful chapel on the Miyagi Gakuin campus. Both Trevor and Nathan were attendants, and little Nathan stood at attention (he was about five, I think) for the whole service, even though Marsha was trying to get his attention to pull him aside. Leave it to Nathan to see the job through to completion!

Tak and Yukiko would laugh later as they shared with me how I had butchered the ceremony, selecting the wrong pronunciations for most of the kanji in the formal ceremony that I had pulled from a book somewhere. "We promised," they said, "but most of the time had no idea what we were promising!"

Now, in the interest of brevity, let me skip ahead about 25 years. Tak and Yukiko were still married, had raised four wonderful children who all knew the Lord. They were all involved in some kind of Christian ministry from professors to missionaries Christian parents with several grandchildren. Tak, as I had feared was no closer to giving his heart to Christ than ever. Then one day, 25 years later, I get a call from out of the blue. "Woods Sensei? This is Takakazu. I need you to baptize me."

"That's wonderful!" I practically shouted. "I've waited so long for this day. Can we get together next week to go over some specifics?"

"No, actually I need you to baptize me before Tuesday."

As we continued to talk, Tak confessed that Yukiko was ready to divorce him, and they were going to see a judge on Tuesday. He hoped that, by being baptized, he could convince her to change her mind. As much as I wanted to help them, and we did meet and he prayed the sinners prayer with a modicum of honesty, I simply couldn't perform a baptism under such pretenses. I invited him to meet with me on a regular basis for a few weeks and then we could talk about it. He said, thanks, but no thanks, and kept looking until he found a pastor who would be delighted to add a baptism to his credit.

To my surprise, Tak's baptism "took", and he was soon a regular at their local church, involved in Bible study and began growing as a Christian by leaps and bounds.

Things were moving along towards divorce, even though Tak was doing his best. On the morning of the second hearing, Yukiko took the time to read her regularly scheduled Bible verses for the day. She was reading in Kings, and she was surprised to see in I Kings 19:15 the section where God says to Elijah, even though there is no promise of anything better, to "go back the way you came".

Feeling this was a direct message for her that morning, she called the lawyer and immediately dropped the divorce charges. She and Tak had some conversations, made some changes in their lives and we still enjoy their fellowship to this day, and of course we love to reminisce about those good old days back in Sendai.

Time for Marsha to talk now:

But now, reverse back to those early days and Yukiko's father, Kazuo. After Yukiko's marriage, we occasionally bumped into her parents from time to time, but I wouldn't have called us friends. He was still dealing with a lot of anger, but time was healing, and he wasn't as opposed to God and Church as he had been initially.

Of course there was the time, a few years after Yukiko had become a Christian, her younger sister Yukari met with a bit of trouble.

When Yukiko was thrown out of the house, Yukari knew only that she did not want to become a Christian after what happened to Yukiko. So in the course of time, she found herself in prison, arrested for selling drugs. Her mother went to visit her, and passed a Bible to her through the bars. "This helped your sister; maybe it will help you," she said.

"She read the Bible, received Christ as her Savior, got out of prison and joined the church. Soon she also was married.

And then, almost 10 years from the initial blow up, Kazuo called and asked if they could come and visit us. We were surprised, but of course welcomed them into our living room. The kids were in bed and the baseball bat was behind the door just in case he tried some of his previous tactics on us, ha.

They came in, sat down, accepted tea and then finally got to the subject.

Kazuo cleared his throat and paused a moment, looked over at his wife, then gazing out the window said almost in a whisper, "When we see our daughters, we know there must be a God. Will you tell us about Him?" What rejoicing we experienced that night to see the meanest man we'd ever known give his life to the Savior! His wife, Shizue was right there with him and I know the angels were rejoicing. As soon as we stopped praying, Kazuo said,

"I have a question, will I have to sing?" we all had a good laugh. Then he continued,

"Will I have to stop smoking?"

I think God gave me quick come back, and by now we were so happy and relaxed, I was able to say, "I'm not your mother! Ask God about that." And he did!

Next began a several month long process, while Marsha and I went to Kazuo's house every week, sharing Scripture and answering questions. Of course this was always accompanied by Shizue's wonderful cooking, so it was good all around.

Incidentally, five years later, Kazuo bought a Cadillac, imported from America. It was bought, he told us, with the money he saved on cigarettes and alcohol. It warms my heart even today to remember how two ornery people became not only happy church members, but wonderful pseudo grandparents to my children, as well as to the many of their own, even now several great grandchildren! How blessed are we all.

And I have secretly spotted him singing in church! Must be the expression of a happy soul.

Back to Tony:

Searchlight Club continued to grow, and when the group got too big for the house, we moved our Thursday night meeting to the downtown church. By now, Rev. Amano had moved on, and was replaced by Rev. Kaneko, a former president of the Japan Baptist Convention and well respected by all. Sitting down with him after his arrival, I was dismayed to noticed that he spoke a kind of Japanese that I had never studied at language school. I think it was some kind of "smart literary" variety, used only by men of higher learning, but he sooned learned that he had to dumb it down if he wanted us to understand what he was trying to say. He also (being extremely well educated) knew a few random English words he would throw in from time to time like "Synchronism" and such.

At our first meeting, I apologized for my poor Japanese, and promised to keep trying to improve so that we could communicate better ... at least better than I had managed with Rev. Amano. Kaneko smiled and said, "Let us pray that your Japanese gets so good we can fight together."

An interesting concept but one I was not anxious to try. In the years to follow, I'm happy to say that we never did "fight" in the strictest sense, although we did come to a point of disagreement over Searchlight Club. It actually began with a theological discussion about baptism. I had always believed and taught the truth of Romans 10:9-10, that is, that the specific requirements for salvation are twofold: believe in your heart and confess with your mouth. Japanese churches, it seemed to me, taught that baptism was a requirement as well. Talking this over with Kaneko one day, he explained, "No, baptism in itself is not a requirement for salvation. But if a person is unwilling to be baptized, then I must question his heart."

Actually, that made sense. I had come across many Japanese who professed to believe, but declined to be baptized, citing difficulties with spouses, bosses and any of a host of other influences. They often quoted Shusaku Endo's novel, *Silence*, a story about a Catholic priest back in the 1600s during a time when Japanese persecution of Christians was at its peak. The priest, not fearing for his life but concerned for his flock, chose to step on a picture of Jesus, publicly denying his faith and thus saving his life. "That's *me*!" people would tell me. "I believe, but I cannot make it public. Please understand."

I did understand, to a point, and many times I would allow them to make a profession of faith to me, in secret, so that they could be assured of their salvation. Many of those, in fact, came to the point where they went public, hanging the consequences. Kaneko and I gave nodding assent to each other's views, understanding and respecting both but never in total agreement.

But there was one point where Kaneko would not bend. I was reporting about the phenomenal success of Searchlight Club, meeting in his church every Thursday night. By now we had up to 70 in attendance, approaching and often exceeding the Sunday morning crowd. We were now blessed with missionary Journeymen, who would teach English, manage the snacks and befriend the students better than we could.

"We have a song service, just like Sunday."

"Yes," Kaneko confirmed.

"We take up an offering, just like Sunday."

"Yes."

"We have a sermon, just like Sunday."

"Yes."

"And we have people coming to Christ, just like Sunday."

"Yes."

"So I'm thinking we should have a baptism some Thursday night."

"No."

Kaneko went on to explain that, as wonderful as the Searchlight Club was, it was not a church. And the church was the only place where a person could be baptized. On that point, we agreed to disagree. Of the new converts at Searchlight Club, some did move on into the church. Others opted for baptism at the nearby river, or in the ocean, sometimes but not always by me. And others put off the ceremony altogether, much to my frustration. We did continue in a good relationship with Rev. Kaneko, though. When he and his wife retired, in fact, they joined our church and became "honored elders", loved and respected by all.

To top off our years together, Kaneko told me one day, "You know, I may have been wrong about Searchlight Club. It really was a church in and of itself. I should have let you have a baptism service."

That was the last thing I expected to hear from this faith giant, and it brought a lump to my throat to find that we had come this far in our relationship. We talked about the good old days, then I patted him on the arm and said, "But you know, this is a lot better than fighting, isn't it?"

He had to be reminded of our first conversation, so many years previously. When he remembered, his face brightened, then he started to bow deeply as a man in his position would do. Then he thought better of it and gave me a big hug instead. I love that man.

Chapter 8

Mentors

So many people were used by God over the years to help mold us into what we were becoming. We couldn't begin to include them all in a book like this, and I hope no one is offended if they don't see their name in the chapter. But as I think about it, the real mentors in our lives would not have expected to see themselves mentioned. That's the thing about mentors, isn't it? They quietly listen, respond when it's appropriate, change the course of our lives and more often than not are never aware of the fact. I'm comforted with the assurance that God knows their years of faithful service and He will reward them in His time, in His way. Below are listed three families whose proximity alone was enough to make them very significant in our lives. The fact that they used that closeness to bless and guide us in ways we couldn't have imagined makes us look at them and think, "Mentor".

Boatwrights

On a wall in our house today hangs a collection of pictures. This is what we call our "Wall of Witnesses". Each picture shows us people who have had a significant part in the tapestry that is becoming "us". There are our parents, of course, and a grandmother … family members who had the most influence on us during those formative years. The rest are dear friends; not necessarily peers, although I'm sure our daily acquaintances are impacting our lives now in ways that won't become apparent except in hindsight.

No, our Wall of Witnesses hangs as a reminder of particular people whom God has used in special ways, and whose memories still direct a lot of our decisions today. Two of the first of these were Bob and Betty Faith Boatwright, who fell naturally into the role of mentor when we moved to Sendai. But it was a role that none of us were particularly conscious of at the time. Our relationship with them was easy going and stress-free, even though they could have taken on a stricter role in our development by virtue of the fact that they were our mission "elders" at a time and place when we sorely needed directing. But their style of leadership was different, in that they would never sit us down as a teacher would a student, but rather by their constant abiding example they taught more than any professor have ever could. I think I can only recall one time when Betty Faith, always the Genteel Southern Belle, ever came close to anything resembling a confrontational side. We were speaking about another missionary family whose lifestyle could frustrate us from time to time. Betty Faith listened while we vented, then said ever so softly, "Well, I'll say this about her… her husband is a wonderful man."

Our son Trevor put it best, even from a preschooler's point of view: "I like to go see Uncle Bob and Aunt Betty Faith. They're always ready."

And that expressed it perfectly. I can remember no time in our long association together when they opened the door, saw us, and looked inconvenienced. It was always as if we had been expected and they had been waiting with bated breath for our arrival. Surely, they had other things to do, responsibilities to take care of, people to meet, but that attitude was never communicated to us. Everything else stopped when we walked in the door. Coffee was prepared and served along with some amazing homemade treats Betty Faith had just pulled from the oven. Before we could even broach a topic of conversation, they sat on the edge of their seats waiting to hear how we were doing. Is Trevor enjoying preschool? Are you getting enough rest? What about your student work? Many were the times when we would leave with smiles on our faces and then recall in horror that we never once asked them about their own lives! Over the years, we've tried to correct that flaw in our host and hostess skills, and if any progress has been made, credit must go to this amazing couple.

The thing that always struck you about Bob was his unchanging sense of humility in everything he did. Never once did he boast about any of his accomplishments, and it was usually from someone else that we learned of them at all. I do remember a time in church when my entire attitude about the Japanese language changed, and it was due to hearing Bob Boatwright preach.

By now, we had finished language school and were just getting established into our new work in Sendai. Mission director Stan Howard's words were coming back to haunt me: "If you get the language, everything else will fall into place; if you don't get the language, everything else will fall apart." I was falling, and quickly approaching terminal velocity. After twenty years in Japan, we shared with people that we had spent the first ten years trying to figure out what the Japanese were saying, and the next ten years trying to figure out what they *meant* by what they said. So, as you can imagine, at about the three-year mark, I was about as discouraged as a missionary could be. At one point I remember telling Marsha, "If I still feel this way in a month, I'm going to start looking for work back in America." That conversation didn't end well.

The next Sunday, though, God gave me a present. He let me go to Bob Boatwright's church and hear him preach. Keep in mind that he was a dyed-in-the-wool Georgia boy, and his speech reflected that. Only a Georgia boy, after all, could make a one syllable word like

"Well" and turn it into three syllables. "Wah-ei-ull, that was kinda fab-you-lous." Go back and read that sentence at half speed and perhaps you'll get the idea.

Bob's Japanese was exactly like his English. If you're reading this and not listening to the audio version, then it might be difficult, but I'll try to imitate his Japanese style: "Ano-neh…wa-ta-shi-wa…bo-to-raito- dei-su.

On that Sunday morning, listening to him preach, I was flabbergasted. Not only was his pronunciation *nothing* like I had ever been taught; he completely ignored the building blocks of sentence construction… those special words we might call object particles, that help put a sentence into context and enable the listener to follow the conversation. I turned to Shinkichi, my Japanese friend and asked (in Japanese, I might add), "Can you understand him?"

"Of course," my friend said. Then sensing my unspoken questions, he went on, "Whenever Boatwright Sensei speaks, we feel the pain he has suffered to learn our language. And we love him for it."

From that moment, proficiency in speaking Japanese ceased to be a top priority for me. I still wanted to communicate effectively, of course, but from now on I would communicate not as some Divinely-gifted foreigner-become-native, but rather as Tony, Texas transplant who is just thrilled to be here. It altered the way I looked at myself, and it changed the way I approached Japanese people. Few things have freed up my life as much as that one decision, and I have Bob Boatwright to thank for it.

Bob's easy-going way with people came across in the way he made friends, and I found myself wishing I could relate to the Japanese the way he did. Not long after that day when I visited his church, I saw him in his element, laughing and talking with Naoki Noguchi, a fellow pastor and close friend. Up until that time, I saw the Japanese as people to whom I ministered, but had trouble imaging them as "soul mates". There were just too many differences in background, lifestyle and of course the language. But here were Bob and Naoki, sharing some private joke and laughing the laugh of real brothers.

How I wanted that!

They must have sensed my apprehension, and tried to include me in their conversation, but there were just too many barriers between us. Finally Bob said, "Hey Tony, Naoki and I are going skiing tomorrow. Why don't you come along?"

"Sure," I answered with a bravado I didn't exactly feel. I mean, I had lived in Colorado, America's foremost skiing capital, and I had mentioned mountain climbing in the Colorado Rockies, but that didn't mean I could ski. But I wasn't about to admit that.

The next day, we drove up to a nearby ski area called "Izumi ga Dakeh", roughly translated "Rice paddy with a spring." I saw neither. Instead, I was confronted with a mountain and a chair lift. After getting our skis on, Bob said, "You and Naoki take the first lift. I'll come along in the next one."

Surprisingly, I managed to slide my way to the lift and get seated before being swept up the hill. Naoki sang old Japanese folk songs and pointed out the beauty under our feet. All I could think of was, "How am I going to get off this thing?"

We reached the top, and I stood up, took a breath, and hit the deck.

Grabbing for the first thing in reach, I pulled Naoki down by his sleeve and together we started sliding toward oblivion. The more we struggled, the faster we slid, and I thought I could see an approaching cliff through the tangle of skis, boots, poles and jackets that was us. Naoki's face was crushed next to mine and the sparkling ice rushing by was giving us both a fresh shave. Just before panic took complete control of my senses, I heard Naoki whisper in my ear, "Sensei, sayonara."

In spite of myself, I started laughing. We did manage to be rescued, thanks to a lift operator with a rope, and from that day, I vowed to be open and honest with Naoki. If I couldn't do something, I would tell him so. If I was afraid, I would share that with him. In return, Naoki taught me things that needed to be learned, from skiing to Japanese conversation to the proper attire for a Christian at a Buddhist funeral. And through it all, he kept our confidences and protected my dignity.

I want to introduce you to Naoki and his wife, but let me say one more thing about the Boatwrights. When it came time for them to retire, we had been together in Sendai for ten years. Saying goodbye to them was one of the hardest things we had to do. They were leaving behind a mission-owned house near the heart of downtown, but the city had negotiated to buy it, planning to bulldoze it down and make a much-needed parking lot. After we saw them off on the train, we stopped by the Boatwright's house to rip out some bookshelves they had offered us. The place was going to be demolished, so we were welcome to scavenge.

Our son Trevor had an unusual request.

"Dad, do you think I could throw a rock through the window?" This is the only time I could do it and it would be okay." I started to say, sure, why not? But then we all thought about it, decided it just wouldn't be a good way to honor the memory of these very special people. It's a good thing we didn't, because the city decided to keep the place intact for several more months, even moving in government employees.

Rather than break windows, though, and because they were going to bulldoze the carefully manicured yard, I suggested we cut down his pecan tree. He and Betty Faith's predecessor, missionary Worth Grant had planted a pecan in their garden nearly 40 years previously. It had sprouted and grown into a huge tree, standing taller than the house.

"That's just too much history to let a bulldozer destroy", I decided. Bringing over a chainsaw, we cut it down, trimmed out as many logs as we could, then carried them to the local sawmill to be cut into lumber. Five years later, when we had built a church north of town, I brought out the boards and made a cross to hang on the front wall. One of our first converts at the church was a man who came to visit. Explaining about the origin of the cross, he got big tears in his eyes and said,

"I knew the Boatwrights and their son, David. We used to climb in that tree!"

So their influence lived on, and was illustrated beautifully in that pecan tree. I mentioned that it had stood in their garden for nearly forty years, but I should also mention that it never produced a single pecan until the year they retired. That's a sermon that will preach itself, and I will, one of these days. But I'm still working on the rest of the analogy. The pecan they planted, you see, was a big beautiful Georgia paper shell. The pecans that were finally produced after forty years were a small, hard native variety. It was then that we all recalled that, when grafted to a tree, the seeds from the fruit from the graft will take on the properties of the tree to which it's attached. Somewhere back in the ancient past, someone had grafted a paper shell branch onto a native pecan tree in Georgia. Like I said, I'm still working on it, but the verse from Luke 6:44 comes to mind, "… for each tree is known by its own fruit…"

Noguchis

Noguchi at 15   and at 84

Now back to Naoki Noguchi, one of the most remarkable men I've ever known. Marsha and I even wrote a book about him called *Sacrificed: Given to an Empire, Found by God.* That will tell you more about his early years and his own life-changing decision to become a kamikaze pilot, but let's start at the place he and his wife Kazuko began to have a direct influence on our lives, earning them a place on our Wall of Witnesses. Kazuko was not your typical Japanese house-wife who sat demurely in the background serving tea. Instead, she embodied everything that was open, honest and to the point. These traits were learned undoubtedly from a very early age by a father who typified nearly every Japanese male of his generation: strict, unbending to the point of cruelty. If you've ever seen the old cartoon character depictions of Japanese soldiers made during the war, he would have been the perfect model. He rarely spoke to the family, and when he did it was usually in reference to something they were doing wrong. This was especially borne out when Kazuko, as a young girl, decided to become a Christian. Learning of it, her father beat her severely and only after a long time of separation allowed her back into the house.

The cycle of dysfunction might have continued through into the next generation but for the end of World War II. Overnight, all the values and expectations Kazuko's father had lived by were torn out from under him. He tried to bear up in typical Japanese stoicism, but eventually suffered a complete emotional breakdown. His family was afraid to bring up the subject, but he himself decided that he had lost his mind and needed to be institutionalized. He looked around, found an insane asylum that would take him and checked himself in.

It wasn't long, however, before he began to have second thoughts. "These people really *are* crazy," he thought to himself. "I don't think I belong here." Approaching the asylum's director, he voiced his opinion, thanked them for their time and bid them goodbye.

But instead of wishing him well, the director replied, "I'm very sorry, but you need to understand that you are a patient here. We can't allow our patients to leave just because they ask us to." What was needed, he continued, was a family member who would agree to take responsibility for him. Then and only then would he be allowed to leave. Not surprisingly, no one in the family was prepared to take on that responsibility.

Finally one day, Kazuko arrived at the asylum. Standing on the other side of a barred gate separating them, she said, "Father, I have in my hand here a paper that says you will be allowed to leave, provided I will be responsible for you."

"Uhmph, let's go," he grunted, but she stopped him. "I'm thinking that I will tear this paper up and go back home. It's very peaceful there now" she waited for the implication to soak in, until the desperate look on his face told her it was time to continue…

"I will, however, let you come home, but on two conditions. First, you must apologize to me for making my life miserable. Then, you and mother must come to church with me every Sunday, sit quietly and listen to what's being said."

Reluctantly, he agreed to the conditions, and as would be expected of any Japanese man of honor, he honored his promises. And not surprisingly, it didn't take long before the Gospel began to find a place in the man's heart. Putting his old life behind him, he accepted the promises of Jesus and was baptized into the church. From that time on, he was an honored elder in the congregation. Even when Kazuko married Naoki and he became the church's new pastor, he remained a humble servant, only speaking up to critique his son-in-law's sermons. Which Naoki appreciated, by the way.

In 1978, Naoki, Kazuko and Naoki's mother Toshiko moved to the far north, settling in Sendai where they soon teamed up with the Boatwrights to do church planting together. A couple of years later, Marsha and I made the scene. We were instantly struck by Naoki's gift as a pastor. His English was passable but not bilingual by any means. Still, he had a way of knowing exactly what we needed and when. The first time I asked for his advice was while I was counseling a young couple who wanted me to marry them. I wasn't comfortable, because the boy was not a Christian. They were both coming faithfully to church, however, and I didn't want to do anything that would drive them away. Sharing all this with Naoki, he said simply, "Keep talking." I started to explain the situation again, but he interrupted me. "Not to me. Keep talking with the couple. Ask questions about their faith. Dig deeper into their reasons for getting married. But never say no. Japanese never say no."

As I thought about that, I realized he was right. Japanese, believe it or not, are very hesitant to be confrontational, a fact that is reflected in their language. In polite conversation, one should ask a question in such a way that allows a negative answer to be stated in a positive way. For example in a restaurant, the waitress will often ask, "Is it acceptable if I don't pour you more coffee?" to which my heartfelt "Yes!" will result in no more coffee.

I tried the tactic on my young couple. We talked, and we talked.... and we talked some more. Eventually, they came to me and said, "We've decided that we need to become more mature before we get married." Which was their way of saying, "Both of us need to be Christians if this is going to work."

Marsha had her own "come to Jesus" moment during one of Naoki's sermons. I was away at another church that evening, so she went alone to hear him preach. He read from John chapter 12, where the woman anointed Jesus' feet with expensive perfume. When the people around tried to stop her for the waste, He told them, "Leave her alone. What she does is a fine and beautiful thing."

Naoki stopped there and said, "Let's think of our missionaries."

Marsha sat up a little straighter and thought, "Hey, I like where this sermon is going!"

"Think of our missionaries," he said again. "They are highly educated and skilled people. They have all left their homes and traveled great distances to come here."

"Yes sir, great message," Marsha thought.

"Then they get here, they open their mouths, and talk like six year olds. We can't understand them, they can't understand us, and sometimes we think, maybe it would better for them to go back where they came from, where their skills could be put to better use."

Marsha slid down in her seat and started looking for the quickest way out.

"But listen to what Jesus said here: "Don't stop her! What she does is a fine and beautiful thing. Think of our missionaries. What are they doing? They're pouring out their lives at the feet of Jesus. And it's a fine and beautiful thing."

From that time on, Marsha and I both began to see our ministry in a whole new light. By now we had learned that we had not "brought Jesus to Japan"; He was there long before we arrived, and will remain long after we have gone. But besides that, we were not bringing a whole lot to the table. We spoke English, which about the only skill we could excel in. What were we doing in Japan, exactly? In short, we were being obedient. God sent us here, and we came. The country is not a lot smarter because of our coming. Spiritually, I suspect that God could have used anything, including the rocks beside the road, to declare His glory, much better than we were doing.

But what we were doing was pouring out our lives. And when you think about it, that's not a bad thing. I hope when we arrive to stand before God's Throne, we will come, completely used up, with nothing left to give. What a waste it would be to hold onto something, like the woman's expensive perfume, until there was no place to pour it.

Naoki exemplified that sermon in his own life. Years went by; Kazuko passed away. His mother passed away at the age of 104. Finally alone, he said goodbye to the church and moved south to be closer to his son. That lasted a few weeks, until Naoki woke up one morning and thought, "Hey! My expiration date is not up yet. I still have work to do!"

Getting on the phone, he called up Yoshioka Baptist, a church north of Sendai that Marsha and I had kick started a few years before. We had moved years before to Australia and were no longer there to be the pastor. There had been another missionary for a few years, but now there was no one to fill the role.

"Hello," he said without preamble to the acting head of the church.

"I hear you're without a pastor. If you'll have me, I can be there by next week."

"That would be wonderful, Sensei! But… you know, we're very small and don't have much money."

"No problem," he said. "I can live on my pension."

"Fantastic! But… but where would you live?"

"I seem to recall the church there has a small study upstairs? That will do nicely."

For the last five years of his life, Marsha and I led countess disaster relief teams from all over the world to his church. Others came on their own or with other leaders. In all there were over 4000 people who got to know him and his amazing stories. They would sleep on the floor, listen to his stories, then he would give them rice for breakfast and pray with them as they went out to work in the tsunami zone.

One day, at home in Tokyo, where we'd moved back to from Australia in 2011, we got a message that 'somebody' was getting married. We naturally assumed it was our best friend Shinkichi who'd lost his wife Kumiko to cancer 5 years earlier, but no, the caller stopped to control her giggles, and then said

"It's Noguchi Sensei!".

He was 'only' 84, and had reacquainted himself with a girl (OF ONLY 80) that he had known back in seminary days. They had both had married and raised families, lost their spouses, but were not ready to be put out to pasture. Yumiko told me that she thought that life with him would be 'interesting'.

We attended their wedding with great joy, ribbing them and teasing him with questions like "Will she fit in the study?" " Do you think she'll like the bunk bed? etc..

They had almost a year of wedded bliss when Naoki felt a pain in his side one day. It was soon diagnosed as cancer. Eventually, he said goodbye his beloved Yoshioka church and he and his new wife Yumiko drove back the length of Japan to Yumiko's hometown of Kyushu, where they'd first met so many years before Not only was his son, Makoto living nearby, but Yumiko also owned a home that they could move into. Another blessing was that Yumiko's daughter was a nurse.

Not one to sit still, Naoki soon found another church nearby that had no pastor and was welcomed with opened arms. He preached there for several months until it got too difficult to move about. Then the church came and said, "Sensei, we've decided that next Sunday we would like to come to your place for church." He agreed, and there from his bed, Naoki preached his last sermon and sang from the hymnbook. He urged the members to tell others about Jesus and continue to grow. A couple of days later, he gathered the family, again urging them to follow Christ first. Then they all had his favorite sushi meal allowing him to eat ate all of his favorites. After the meal, he played his shakuhachi (wooden flute) one last time, and while they all sang "Jesus Paid It All" in Japanese, he went to be with his Lord.

There is so much more to this man's life than we can share here. If you get a chance, find or download a copy of *Sacrificed* and read more about this remarkable man with a remarkable family.

Itos

Kumiko

Shinkichi

The last couple we want to introduce you to are Shinkichi and Kumiko Ito, a couple who are a little younger than us, at least in body, but not maturity, who were led to us by the Boatwrights. They knew we needed good Japanese friends, and assigned the job to this newlywed couple when we moved to Sendai

What began as a case of obedience to Bob and Betty Faith soon blossomed into a true friendship that has stood the test of time. Their children played with our children. When we moved to the north of Sendai to build a new church, they joined us, faithfully serving in any and every capacity. Kumiko was the confidante Marsha needed to help her understand everything feminine about Japan.

Shinkichi was my rock solid truth-teller who would never fail to let me know if and when I messed up.

One of the biggest contributions he gave was his ability to correct my Japanese when out of respect for the pastor no one else would. I remember one day I was preaching about the Pharisees and how legalism was their vice. The word for "legalist" In Japanese is "Ripoushugi," but somehow my tongue got twisted and it came out "Shipousugi" which roughly translated means "too much tail."

After the message, everyone complemented me on a fine sermon, but Shinkichi waited his turn in line. Stepping right into my face, he asked, "What were you trying to say??" I explained, he gave me the correct word, and I turned immediately to a lady who had just told me how the message had blessed her.

"Why didn't you say something?" I asked her.

She turned several shades of red, then said, "Well… I thought it was a Greek word. But very inspiring!"

Kumiko and Shinkichi proved themselves over and over again to be the finest friends we could have hoped for. In retrospect, we remember that they were some of the fewest friends we had that were as spontaneous as we were. One very formal New Years worship day, as we duck walked out of church in our tight kimonos, smiling and bowing, we then brightened to hear Kumiko say, "If we hurry, we could hit the ski slopes in an hour!"

We all raced home, threw some rice balls together, flung off the layers of kimono to exchange for the layers of snow clothes and raced for the slopes to spend the afternoon enjoying sledding. True friends.

Even when our son Trevor was diagnosed with leukemia while we were in America, Shinkichi flew over for the express purpose of helping little brother Nathan celebrate his birthday. He knew that in all the chaos of trying to deal with the situation Nathan would be ignored and he just wanted to make sure that didn't happen.

A few years later, their daughter Yu Chan was to be married to a young man she had met at Dallas Baptist University. She called me up and said, "Uncle Tony, could you please come do the wedding? After all, you speak Japanese AND Texan!" I was thrilled to take on the challenge.

But the day came while we were working in Bangkok, Thailand that we heard Kumiko had cancer. She didn't have to suffer long, and we got the news that she was on her deathbed. Boarding the first plane we could, we raced to be with them in Sendai, but were too late. Something amazing happened however that I'm going to be processing for a long time. Kumiko had been in a coma for several hours, surrounded by her family. Suddenly, she opened her eyes, looked to the ceiling and called out, "Oh look! Shepherds!" Then she lay back down and slipped away peacefully. Yep, we've got a few questions when we get to Heaven.

Chapter 9

New Directions

B y the late 1980s, things were getting tight all over the world.
As financial support began to falter, missionaries were pulling up
stakes all around us, leaving behind thriving ministries simply
because they couldn't afford to stay in a country as expensive
as Japan. Our mission still took better care of us than any we

knew, but the handwriting was on the wall. At first there were subtle cuts in budgets. New projects and big developments were put on hold. Housing and transportation allowances were slashed, affecting our ability to move into new areas.

Finally at one mission meeting, the higher ups began verbalizing what we knew all along: opportunities were going to suffer because of a lack of funds. The Southern Baptist Cooperative Program was truly inspired as it allowed even small churches in the States take part in global missions. Wherever we went in America, whenever I was invited to speak at a Baptist church, I was able to begin by saying from the heart, "Thank you... thank you enabling us to do what we do." Now that had to be qualified.

On a global level, it meant that priorities needed to be shifted, with appointments and outreach projects considered in light of money available. One well-meaning but totally unappreciated representative from Richmond even shared a chart that evaluated each country's cost-per-soul. We in Japan were horrified to hear that it cost us more per baptism than any other country in the world. How could anyone say such a thing! We implored. How can you put a price on a new Christian? But desperate times call for desperate measures; someone began a sliding scale that measured not only the cost of new converts; but their intrinsic value in terms of their ability to contribute to evangelism world wide. From that perspective, A Japanese Christian might be considered more valuable than someone from an African village, in that he or she would be more likely to impact others around the world.

Such discussions were ludicrous at best, but then it finally came down to a personal level. At that mission meeting in 1990, we were told,

"If anyone would consider transferring to any other country where it's not so expensive, we'll work with you to make it happen."

I don't believe anyone took the offer, at least not right away, but in that instant a cloud of guilt and depression settled over the mission family. How could we continue in the work, knowing that global missions would suffer because of what we're spending? Then right on the heels of that thought came the other: how could we possibly STOP doing what we're doing, knowing the eternal impact it would have on those Japanese closest to us?

By the end of that mission meeting, a new spirit invaded us all: a spirit of despair held up by the gossamer wings of Pharisaical accountability. No one dared suggest a new project for fear it would require more than the budget could allow. We now started counting the cost for everything we did, and to our shame found levels of justification for the things we did.

Transportation budgets were slashed, so that personal miles driven in a mission car were counted precisely. But if something "ministry related" were included in a personal trip, then it wouldn't be counted against us. Case in point, if you go on a picnic with the family, it's personal. If you stop at the church on the way home, it's business. No longer were we to be so generous with ministry food budgets either. We don't buy food for distribution; leave that for the homeless shelter. If you have a sandwich, it's a meal, but if you cut it into fourths, it's a legitimate snack to be served at a ministry function.

With those thoughts swimming in our heads, the question had to be asked: would we ever consider leaving Japan, moving to a new country, a new people … a new calling? My immediate reaction was, thanks but no thanks. God had called us to Japan, and that's where we would stay. True to the promises we had made to the people we worked with in Sendai, we had every intention of "burying our bones" in Japan. Thanks … but no thanks.

But the thought wouldn't let go, and in hindsight, I have to believe that the Holy Spirit was involved in the process. Reminiscent of my call to full time service so many years before, it seemed as though God once again was speaking to me in questions rather than commands.

"What is your call, Tony?"

"To Japan, of course."

"Is it in fact to Japan, or to the Japanese people?"

"Well, I .. don't know."

"What if I show you something that's neither Japan nor a Japanese person? Will you refuse to go?"

"No! Of course not. But…"

"Let me ask you again, Tony: what is your call?"

"I…I…I…"

"Let me help you, Child. Your call is not to Japan nor to the Japanese; your call is to obedience."

So the ground, like my heart, was broken. I was now more open than ever to listening for God's call, unhindered by any preconceived notions of what I thought I was "supposed" to be doing. The soil would still need to be tilled for some time before anything so drastic as a major move would come about. Our student ministries were going great, but were rather fragile in terms of leadership and commitment levels from those involved. The area north of Sendai was in desperate need of a church, and people were beginning to look to us for direction.

And before any of those things would be accomplished, a horrible sacrifice would be made. Our hearts would be ripped out, and our lives changed forever. And then in the healing process to follow, God would accomplish things we would have never thought possible. The time for turning southward would come, but not today.

Now jump forward with me to where we left off: Sendai, Japan, the early 1980s.

By now, Searchlight Club had grown into a life of its own, filled with students from all three of the colleges and high schools where we had contacts. Responsibilities for the programs were handled mostly by church people and by Journeymen missionaries that we requested for just that work. Marsha and I continued to participate, but it was mostly in the role of "honored elders".

We did hang onto an annual homestay program, though, where we would send 12 to 25 students to America for one month, visiting in the homes of Baptist church members we could recommend. We would tell the hosts, "Don't try and shove the Gospel down their throats; just live the Gospel in your homes."

The results were incredible. When the kids arrived back in Japan, they were thrilled with the experience and mystified at the concept of "Christian home". During de-briefing, we would explain again what they had witnessed, and talk about the loving attitudes that come from belonging to a loving God. Overall during twelve years of Searchlight Club's Homestay program, scores of young people came to know the Lord; more in fact than all of our other ministries combined.

One added bonus was the fact that, by paying for the program (which was incredibly cheap due to the fact that the host families never charged for the service), there was enough left over to pay for two Christian leaders to accompany the group and make sure everything ran smoothly. This gave us an excellent opportunity for discipleship, and many solid leaders came out of the program, several of whom still serve in full-time ministries to this day.

All that is to say, Marsha and I began to detect subtle changes in the nature of our work. We seemed to be spending less time with students and more time with adults. That was a reflection, I suppose, of the fact that we were moving more into "adulthood" ourselves.

Anyway, we (and by *we* I mean us and the five pastors we served with in Sendai) were all being led to the need for a church north of town. The city had grown in that direction for several years now, especially after a big earthquake had devastated the southern side a few years previously. Looking around, we discovered what was left of a small church in the village of Yoshioka about 15 miles north. A Christian doctor by the name of Abe (pronounced *Ah-beh*) had begun a Bible study at his clinic many years ago. Both he and the clinic had passed on, but a preschool had sprung up among the participants and was continuing with occasional support from the Sendai churches.

After meeting with the two teachers who ran the place, it was decided that I would come out every week and sing a few songs with the kids, followed by a short devotional for the mothers. It was here that my Japanese began to blossom, since NO ONE in the area spoke English, nor did they have any interest in it. The village had been known as a sake-making town (that's *sah-keh*, as in rice wine) for the last 700 years or so, and the area was seeped in tradition. I discovered that by learning a few simple preschool songs in Japanese, I could communicate the Gospel to both kids and moms.

To our delight, we found that Little Nicki (you'll meet her soon) thrived at the preschool. It looked a lot like her orphanage, and all the kids there super charged her. By now she had been with us only a few short months, and her English was still fairly lacking. But when I first took her with me, she walked in the door and said something in Russian that sounded a lot like, "Now THAT'S what I'm talkin' about!" Sizing the place up, she grabbed a kid-sized chair, drug it to the front row and began her real transformation.

She did have one small setback when Christmas came around. I was asked to come be Santa Claus for the kids: sing some songs, hand out some presents and share a word about the true meaning of Christmas. I figured Nicki would love it, but when I came out from behind the curtain decked out as Old Saint Nick, she started screaming! I realized then that she probably had never seen Santa Claus, never heard the story, and somehow imagined that they were being invaded by some kind of red child-eating monster.

Trying to salvage the moment, I sang out, "Ho ho ho!" then raising my beard a bit I whispered sotto voce, "Nicki! It's me! Don't cry!"

"Merry Christmas everyone! Nicki, it's me, your Dad!"

Thanks to the reassuring arms of a nearby teacher, she managed to stay in her seat, but covered her poor face with her hands, not wanting to see what would come next. I made it a point to give her a big candy cane, and with a last "Ho ho ho!" slipped back behind the curtain. From the audience, I heard her frightened voice.

"Good bye, Daddy! Change clothes!"

Pretty soon, a Bible study had been established at the Yoshioka daycare center, and little by little, folks were coming to know the Lord again. The Bible study grew into a proper Sunday morning worship, and things began to take off.

The only distraction was an old 700-year-old temple that stood next door. Hardly anyone ever visited it, but when they did, invariably it was on Sunday morning just as we were getting started. They would ring a huge bronze bell and start chanting prayers to whichever god happen to be in attendance.

After services one morning, we talked about the temple over tea. "What do you think we can do about it?" I asked.

"Let's burn it down!" one of the men suggested.

"No, I don't think that would be appropriate," I said. "But we could begin by praying around it." The place was empty by now, so we walked next door and checked it out. In the front stood a huge carved stone, about twenty feet high, three feet wide and one foot thick. On the front was carved some ancient prayer that even the Japanese couldn't read completely. Stepping around to the back, I looked up and was shocked by what I saw. At first glance, it appeared to be a big cross carved into the back! Looking closer, I realized that it was actually two stone cutters' marks, one horizontal and one vertical, making an almost perfect symbol of a cross.

"This is it!" I said excitedly to the group. "Seven hundred years ago when this stone was fashioned, God placed His mark on it. Whether anyone knew it or not, He had a plan for this place, and gave us a hint in the kind of symbol only His children would recognize." We gathered around the monument and I prayed, "Lord, thank you for Your faithfulness. Thank you for the encouragement we feel today as we see this sign of Your Presence. In that assurance, we pray together against the enemy, who would lead yet another generation away from Your truth. May the enemy's plans be foiled from this day on. We look forward to the day when this temple no longer stands here, and Your people are free to worship here under Your watch care."

Not long after that day, our family returned to the States for a one-year furlough (which we'll talk about soon). While we were away, a man from Tokyo came to visit the church leaders. As it turned out, the property the temple sat on was owned by no one, having sat there for at least 500 years unchallenged. The visitor explained that he had now bought the land from the government for back taxes. "I'd like to sell it," he said with a hint of sarcasm, "but no one here would be brave enough to buy it, since it's full of all kinds of spirits." He took a sip of tea, leaned back in his chair and said, "I'm thinking Christians like you wouldn't be afraid of something like that. Want to make a deal?"

How I wish we could have bought it! The asking price was several hundred thousand dollars, and no one there had that kind of money. The man finally sold it to an out-of-town developer who brought workers up from Tokyo. They carted the monument away, tore down the temple and built an apartment house.

$$\gtrsim$$

As we spent more and more time north of Sendai, the pastors and the mission all agreed that we should consider moving out that way, to be on the cutting edge of the city's expansion.

We started looking for property, and one day as we were driving home from Yoshioka, Marsha noticed a lot of bulldozer work going on just up the hill on our right. A sign at the bottom of the hill marked the place as a construction zone along with big "Keep Out" warnings.

"Go check it out," Marsha insisted.

"Did you notice the big *Keep Out* sign?" I offered.

"Oh, we're gaijin (foreigners)," she said. "Everybody knows we can't read."

So I pulled off, made my way around the sign and proceeded to the top of the hill. There stretching before us was a huge open area about two miles square. Streets and curbs were being laid out and it looked to be the makings of a major housing development.

"Cutting edge," we thought to ourselves, and began looking around. Soon we spotted a temporary hut with a sign outside that said "Sales office."

Realizing this was a time for the Big Guns, we went home and called up Noguchi Sensei. If anyone could succeed in getting past the front lines, it would be an ex-kamikaze pilot.

The next day, the three of us made our way back out, around the *Keep Out* sign and over to the sales office. We let Noguchi take the lead, as they exchanged business cards and got down to the nitty gritty. Noguchi explained that this fine young couple were Baptist missionaries and were looking for a place to start a church.

"Sorry," the sales rep answered a bit too quickly. "All lots are sold already."

I looked around and saw a poster on the wall. "But it says here that sales don't begin until next month. How can you be sold out already?"

The man mumbled something, said sorry again, and we were ushered out. Marsha was thinking that Noguchi may have made a mistake by being so honest with them, telling them outright that we were going to build a church. We were discouraged until…

Two days later my phone rang. It was the sales rep. "Were you serious about building a church?" he asked right away.

"Yes, of course. But we would need to gather enough people first before a building could go up."

"The committee met last night and decided a church would "image up" the place. Come down tomorrow and pick any lots you want."

We came with Noguchi and picked a perfect place for a church, right at the entrance just as you come up the hill. The mission bought three lots together in an "L" shape to invest in for later use. Then we found another lot on the back side of the project, up against the woods with a view of the valley below, that would be just perfect for our house.

As it turned out, the mission was ready to experiment with a new construction method. It seems we could take a mission-approved house plan to a contractor in America. He would draw up a parts list for everything needed, from trusses to windows to carpet. All that would then be placed into two shipping containers and sent to Japan. When they arrived, we would ask for a team of volunteer carpenters, partner them up with Japanese carpenters to make sure everything fit with local codes, and voila! House built for half the cost of having it done with local supplies and labor.

The biggest challenge was insuring communication between the two teams of carpenters. Our volunteers were some Idaho good old boys, laid back but very competent. The Japanese were very typical of the trade, decked out in matching uniforms, hard hats and goggles. Each day as the American team enjoyed a second cup of coffee from their thermoses, the Japanese would line up for morning exercises and a pep talk. All went smoothly, especially when Marsha and I would show up each day about mid-morning with cookies to check on progress. The Japanese had the same question every day: "What doing?"

Together we'd look over the blueprints, talk about everyone's responsibly, and clear up misunderstandings, such as the fact that while the Americans were working with feet and inches, the Japanese knew only metric. There were a few bumps as would be expected, but the house rose up and stood proud, the very first one in the neighborhood.

My main job now was to watch for trucks loaded with household goods. When I saw one come in, I'd follow it to the new home going up, meet the owners and introduce myself as their pastor for "Taitomi Danchi", the name given to the area. We observed an interesting phenomena: practically every resident was gaijin (foreigner) in that while they were Japanese, they had all come from someplace else, with no local traditions to tie them down. Many were young families, most looking for a new life, and just about everyone we met was open to hearing the Gospel. It wasn't long before our house was throbbing with the sounds of a new church in the making.

The downtown church, under Rev. Kaneko's direction, organized a "kabuwake", a special word meaning "core group" who came to Taitomi to help us with our new church plant. They were a great help, although at times they seemed bent on reproducing the downtown church here in the new area. Noguchi was the perfect person to vent my frustrations, and he was very helpful, acting as go-between to Kaneko and communicating our desire that the new church reflect the young attitudes of the people around us. One day, Noguchi made a comment that I'll never forget. He said,

"Kabuwake are a wonderful help to a new church. But sometimes they can become a cancer, when they keep calling back to the 'way it was.'

But in our case, the kabuwake remained indispensable. Even after the church was organized and they were released to go back to the downtown church, most of the group opted to stay at Taitomi, where they and their children remain to this day.

And that leads me to the next Big Thing in our lives that I like to call "Signs and Wonders 101".

It was 1990, about a year into the church plant. Something happened over the next twelve months that we are convinced was God-ordained. We call it our "Signs and Wonders 101" year. It began when a feeling of discouragement started being felt among all of us at Taitomi.

By now, we had hoped that the church would be strong enough to incorporate and buy the property that was earmarked for a building, but things were moving slowly, both from the mission and from the people coming to church. This was a huge step, we were reminded; a big investment where failure was not an option.

I can point to the exact moment when our "101" course began. It was a Saturday morning, and I got a surprise visit from a Lutheran missionary friend, Gaylen Mathesian. We had met socially, but had never spent a lot of time together. He came ostensibly to check out our basketball net, to see if he could build something similar at his place. The conversation quickly moved to the topic of spiritual depression, and Gaylen said,

"I don't know… I just think something has to happen around here before things are going to bust loose."

"Come inside," I said. "We need to talk."

Long story short, before the week was out, eight tired, broken missionaries were meeting at our house for the sole purpose of praying. At first all of our prayers were selfish.

"Lord, help me. Lord, encourage me. Lord, fix me. Lord, forgive me."

Then after a few weeks, we lifted our eyes a bit and started praying for others in the group.

"Lord, encourage him. Lord, lift her up. Lord, heal him."

I guess we shouldn't have been surprised, but I confess that none of us saw it coming: the Holy Spirit began to move in our midst in ways that none of us had ever experienced. It started with simple things, like a case of the sniffles being cleared up suddenly. Then a fever. Then a rash. When we prayed, people were healed!

We knew something was happening, but no one wanted to say it out loud. Then Gaylen's son was taken to the hospital with acute appendicitis. Could we please come and pray for him? We gathered around as doctors and nurses were prepping him for surgery. We prayed. It took several hours of head scratching before the doctors finally concluded that he no longer had appendicitis and he should go home.

Something like that couldn't be kept secret for long. Before we knew it, people started showing up at our weekly prayer meetings to ask for prayer. At first we said, "No, we're not a healing ministry; we're just looking for God's direction." Finally we decided that we simply could not refuse anyone who asked for prayer. Things started small, then went semi-ballistic. Children were healed instantly of things like eczema, coughs and fevers. Adults were cured of chronic symptoms from which they had suffered for years.

Then one day we got a call from Noguchi Sensei. A member of his church, an elderly fellow, had liver cancer and was in the hospital. Could we come pray? My thought was that we could offer some comfort for him and his loved ones, but soon learned that God's thoughts were not the same as my thoughts. Arriving at the hospital, I found the gentleman in a room by himself. As I placed my hand on his forehead, I immediately jumped back. He was burning up with fever and semi conscious. Putting my hand back on him, I started to pray, and after a few minutes noticed that he had grown icy cold. "Oh Lord," I thought. "I've killed him."

I opened my eyes, and saw him staring back at me.

"Are you okay?" I asked.

"I think so," he answered.

And he was. A few days later, he was released from the hospital, and lived many years after that. When he finally passed away, it was simply from "old age" and most certainly not from liver cancer.

The feeling that our group was beginning to have went from ecstatic joy to sheer terror. It was voiced by the husband of an elderly lady one morning. His wife had suffered a stroke and had lain unconscious at their home for months. A few of us went to their house and prayed for her. Nothing happened, but we all agreed to come back a week later. That time when we prayed, her eyes opened, but she was unresponsive. We kept going back, and each time there was noticeable improvement, but still far short of what we would call "healing". Sitting with her husband one morning over tea, I commented, "Isn't this wonderful, to see God at work?"

He hesitated a moment, then said in a low voice, "It scares me to death."

I was confused, and he explained: "Every time I come into the room now, she turns her head and looks at me. I realize again that there is a power here that I don't understand. It terrifies me."

As he spoke, I felt the hair on my neck rise up. We kept going back and praying for some time, but she never improved beyond that. What had we gotten into? Where was all this going?

We were soon to find out when we were approached by a man who was obviously demon possessed. None of us had come across anything like this, were totally unprepared for it, and not even sure we believed in it. But at the end of the day, when we prayed, demons ran.

Then there was that time when I was in downtown Sendai, walking along the sidewalk. About 50 yards in front of me was a man yelling at the top of his lungs. He yelled at the cars, he yelled at the storefronts, he yelled at the passersby. I couldn't understand his words, but his meaning was crystal clear: this man was not alone.

As he started to cross the street, still about 50 yards ahead, I looked at him and prayed to myself, "In the name of Jesus, come out of that man."

What happened next is hard to describe. It was like the whole scene was freeze-framed. I was aware of nothing except that man standing in the street. He was facing away from me, but he suddenly stopped in mid shout and remained motionless. Then he started turning, looking this way and that, until he had come all the way around and was directly facing me. He looked no further, and immediately his eyes bore into mine. I've never seen such a look of pure hatred.

What did I do? I looked down at my feet. As soon as I did so, the man turned back and continued walking, shouting at anything and everything. Sharing the experience with our group, one of my friends, Bob Schnackenberg, whose opinion I still treasure said at once, "Simple. You sent a challenge; he accepted the challenge; you backed down. End of story."

But what was I supposed to do? Perform an exorcism right there in the middle of the street? None of us had any good answer to that, but we did conclude that when it comes to demons, we need to pick our battles, and let the Holy Spirit lead. Without that formula, any one of us could end up like the seven sons of Sceva in Acts 19:15, "Jesus I know, and Paul I know; but who are you?"

During the course of a year, we had confronted just about every malady imaginable and experienced every gift of the Spirit listed in 1 Corinthians 12. Words of knowledge came to me when I least expected. The first time came as a definite impression that when we got to our ladies Bible study in Yoshioka that morning, one lady was going to ask for prayer for her son who was at home with a fever. I wrote it down, put the paper in my Bible and headed out the door. When I asked the group for prayer requests, the first lady to speak said, "My son couldn't go to school today because of a high fever. Please pray for him."

I felt a tingling as I pulled the paper from my Bible, handed it to her and said, "Don't worry; he's okay." She raced off to the telephone and came back crying tears of joy. Yes he was okay and enjoying his day off from school.

Another time as I was praying for the Searchlight Club meeting that evening, I had a clear image in my mind of a young man I didn't know. He was wearing a gray and white checked shirt and white socks. In the heel of his left sock was a hole about the size of a quarter. I wrote that down, and went to the church in anticipation. About 70 kids were in attendance, but there was no sign of the young man. I was disappointed, but figured I had just gotten it wrong. After the classes were finished, we broke up for snack time, and I wandered around speaking to the kids.

There he was, sitting facing away from me with his left leg crossed. The shirt was unmistakable as were the socks. Edging slowly around so that I could see, I saw it: a perfect hole in the heel of his left sock.

"Hello," I said, trying to keep the tremor out of my voice. "I don't believe we've met."

"How do you do?" he stood and introduced himself. "I was passing by when it started raining, so I came under the porch for shelter. Some people invited me in. I hope that's okay."

Of course it was okay. At this point, I'm not sure if I did the right thing or not. Rather than show him the paper folded up in my Bible, I just talked with him. He wasn't a Christian, but seemed to like what he saw. He kept coming, made a profession of faith, and today is involved in full-time ministry.

It would be hard to assess that year of "Signs and Wonders 101". Looking back on everyone we prayed for (we kept extensive notes), some became Christians and even full time ministers as a result of their experience. Most, although healed, did get sick again, and many of those who were pulled from the brink of death eventually died of something else. The exorcisms were the most exciting, but even many of those found themselves back in the enemy's grip, reminiscent of Jesus' warning concerning the spirit that was driven from a man in Matthew 12:45, "Then it goes and brings along seven other spirits more evil than itself, and they enter and live there; and the last state of that person is worse than the first. So will it be also with this evil generation."

If I were to assign any real meaning to the experiences of that year, it would be described in one word: "preparation". Although Marsha and I did not know it, a valley more horrendous than any we had ever experienced was waiting just beyond the next hilltop. Many who walk through that valley never return, and if they do, most are scarred beyond recognition. As the day of our descent approached, the Spirit was preparing us. We were surrounded with faithful friends who would soon be called upon to reach out to us in Christian love. We rejoiced in the assurance of God's call and purpose for our lives, even though both would soon be brought into profound question. We enjoyed the daily affirmation of a loving family, unfettered by any of the difficulties that plague so many of our peers, even to this day. But most importantly, we were being strengthened daily by a constant succession of demonstrations of Christ's Presence and Power, even though, in the words of C.S.Lewis in *A Grief Observed*, "It was not that I came to disbelieve in God, but that I began to believe dreadful things about Him."

Chapter 10

Trevor

Trevor

W e mentioned earlier the possibility that our time in Zambia had placed our unborn son, Trevor, within the reach of the newly-discovered Burketts Lymphoma virus, leaving him infected with a ticking time bomb on a genetic level. We won't know for sure this side of Heaven, but one thing became agonizingly clear following our "Sings and Wonders 101" year: the Bear reared his ugly head in 1991, and we would never be the same again.

That year found us coming to the end of our year-long furlough in the States. In 1982, on our prescribed furlough, we had enjoyed the role of "missionaries-in-residence" at our orientation center in Pine Mountain, Georgia, followed by helping in the move to the "Missionary Learning Center" near Richmond, Virginia. Now for our second Stateside Assignment (as it had come to be known), we would serve again as missionaries-in-residence, this time at our own alma mater, Golden Gate Baptist Theological Seminary in Mill Valley, California.

It was a bittersweet year. I still cringed whenever an ambulance went by, bringing to mind the career crisis that had settled me once and for all on our God-given path. I sometimes wondered if any of the same people still worked for the ambulance company, and if they would remember me if I dropped in to say hello. But even after fifteen years, the scars from that experience still hurt, and I decided to just put all that behind me.

The job of missionary-in-residence was fun and challenging. I couldn't believe I was seeing the school now from the other side of the teacher's door, serving on a peer level with many of the same professors who had helped shaped my theological understandings. Some confirmed my great respect for their hard work and dedication to the task; some raised a few questions that I had not yet formulated before my time in the crucible known as the "mission field". It was an unprecedented opportunity to talk with these great men and women of God about the things they had taught me, and profoundly humbling when they asked me to affirm the knowledge they had imparted in the class room, and to talk about how those things manifest themselves in the real world "out there".

Our year was also marked by the experience of my Mom having a heart attack during a visit by her and Dad. They were serving as missionaries in Taiwan, and decided to take some vacation time to come and see us. They hadn't decided if they would stop by Hong Kong on the way back but determined to have the time with us first and then check the ticket situation along with their pocketbooks in a few days.

It was a God thing that they decided to come see us at all and it turned out to be a lifesaver, since she suffered complications that few medical centers would have been equipped to handle. Emergency bypass surgery resulted in septic shock, which led to her going into a coma that would last for over four months. No one expected her to survive, but we never gave up hope, praying and anointing her with oil with as much courage as we could muster. I should be saying we never doubted, but I'll admit we were pretty worn down by four months of highs and lows, hope and despair.

And so it was a double shock when she woke up one day, fortunately while Dad was sitting by her bedside.

Yawning, she turned towards Dad and said casually, "So what about Hong Kong?" Dad was speechless, trying to find his voice while fumbling for the call button by her bed, "Uhm…uhm…"

"You know," she continued, "we talked about stopping in Hong Kong on the way back to Taiwan. Should we think about that?"

"Ahh …."

Slowly, Mom began to take in her surroundings, and as the doctors and nurses were racing into the room, she asked, "What day is it?"

"Ah … Wednesday."

"Where am I and how long have I been out?"

" Uhm" he searched for words not wanting to send her into another coma because of shock, " Oh, it's been awhile, I think" and sensing no visible shock, he continued, … "we're coming up to four months now."

What followed were several more months of joyful 'reunion', rehabilitation, early retirement, and the blessed opportunity to retire back in Texas, surrounded by family and friends until she died peacefully five years later, the result, it seems, of a reaction to a flu vaccine.

Marsha's take:

But with the end of the school year, and the resolution of the drama with Jody, we were anxious to get our family back to Japan and settled in before Trevor would be leaving for the dorm in Tokyo to finish his high school years. We made sure Jody was well ensconced and on her way in the rehabilitation center and we packed our crate and said our goodbyes. We wanted to spend some time as just a family after the four-month drama with Jody, and we thought, what better way than to head north?

We decided to drive the old Subaru we had been using all the way to Anchorage, Alaska. There, we would sell the car and pick up a flight to Tokyo. It was a magical time for the four of us, surrounded every day by breathtaking beauty and unending wilderness. For Trevor, it was a dream come true, since the open roads and sparse traffic gave opportunities every day for him to try out his learner's permit behind the wheel.

After about a week of camping, just outside of Anchorage, we knew something was amiss when Trevor said, "I don't think I'll drive today."

"Why? What's wrong?"

"I don't feel so good, and my back hurts."

By the next day, we knew he was unwell. We decided not to camp and after getting a cheap motel and unloading our stuff, we took him to a local clinic for a checkup. Our flight left in three days, and we didn't want to start a long trip with a sick child. That night back at the motel, the phone rang. It was the doctor. "Mr. and Mrs. Woods, I need you to come back to my office right away, and bring Trevor."

We arrived at the big city hospital and were ushered without Trevor into the office. It sounded serious, and it was. "I'm sorry to tell you this," he began, "but Trevor has tested positive for acute lymphoma, a type of leukemia."

"But that's impossible!" I began. "He was fine just the day before yesterday."

"That's why they call it 'acute'," he said gently. "What you need to do is this: get on the next plane for the lower 48; any state down there will be better equipped to handle something like this. I would suggest a place where you have family or friends. This is going to be a long ordeal. I'm keeping Trevor overnight and I want to talk to him alone".

While Tony and I exited the office to cry into each other's arms, Trevor talked to the doctor. After a few minutes, we had pulled ourselves together enough to be ready for him when he came out. As a typical teenager, he wasn't too upset, but rather had a look of getting a big challenge on his face.

"Mom, Dad" he fairly beamed, "The doctor said I have a bad disease. They can fix it, but I'm going to feel like SHIT!" I think he was so 'flattered' that the doctor had talked to him like a man that it covered the terrible news.

Later that night as Tony was getting him settled into his hospital bed, Trevor turned serious.

"Dad", he said, "I want you to know that I'm not afraid to die. But whether I live or die, I want to do it with grace and humor......... and I want to be in Japan."

The next 24 hours were a nightmare that we kept hoping would end. We contacted the local Baptist church, and they were wonderful, taking our car and camping gear to be sold. We managed to get plane tickets to San Francisco, to be near Mom and Dad, figuring we'd decide about long-range plans later.

Something very interesting happened that night as we were packing to head for the airport. Dad had been with Mom all day at the rehab center, then said good night and went to the house the mission had set up for them. Just before going to bed, he decided to call Mom to say good night once more. As they were talking, Dad noticed the message light was blinking on his phone. He turned it on so he and Mom could listen together. It was Marsha.

"We're flying back to San Francisco in the morning. Trevor has leukemia. We'll call you when we know more tomorrow. Love you."

Mom and Dad were both speechless. Finally he said, "I'll come back to the rehab center so we can be together."

"No," Mom insisted. "We need to rest. The kids will need us more than ever tomorrow."

They prayed together over the phone, said good night, then each began processing this tragic news. Mom was lying in bed, unable to move, so she pulled the sheet up over her head and began to cry. Almost at once, she felt a soft hand on her arm. Pulling the sheet down, she was surprised to see a woman with snow white hair, backlit by the light out in the hall. Before she could say anything, the woman gave her arm a pat and said,

"There there, dear; it will be all right."

Rather than say anything, Mom closed her eyes, a peace sweeping over her like never before. She slept, but every time she woke up in the night, the woman was there, her hand on Mom's arm and a smile on her face. Daylight came, and the sound of a nurse opening curtains and checking meds woke her up. Mom looked around, then asked,

"Where is that wonderful lady?"

"I'm sorry Mrs. Woods, who are you talking about?"

"That sweet old white-haired lady. She stood by my bed all night long."

The nurse look confused a moment, then starting checking her medications.

"Mrs. Woods, I've been right outside your door all night long, and I can assure you that no one was in here last night."

Another 'coincidence' was on the plane. Because we had booked only the afternoon before, we didn't have adjoining seats. Trevor had spent the night in the hospital and had been released, but was pretty miserable, so we were trying to get him comfortable by asking passengers to swap seats, etc.

One lady moved so that he could recline his seat better and we got to talking about our situation. She seemed very attentive, and as I was pouring out my soul to her, she produced a thermos and a large coffee cup. "Here" she said, "It sounds like you'll need this".

There on the cup in bold letters were the words "God will take care of YOU!"

We landed and went straight to the hospital where they were waiting for him. Everyone was upbeat including us, who after the signs and wonders year, as well as all the affirmation we'd got since the diagnosis, we couldn't help but think,

"We've got this!"

The next eight months were a roller coaster of faith, hope and a living hell, but whenever we felt total despair taking over ... whenever the Bear was at his worst ... all of us drew back on that experience and the message that had certainly come from the Throne of God Himself:

"It will be all right."

Of course, "All right", we knew, does not necessarily mean physical healing. In fact, Trevor suffered horribly as tumors along his back invaded his central nervous system, bringing pain that no amount of anesthetic could touch. He was soon restricted to a wheelchair and then bed, the worse that could happen to a 15-year-old in the prime of life. He did manage to hold onto a sense of humor, though. One day after what seemed like an endless stream of well-wishers, he commented,

"Go figure; people used to remark about how tall I was. Now they talk about how *long* I am."

Finally he was between rounds of chemo and we were able to take our "make a wish" trip to Disneyworld. We were briefed by the doctors, who reminded us that some children in his condition got there and had to spend the entire time in the hospital.

"Enjoy as much as you can while you can," we were told.

All in all, it was the best vacation ever. Make a Wish kids, we discovered, are given the moon. Everything we needed was provided, including gift vouchers to fancy restaurants. The park was crowded as always, but Trevor was ushered to the front of the line every time. Of course he was miserable and in pain much of the time, but he kept to his promise to do everything with style and humor.

If we'd known he had only weeks to live, we would have skipped the fun and tried to head for Japan, but I realize now that it could never have happened. We returned home and went into the clinic for the next round of chemotherapy, but it was decided that he was too unwell to take it. The pain and disability continued to worsen until one day a team of doctors came and asked us to leave the room.

"He needs to hear this from us without his parents," they said.

It would be impossible to put into words what Marsha and I were feeling as we left our son with people who were about to tell him he was going to die.

The doctors finally came out of the room, and each one carried a look of incredulity.

"We've never seen such a response from one so young," they whispered. "When we told him the medicine wasn't working and he had days to live, he said, 'Well, I'm a Christian, so I'm not afraid to die. But what I really want is to go back to Japan, to see my friends.'"

After so many months of hope and despair, I confess that it was almost a relief to see him slip into a coma. I just couldn't believe that we were going to lose the battle. I stepped outside the hospital, supposedly to get a breath of fresh air, but actually to try one more time with God. As I walked in the darkness, through a nearby park, I started pleading with Him. Then my attitude turned to helpless frustration, and finally to anger.

Remember that story in Mark, chapter 4? The disciples were out on Lake Galilee, and had gotten caught up in a storm of biblical proportions. They knew this was no ordinary squall, and I'm convinced they were correct. Running to Jesus, they were horrified to find Him asleep in the back of the boat. That's when they crossed the line.

"Teacher," they shouted over the storm, "don't you care if we die?"

Jesus stood up, rebuked the storm, and it got quiet. I think the only sound would have been that of the disciples' heavy breathing. Then Jesus turned and rebuked them.

"Why are you afraid, you men of little faith?" (Mark 4:40)

That passage has always had a special significance for me, and especially since that night in the dark, outside the hospital. As my prayers moved from desperation to frustration to anger, I too, like those terrified disciples, gave vent to my emotions. If anyone had been watching me that night, they would have given me a wide berth as I stood shaking my fists at the sky and calling out at the top of my lungs,

"God! Don't you care if my son dies?"

In the moments that followed, I have to say that there were no banners across the sky, no heavenly hosts singing, not even a white-haired lady to smile and tell me that everything was going to be all right. What there *was,* was an almost palpable sensation of a Hand on my shoulder, and an almost if not quite audible Voice. And the words were unmistakable.

"Peace. Be still."

I've thought a lot about that night in the years since. Admittedly, I still have a lot of questions, and there are times when I join in with C. S. Lewis in saying, "It was not that I came to disbelieve in God, but to begin to believe terrible things about Him."

Trevor remained in a coma for the next three days, mystifying the entire medical team. One doctor observed,

"It's almost as if he's waiting for something."

It was Marsha who finally realized what that "something" was. She organized for a phone to be brought into the hospital room, then called Makoto, one of his three best friends in Japan. She told him to get the others, Jun and Katsuya, and gather at his house. We would be calling in the next thirty minutes.

With all the boys together, Marsha held the phone to Trevor's ear while, one by one, they each said goodbye. He made no visible response as they shouted happily into the phone in the slangy Japanese dialect that they had grown up with.

"It's been great, Trevor!" they yelled. "We'll see you in Heaven!" "Thanks again for the fun times!"

We hung up the phone, and Trevor's pulse, which had been racing at 140 beats per minute for days, gradually slowed to 60. We watched as the muscles in his legs relaxed after having been drawn up in pain for so long. As we held him in our arms, I cried,

"Lord, have we missed anything?" A peace settled over the room and we let our baby slip into the arms of Jesus.

And Heaven became an even more precious place.

Chapter 11

Nicki

W ow, where to start? I have to apologize at the outset, because this chapter is going to be a long one. But I have to include all the details here, because if I don't, one of the most amazing stories of all time might be lost forever. The loom is set, the sunlight is shining through. The Weaver works His magic...

Before Trevor got sick and died, we had been writing letters to the

Arkansas lawyer asking for a baby, preferably a girl. Each year the answer was the same.

"Arkansas at this time no longer allows international adoptions, and so we're not doing this anymore."

Still we persisted, but finally I was beginning to accept that I'd be the mother of two boys, like so many others, happily waiting for my girl in the form of daughters-in-law. I even had two pictures of little girls hanging on my wall with the words from that song, "Somewhere in the world today a little girl goes out to play…" I would look longingly at the pictures as I prayed, wondering where those girls were. When will they meet our sons?

And then Trevor died, and our world was shattered. We had beautiful Nathan, a real "Gift of God" as his name suggests. He was now 11 years old, but not once had I ever envisioned him being an only child.

We began to make discreet enquiries. Trevor's death was still a shock to all and we didn't want to seem that we trying to adopt a child in order to 'replace him', especially because that was the last thing on our minds. But the fact was that we were getting on in years (40 and 42), and most days we still felt like the life had been sapped out of us. I remember one day Tony saying, "Heavens, if we adopt now, she'll be 20 when we're like, 65 or something! We'll be old!!!"

To which I countered, "And if we *don't* adopt a child, 'he or she' will still be 20 in a few years and we'll still be 65, but will either of us have had the life the Lord intended?"

And so we proceeded carefully and quietly. We were called for an interview at an international agency in Tokyo, and I remember standing in the kitchen talking to Nathan, who was in on what we were doing.

"I'm just so scared," I confided in him (he was 11, remember).

"Oh," he popped back happily, "Scared you'll lose me too?"

OH MY GOODNESS! Who can imagine the minds of children. I had heard of others who'd had lifelong scars because of misunderstanding their role in the death of siblings, etc. How on earth had he come to this conclusion? I grabbed him, dropping to my knees as I pulled him in close, "Oh no, Sweety, we'll never lose you! We're not afraid that that could happen, not ever!"

He shrugged his shoulders and skipped off to play but I was sobered by his thinking, and determined from that point on to be sure and keep him in the loop with what was happening.

Then came the fateful day when we received a letter from my niece. She had met a 'friend of a friend' who was getting children out of the fallen Soviet Union and we were being urged to just 'go and get some'.

That prompted a blur of activity resulting in $5000 being paid to a lady aptly named "Natasha" (I always think of the cartoon Natasha and Bullwinkle, where Natasha is the wily evil lady). She had recently come to the States, and was confident that she could get us countless children just by snapping her fingers. She began by helping us with the preliminaries, such as obtaining a visa to visit Russia. In those days, tourist visas were not readily available, but she arranged for us to visit a hypothetical "marble factory" in Moscow on behalf of a (fictitious) American investor. Before we knew it, we were on a plane to Russia.

We would be met in Moscow by a translator, an assistant and a driver, all arranged by Natasha, and would have two weeks room and board included with Natasha's parents as well. The U.S. Embassy, in the meantime, had provided us with the paperwork necessary to get "permission" to search for an orphan.

If what Natasha had told us was true, we would have plenty of time to locate and pick up a lucky orphan or two and be back on the plane for home before anyone was the wiser.

We were euphoric but scared spit less at the same time. Taking personal leave time, we headed for America and grandparents, where we dropped off Nathan and picked up three huge boxes of children's clothes to take along as gifts. Natasha assured us that she would be at the Denver airport to meet us and help with final paperwork.

However, she didn't show up, and that should have been a clue. I'll always wonder what my parents thought to see us pouring our hopes and dreams into this risk, while taking the boxes back home because we didn't have the paperwork to ship them.

To our great relief though, we *were* met in Moscow by Vitali, the driver, Nadia, the translator and Alla, the..... we were never sure what her role was. They took us to Natasha's parents, who were kind, but obviously confused.

Nadia finally voiced everyone's concern.

"Actually, we're not sure why you have come," she said uncomfortably. "As far as we know, foreigners are not adopting children here. But as long as you are here, we would be happy to show you the sights of Moscow."

The next day dawned cold (it was late September and already looking like winter). Nadia was the only one who spoke any English, so she explained that we would be sight seeing today. We were frustrated but figured we better get it done, so off we went. All the basics: Red Square, St. Basils, etc. We began to notice the lack of cars on the street. Vitali, our driver was a handsome man and we were told that he'd taken off work to drive us around. We were paying them (included in the $5000) $10 a day for their individual services. At that time a month's wage was about $10, so everyone was happy...... or so we thought.

The second morning Nadia met us and said,

"I'm sorry, but we have to have more money, we cannot work on this small amount." We weren't too surprised because we thought $10 a day was pretty cheap too, but then when we said something about the $10 a day thing, her eyes widened.

"Did you say "$10?....EACH?"

"Yes" we assured her. "We gave Natasha $5000 and that included two weeks of $10 a day for each of you."

"We call Natasha tonight."

And on we went, wondering just a bit what was going on.

As we went we noticed something else. Because there were so few cars on the street, we thought it was odd that we were invariably stopped anywhere there was a soldier or policeman present. They would approach the driver's side, always looking very scary with their angry scowls and automatic weapons. We would sit meekly, three girls in the back with Tony in the passenger's front seat, and wonder what would happen next. But what happened was always the same. Approaching the car, the policeman/soldier would either look at Vitali's identity card, or else recognize him from a distance. In every case, there was a quick snap to attention followed by a frantic wave to urge us on.

Alla and Nadia would look at each other and roll their eyes suspiciously, a look of fear on their faces. Pretty soon they were mouthing "KGB" to each other silently as he 'dealt' with the frightened police. By the third day we were getting anxious to get started and Vitali, the driver, announced that he had found an orphanage that would get us everything we wanted. Off we went. He did explain that we would probably be asked for a $5000 bribe if we got an orphan.

I always struggle when I try to explain what we saw when we arrived at the orphanage. It was a very large, pristinely clean building. We were told that there were hundreds of children there, but we never saw a single one. We were met by a guide, who told us that the children were "resting" and ushered us instead into the most pristine 'playroom' we had ever seen. Each toy was shining clean and arranged in perfect order. I had seen more casualness in department store windows. They not only allowed us, but encouraged us to take pictures. Something was definitely suspicious. The next day we were told we could 'visit' with a four-year-old girl named Katerina. Thinking we could get our hands on her and be on our way, we told them we wanted to take Katerina to the US embassy for a required medical exam. They agreed.

She came out of the seemingly empty orphanage and got into the car with her attendant. Immediately I was suspicious. She was blonde and normal looking, dressed adequately, but she didn't make eye contact at all.

"She's just shy", the attendant said as she sat on Tony's lap, ferreting thru his shirt pocket like a mouse with quick furtive motions. Then suddenly her eyes rolled back in her head and she coughed and then cried. By then we were waiting to see the American doctor.

"What was that?" I jumped out of my seat and ran over to her, along with the attendant who scooped her out of Tony's lap.

"She's just upset," she said quickly as she spun away from us to hold and shush her.

Yeah, right, I thought. First she's shy and then she's upset. I may not know much about kids, but I've never seen them roll their eyes back in their head, no matter how 'upset' they are. We were ushered into the doctor's office and sat nervously as he scanned over her medical report. Nadia leaned forward and pointed at the comment section where it said (in Russian) "Suspected Oligophrenia".

I asked what that meant, to which he replied, "I don't know, but she looks OK to me. Just take her home and love her." I questioned him further about what I supposed to be a seizure, but he brushed me off, looking at his watch and stood up to leave. After all, I supposed, at $600 a consultation, you couldn't take too much time with these US Embassy required examinations (I may still be a bit mad about this).

We returned Katerina to the orphanage and went home. Nadia was visibly upset and seemed to be searching for words. When we got back home I said to Tony, "Do you suppose love has to grow, because to be honest, I felt nothing."

He agreed that she might be a challenge… and that hyperactivity had seemed a bit 'odd'. We talked about the possibility of adopting her, or another child who came with a serious medical condition. As much as we might have been tempted to take on the challenge, we were reminded that our mission's insurance would not cover the expenses of any "pre-existing condition". So if we were looking at a lifetime of special treatment, it would be at our own expense.

The next day we tore off to see a group of kids, three siblings, who apparently needed to be adopted. As we wound through the traffic, thinking we'd hit the jackpot, someone in the front seat mentioned, "Oh, and they're all boys!" Like that was a good thing. Tony and I slumped in the back seat in despair, whispering to each other about how we were going to get out of this one.

But no worries, after a nice cup of tea and some cookies with the boys running circles around our feet, the grandfather said that he may have mentioned that life was busy, but he had no intention whatsoever of giving any of them away.

By now we'd been in Russia almost a week and were beginning to feel a panicky despair. Tony and I had to admit that we might have just bought a very expensive 'Tour of Russia' and would return on the last plane and accept our fate. Then there was a knock on our door. It was evening so that came as a surprise, but we carefully unlocked the deadbolts, opened the door, and there stood Alla and Nadia. Nadia translated for Alla.

"I've found a little girl; she's just turned three and the orphanage's government support will not allow her to stay where she is for long. She's cross-eyed and so has no hope of being adopted locally. The director says if you come, he will work with you to get all the necessary permissions."

"That's great!" Tony exclaimed. "Can we go see her tomorrow?"

"Yes," said Nadia. "But pack a suitcase. We need to go by plane."

"Just where is this orphanage?" I asked.

In a little town called Armivir, in the state of Georgia. It's about one thousand miles south of here."

"One thou… no way! We can't go off on a wild goose chase like that. I'm sorry but …"

"The girl's name is Marsha," Nadia added.

"We're in," Tony said, looking at me. "What time do we fly?"

The next day we stood in line for an interminable length of time and bought four tickets on the next plane to Krasnador, the capital of the province and about an hour by taxi to Armivir. Soviet tickets were $5 and foreign ones were $100. Since we'd be nothing without Nadia and Alla, we bought four tickets at the foreigner price and they threw four innocent and unsuspecting locals off the plane to make room for us.

I was ashamed enough, and then I found that I couldn't physically lift the huge box of orphanage clothes up the stairs onto the plane. The stewardess yelled something in Russian to the tune of "Are you going to pick that up and get up here or shall we throw you and it off the plane as well?"

I found that extra reserve of energy. Talk about being 'persona non grata' as we all found places to sit and nooks to add our luggage around the live chickens and what not. I was shoved into a seat that I think I was next to the wife of a man who had just exited and who was gesticulating wildly from the tarmac, suitcase in hand. I just bowed my head quietly and reached for my seatbelt.

No seatbelt, OK...I'll just lean back. Oh wait, the seat keeps leaning all the way to the lap of the person behind me. I better sit up straight. Whatever I do, I don't want to make eye contact with anyone, especially the stewardess who looked like she'd just retired from the pro wrestling circuit. This was going to be a life-threatening adventure. I had no idea where the rest of us were, but since I was on last, I knew they were somewhere back in the plane.

Happily, after a two-hour flight during which we were given lukewarm water in a battered plastic cup (for which we were thankful), we landed without event and were told by Nadia sternly to keep our mouths shut till we got a taxi. One advantage to being what we call "Caucasian" was that unless we spoke, no one knew we weren't Russian, except possibly the people who'd been thrown off the plane.

We got into a taxi and left the airport. Oh, but wait, we've just had a flat tire, so now we're back at the airport because apparently there's no spare tire. We still haven't spoken in order not to give our subterfuge away. A look of panic was in Tony's eyes. He's the kind that would prefer TWO spare tires for a trip of just under a hundred miles. Finally, the driver was able to beg a tire off of a friend, and although it looked pretty questionable, we took off again.

Suddenly Tony got very sleepy and since there were no seatbelts, he hunkered down in the corner and pulled his leather jacket over his head. I still chuckle to think of my 'Knight in Shining Armor' being so afraid. But then I had to remember my own "nap time" in the floor of a VW van driving through a Rhodesian war zone. I had no recourse except to just sit, mute, in the middle seat and pray.

It really was a rather beautiful drive in the moonlight and after a couple of hours we came into a small town and were dropped at the front door of the orphanage. A staff or several scrubbed and smiling people greeted us at the car (which by now had yet another flat tire) and ushered us into a warm and cozy office. Before we could fully appreciate the huge picture of Stalin glaring down at us, we were handed steaming cups of sweet tea as everyone gathered around to talk. The doctor, who was introduced as Vegislav, spoke up after we'd all had a few sips.

"Marsha has crossed eyes," he said softly. We indicated that we knew that. "She's got dark hair as well." Hmmmm ... I didn't know that, but OK. Leaning back in his chair he continued, as if talking about the love of his life. "She's really very smart, little Marsha is". The others nodded and smiled.

After a long rush of un-translated and animated Russian with smiles and laughing, we were led to the door and told we should come see her in the morning. Nadia told us some of the things that had been spoken of when there was no translation. "Dr Vegislav says Marsha loves to come to his office when she's either sick or feigning sickness because she's given an apple (yablushika) when she does. They also spoke of what a little mother she is to the whole class, making sure they're all ok and following the teacher correctly. Apparently her father was 'White Russian' but the mother Armenian, and that's why she's dark."

We checked into our hotel, such as it was. It definitely had seen better days, but at three dollars a night, we couldn't complain. It had two twin beds, each nailed to opposite walls, and a thin blanket on each. There was a cold water pipe where the shower was supposed to have been, attached to the ceiling right above the toilet, which had no seat. There was a multi colored plastic phone in the room that unsurprisingly didn't work. The week we were there I never removed my coat. At one time I decided to splurge and get my hair washed (since I wasn't too fond of the shower). It was only thirty cents, but I didn't get my money's worth. The girl motioned for me to lean head first over a trough in the floor and without warning doused me with a bucket of cold water. Then she handed me a dirty comb with broken teeth and collected my money. Done.

The next morning, with our hearts in our throats, we made our way to the orphanage, a small house in a neighborhood with a big wall around it. We had been told that the children would be having their music lesson today, and part of the festivities included dancing around the room while picking up fall leaves they'd made of colored paper. We walked up some steep stairs into the room and Tony may have to write this part, because he swears that as we stood at the doorway, he saw a bright arrow-shaped light shining right down over her dark head. She was facing away so we couldn't know it was her (the crossed eyes would have been a giveaway), but I'll never forget his exclamation of "Oh YES!" The look of love. Sure enough, she turned around, looked directly at us and smiled. Clever girl, we were hooked!!

What was to be overnight trip turned into several days. First we had to get a passport picture made, which meant we had to ride in a "machinka" (car), something little Marsha had seen in books but never experienced. She was thrilled beyond words but then slipped into a punk when she was removed and ushered into a boring old office for the picture. Because of missing her beloved car, she refused to cooperate and finally we had to resort to just snapping and going. The ladies all agreed it would help with getting her out, because she was anything but charming in the picture.

And then started all the official visits to official people, starting with hour's drive back to Krasnador. At the prefectural office there, one lady said vehemently that we had the wrong paperwork and the adoption could not under any circumstances continue but she would try to call Moscow. That was like saying she would try to call the moon, because by then we realized that her phone had about as much chance of working as the plastic one in our hotel. I stood on one side of the room and Tony on the other as the mean lady with the bleached blonde hair picked up the phone and yelled in the number. I was praying so hard, I noticed that I was fingering a piece of string in my pocket like a rosary.

Tony looked like he was going to be sick, we were so hopelessly in love with this little mite. And then the blonde's voice broke the reverie, and she was talking and taking notes. She slammed down the phone and threw back her head and laughed. It was all okay. She stamped some things on the paper and handed it to us to take to another office.

Buoyed up with hope, we rushed across the street and barged into the last office. The man took the paper, slammed it on his desk and got another sheet out of his desk. It was covered in bold lettering and red ink. The doctor read it and the color left his face. That's when Nadia, the translator jumped up and started shouting at the man. Of course we had no idea what she was saying, but he dropped his head like a whipped puppy and proceeded to stamp our paper with the requisite permissions to adopt.

We sailed out of the office on air, slapping backs and shouting victory. We had actually adopted Marsha Nicole Woods! During the ride back to where we were staying, I asked Nadia, "What was that in the last office when you jumped in and started talking?" As a translator, she was never asked to offer her opinion in any of the discussions.

"Well, he showed the doctor a letter that had just arrived that said no foreigners could adopt any more. He said it's the law."

"And that's when you jumped up?" I asked.

"You're right, I wasn't going to accept that. I told him I saw LOTS of foreigners adopting kids in Moscow"

"But Nadia, you didn't." I said cautiously, not wanting to spoil the moment, "You saw foreigners lined up at the doctor's place getting physicals. That had nothing to do with the adoption process."

"Oh," she said and bowed her head for a moment. Then she turned to me and smiled and we both hugged each other. Another case of the walls come a'tumblin down!

That night in the hotel room I took her in for her first bath. She was just too, too cute. The three of us had a sweet snuggle and she slept, like the baby she was. After she was asleep, we were reviewing the day and the terror we had felt at the blonde lady's office. I mentioned praying so hard that I was fingering a string.

Tony said softly, "I was putting together escape plans. I just told God I'd watched one child slip away and I couldn't survive another."

"You said that to the GOD OF THE UNIVERSE?" I shouted in shock.

"Well, it was true," he said.

And then I remembered what I had first loved about him. He was humble and honest. It WAS true. Our hearts were too far gone to give this one away.

The next day dawned bright and early and we all headed for the airport. But there was a problem. There was only one seat, foreign or otherwise, for the next several days. Well, that was an interesting math problem. Of course little Marsha would fly free without a seat, but which one would take her? I could go, but then Tony would be left with two women. Finally we all decided that Tony would take her and get her far, far away before somebody realized the rather flimsy loophole Nadia had accidently created. Off the two of them went, smiling and waving back at us while I prayed especially this time for a safe journey. Tony said Marsha held my business card the whole way to Moscow, sitting on his lap with no seatbelt and saying, "Momma? Momma?" the whole time.

I moved into Nadia and Alla's room at the hotel and we had two days of carefree sightseeing and visiting. Tony arrived in Moscow safe and sound and Natasha's folks were delighted to love on little Marsha. She was pretty happy, especially to find somebody who spoke Russian!

Three days later, we arrived in Moscow late at night to find Vitali waiting. There was no conversation, and I had to wonder if he knew we were 'on to him'. We traveled along without incident, but as he dropped us off at our respective residences, I began to realize I would be the last. When Nadia exited the car, I jumped out and ran to the back where she was getting her bag and said in a whisper,

"Which way should we be driving towards my home?"

She gave me a chin nod in the direction we should be going and squeezed my hand. We both knew I'd be jumping out of a speeding car if he made a turn.

As I sat as tense as a spring in the back seat, he looked in the rear view mirror and said, in his best English,

"You like lil' girl?"

"Yes," I answered enthusiastically, and remained silent until he reached our destination….safely.

Now our last step was the US Embassy. But first we had to verify the passport we were given in Krasnador. Off we went to a fancy office to do that, and like so many others, it was now operating out of a crumbling mansion of bygone days. I think it had probably been some bourgeoisie royalist home before the 1917 revolution. We entered and stated our wishes, to which there was a kafuffle around the window and Nadia rushed back to us. "They say this is just a passport for domestic travel and she is not to leave the country. We may have to return to Krasnador and get another passport."

How many times could we hit the wall with this endeavor? She was OURS now and we'd live our lives out in Russia if we had to, but I'll have to say we weren't keen to do so.

Suddenly Vitaly must have noticed our body language because he pushed into our huddle and we could tell he was asking what the problem was. Then he spun on his heels and walked up to the biggest, leather padded door and barged through without even knocking. As the door swung shut Nadia said, half under her breath,

"We're going to the Gulag."

After a while, the door burst open again and Vitali and someone who looked like an officer, festooned with medals and ribbons, charged out and up to us. We rose to our feet in time to catch his hand as he reached to shake Tony's. He said, in accented English,

"Mr. Woods, we have new passport ready in few minute. I just want say you do fine thing." He turned and then reconsidered as he called back over his shoulder, "Oh, you like tea? Coffee?" As we sat in wonder, little Marsha's new passport arrived with bows and smiles and we were on our way. In the car Nadia ventured a question to Vitali. There was much talking and then she translated,

"I asked him what he said to the official and he said,

"Oh I showed him my ID and told him you were my boss living in America."

We dare not laugh in the car, but when we reached home and were out of Vitali's hearing, we all burst out in laughter. Imagine Tony a KGB mole wanting a 'lil' girl.

So......all that remained was the US Embassy. Should be a no brainer, we had all the requisite paperwork except for the 'permission to search for an orphan' but we understood that it was in the works. We had three days before our tickets became null and void, so we were good.

Or so we thought. I called the Embassy and on the 4th try got through. That in itself was a lucky omen I thought. "Yes, of course, we can book you in for your interview in, let's see, three weeks, how's that sound?"

"WHAT?" I yelled into the phone, "We need to leave in three days!"

"Sorry," came the not sorry voice on the other end. "We're very busy, your agent should have made the appointment weeks ago". Well, I guess we should have had an "agent".

I began a daily phone call, starting about 30 minutes before the Embassy opened in the hope of catching a cleaning lady or somebody who'd hear my plight. I became amused at the answering machine response, in perfect icy English,

"This is the United States of America Embassy. All of our offices are closed. If you are an American in trouble, please call back during business hours." So we had to make some decisions. TWA was stopping service to Moscow the next day, after which our expensive tickets would be null and void. Tony would leave on his plane ticket as planned, joining Nathan at my parent's place in Colorado.

It was also time to vacate Natasha's parent's apartment. They'd been paid (supposedly) by their daughter and were anxious to move back in as they had been staying with the neighbors. In addition, Vitali had begun harassing us for money. My guess is that when Alla made the phone call weeks earlier, Natasha had come through with more money, but because she'd blown the first $5000 on who knows what, she was now trying to scrape up more, starting with my Dad. Daily phone calls reminded him that we were in real danger, and only more money could fix the problem. While Daddy was a loving and wonderful father to us, and wanted this to succeed, he was no fool and Natasha was barking up the wrong tree.

When Natasha called again, this time to tell of a horrible bombing at the MacDonald's in Moscow (never happened), Daddy suggested that they might continue their conversation down at the Immigration office. We never heard from her again, and are pretty sure she was in the US illegally.

Nadia had a friend with a sick boy and it was decided that little Marsha and I would go there secretly and pay her $10 a day in cash for a place to sleep, away from Vitali's clutches. The mother needed the money in the form of the 'hard currency' of US dollars for medicine, so it was a good move for all of us. We kissed Tony good bye at 4:00 AM and by 6:00 AM I got a phone call from Vitali and his 'translator'. I was never sure if the translator was a man or a woman but he definitely couldn't speak English. The conversation went something like this:

"Husband tell he give $1000 when he leave."

"No," I corrected kindly, "we both talked to you and said we would give you 100 dollars as a bonus when Tony leaves."

"One thousand dollars."

"No, 100. One Zero Zero," I maintained. "I'm leaving it here at Natasha's parents for you to collect."

Long pause with Russian discussion going on. Then, "When you leave airport, you have trouble, I be there." And he hung up. I was glad we were moving quietly to another section of town.

And so Little Marsha and I began our 'bonding', sleeping on the floor in a quiet and safe place. Nadia would visit every day after I would fail to get the Embassy and we would wander around Moscow. Little Marsha was beginning to tire of this game of having a nice lady who couldn't speak Russian trying to take charge. Of course she enjoyed Nadia and the family we were staying with, but I think she was beginning to grieve the loss of her 'family'. We would go on outings where she would throw herself on the floor screaming uncontrollably, and we would both shake our heads. She called me 'kaka' on numerous occasions but her favorite seemed to be "Ni nada", said angrily with her hand on her hip. I knew enough from the gesture it was not kind, and Nadia wouldn't translate. Only years later we understood that it meant, "None of your business," perhaps in a more crass way, like her kaka word. So cute, so sad.

During these two weeks, Nadia and I had attended the Bolshoi Ballet one night, leaving Marsha in the care of our host family. Earlier in the day we had gone to purchase the tickets. At the kiosk Nadia was about to pay when they heard me say something to her in English. Suddenly our two dollar tickets were fifty each! She excused herself and said sternly to me,

"Haven't I told you to keep your mouth shut?"

At the next stall, I was silent and we forked over two dollars each to see this world class ballet. I'm not sure if I was more impressed with the ballet (Giselle) or the building itself, something the Communists had somehow not destroyed.

It made me sad wherever we walked to see old men sitting in the cold with their war medals spread out on a handkerchief for sale. People lined up to enter grocery stores for the few remaining cans on the shelf.

Before Tony left, he was out walking one morning, under strict orders from Nadia to keep his mouth shut. He noticed a long line leading into a shop, stuck his head inside and saw that it was a bakery. As he turned to walk away, someone in line shouted something to him in Russian. Tony, not understanding, shrugged his shoulders and lifted his hands in a "I don't understand you" gesture. The man slapped his forehead and broke out of line, but not before several others looking on did the same thing. Tony could only wish that he could understand and communicate. There had been plenty of bread in the store.

Finally, after two weeks, I was given a 1:30 appointment with the consular who would grant her a visa for the USA. We were excited. The day before the interview, I made Nadia take us to the one Baptist church that I knew existed in Moscow. She didn't want to go, saying she was afraid of "Baptists" as it was rumored that they drank blood (poor understanding of "communion" I suppose).

I insisted. Russia was experiencing a mass return to the church after "Perestroika" had happened a few months earlier. With the dissolution of the communist regime, people were free to do as they wished, and no one really knew how long that would last, so.....

We got out of the taxi several blocks away because it couldn't get any closer due to crowd surrounding the building. There were literally thousands of people, all clamoring to get into the door. I spoke English, and either that or the fact I was holding an adorable little girl in my arms, the crowd parted like the Red Sea and we were ushered to an office on the second floor. I untangled Marsha's arms from my neck and set her on the floor and she began screaming like one possessed. She could not be shushed or comforted and I even thought to myself , "Is this the work of the devil?"

Then a kindly lady stepped forward and led us up into an office. We had to step over hundreds of people lining the stairs, and Marsha still screamed on. Then when we got inside, the lady came forth with the ultimate weapon.

"Yablushika?" she said, offering little Marsha a shiny apple. She reached out, took it and the screaming abruptly stopped. We visited a moment while Marsha devoured the apple, core, stem and all, and settled into a comfortable chair.

There was a stirring outside the door and the lady indicated that we were welcome to move into the sanctuary as another service was starting. I scooped up the little angel and we hurried out the door .... only to be met with a wall of humanity, still standing and sitting on ever step and crevice all the way up and down the staircase. Again the mass parted and we went to the door where I looked in.

I will never forget the sight of literally thousands of people, standing cheek to cheek, waiting for the service to start. There were no chairs, no aisles, just people. Forget the 'drinking blood' part, I was freaking out when I told Nadia, "We can't do this," and we beat a hasty retreat.

Muscovites: so hungry to hear the truth that they would stand for hours to hear the Gospel. Also during those empty days waiting for the embassy, we went (again against Nadia's will) to the Billy Graham crusade that was in a Moscow stadium. It had a capacity of 60,000 but there were an estimated 80,000 there.

This time we left the baby home and went alone. We found seats but just by luck. Every inch of every step, nook, everything was filled with people.

As the evening began, Joni Erikson Tada took the floor. Her talk was about asking God the "Why" questions. I tried not to burst out crying because Nadia was obviously freaked out enough, but I so resonated with what she was saying. Trevor hadn't been gone a year and I still had a lot of questions. Nadia squirmed through the message, always the same, of Billy Graham's call to Christianity. When the altar call was given people absolutely surged the platform and I thought there was going to be a stampede, but finally they got it under control.

I'll never know the outcome with Nadia and Billy Graham. When we left some days later I gave her my Bible and even though we soon lost track of each other and her letters were returned, I pray often that she and her family found Christ. On a side note, as we were leaving with the masses, an obviously extremely mentally disabled girl stumbled across our path. Nadia pointed and said, "Like that,

Oligophrenia".

Thank you Lord for your protection, and as I continually do, I pray that little Katarina was able to experience your love somehow.

The very next day, we were at the Embassy by 1:00 for our 1:30 appointment. I began to realize that 40 or 50 of us had all been given the 1:30 appointment as the waiting room filled up with wild eyed parents and confused children of all ages.

Little Marsha was contentedly playing with the blocks and the other children, all rattling along in Russian. Nadia excused herself for a quick trip to the bathroom while we were waiting. The plan was for her to watch Marsha until she was needed to see the consular, since I figured there'd be some preliminary paperwork etc.

At 1:29 sharp a small hole in the bullet proof glass pulled back and a gruff looking woman shouted out,

"Who's first?"

"I am!"

I jumped up, grabbing Marsha by the arm. Nobody was going to beat me out of this, I'd waited three weeks and I had HAD it with it all!!!

"Nyet" said Marsha, who naturally didn't want to finish up her playing, whereupon she twisted her arm and plopped down on the floor. I hadn't let go of her when this happened. And then she started the screaming again. Loudly.

I scooped her up, grabbing a lolly pop out of my bag and handing it to her. She kept screaming.

"Next!" the lady said with irritation. "Madam, stop your baby crying," she glowered as she craned her neck to look around me. "Next!" she called again.

I stepped back into her vision and said loudly, "The baby's fine, we're having this interview now!" Thankful that the lolly was muffling the screams by now and she settled into my shoulder, winding the candy into my hair.

I wasn't invited into a room or anything, but stood there fighting down rage that I had waited three weeks for this woman to talk to me thru a little hole in the glass while leisurely browsing thru my paperwork, saying to me, as if I didn't fully know, "Ah, this is your application, here is the letter from the birth mother, and on and on."

Finally Nadia reappeared and I said carefully, "Excuse me for a minute," and walked over to Nadia. "Hold the baby and don't let the consular see that her right arm isn't working." I'd come to that conclusion as I was holding her.

Nadia looked at me in shock with an accusatory stare that said, "I can't leave you for a moment can I?" and settled Marsha on her lap. She, by then, was too interested in her lolly to resume playing with the kids.

Within minutes we were all stamped, sealed and ready to go... to the hospital. Neither of us could figure it out, but the right arm was hanging limp and Marsha didn't want us to touch it. "I'll take her to my hospital, maybe they won't remember that my little girl is actually six and see her for free. You sit outside and behave till I'm done," she chided gently.

Within an hour she came out with a shocked look on her face. "The doctor says her arm is broken. What on earth did you do? We have to go home and get some bandages and then go to the city hospital to get it set."

I've felt remorse before, but nothing like this. How on earth had I managed to break her arm by just pulling her to answer the consular's call? We went back to the apartment and loaded up on our landlady's tea towel supply. In the car I remembered the stores I'd seen near hospitals selling various things including clean needles. Faced with a growing AIDS problem, clean needles were essential but not always available, like now that the stores were closed.

"Nadia," I said in the taxi, "We've come too far for me to let her get AIDS. We can't let them use needles." She nodded her head thoughtfully.

The taxi pulled to a stop and we got out. Marsha was whimpering, still in pain, now exacerbated by exhaustion since we'd clearly missed her strictly enforced nap time. I didn't see anything but a junk yard with a dirt path thru the middle. Nadia started walking and finally my eyes focused on a huge sprawling brick building. The City Hospital…..in the dark.

We tried several doors, and they were all locked. We knocked and then we pounded. Nothing. I was glad this wasn't really an emergency. Finally we saw a light on several stories up. There was a fire escape so we thought,

"Well, I guess we'll give it a try" and started up.

On the second flight, I, who was carrying Marsha, stepped onto the hem of my coat and we both tumbled forward onto the stairs. They were wet with ice by now. Instead of scolding me this time, we all broke into helpless laughter with Nadia saying with exasperation,

"I can't take care of BOTH of you; give me the baby.

Finally our knocks were answered and we were led the corridors to an outpatient sort of area, back on the first floor. A young doctor bounded in with a bright colored kerchief wrapped gaily around his head. Little Marsha shouted "Clown" and warmed to him immediately. Nadia later explained that the headdress meant he was a qualified doctor. Never saw that in the movie, "Dr Zhivago". He began to have a lively conversation about something with Marsha, and before anyone knew it, he'd taken her arm, gave it a good 'pop' and everything was fine.

Nadia translated what he said to me, as he was looking directly into my eyes, with kind tenderness. "You see, little girls have weak elbows until they're about five. We must never pull them or exert weight on them, but rather 'lift' them. If we're rough, they'll dislocate their elbows and it's quite painful."

The day at the church and then the embassy now made sense. She evidently had popped it back into place when she reached for the apple but the Embassy was just too much. The doctor bid us a fond farewell and left the room. We began to gather ourselves for the exit when Marsha realized she was no longer the patient. Suddenly she coughed and said,

"I'm sick," to which we both laughed heartily and headed home.

The next day we practically skipped to the defunct TWA office, who, when they heard our plight, directed us a few blocks over to the DELTA office. For a fee, they would take my invalid ticket and put me on Delta as far as Frankfurt, whereupon I'd continue back onto TWA. They couldn't fly the next day but the next for sure. I returned to TWA to wrap things up and the agent quipped, "So then, I guess Delta isn't 'ready when you are." That was Delta's commercial jingle at the time.

So now all that remained was the possible hurdle with Vitali who's last words to me had been a not-so-veiled threat of trouble at the airport. I patted my money belt. It had been on my person, keeping me warm for almost a month. When Vitali said that the first orphanage we visited would require $5000, we thought this would be the norm and went to Western Union and got that much more money. It took two days to get it, standing in line, filling out forms, etc. Nadia indicated that she didn't want to know anything about how much or where it was because someone might get the information out of her.

I noticed that after years of Communism, the Russians had no trust of anyone or anything. Having Vitali in the mix was even more scary and the girls, Nadia and Alla took precautions to keep things more secure that we could ever imagine doing in America. Anyway, because we had a decent normal orphanage where little Marsha was loved, not exploited, we had paid out very little, so I still had enough to get us out of the country with the KGB if necessary.

The next day, after mountains of hugs and kisses, we went to the airport. But wait! It was the DELTA airport and not the TWA one, (at that time there were several 'international' airports in Moscow), so we'd definitely given Vitali the slip.

The last gate was through Passport Control. I remembered Tony calling me just before boarding his flight to say that they had grilled him about his "visit to the marble factory" that had been the reason for his visa. After a few anxious moments, Tony, quickly thinking on his feet, produced a business card from his father that he still had from when he was a salesman, and they were satisfied and let him go on through. Tony left with a renewed determination that he would never, ever be a spy.

In my case, I wasn't in possession of any such business card, but perhaps as I was holding a wiggling child, the subject never came up, and we were soon on a plane for the four-hour flight to Frankfurt. Our wonderful host wished us a safe journey and as a departing gift handed me a bag of six beautiful apples.

We settled into our seats next to a NASA scientist. He was pleasant and kind to Marsha, but as she powered through the apples (she weighed 10 kilos at the time, 22 pounds); he was doing the math and we both realized that this lil' girl was going to explode soon. We smiled and distracted her and then hid the apples. The next three hours she spent screaming "Dai!" (which means 'give me'). I had to admit, she had a set of lungs on her!

Arriving in Frankfurt with Marsha firmly strapped in her stroller, I tried to avoid the stares of condemnation from fellow passengers. I hurried to my connecting gate for my TWA plane. The agent, looking annoyed, said, "You're too late, we've closed the gate. You can try again tomorrow."

You can imagine after four hours of screaming, I wasn't looking my best and I teared up as I wondered if I had enough energy to cry. "I can't spend the night alone in Frankfurt, I have this screaming child I can't control," I whined. The agent stood up and looked over the counter into the face of an angel, fast asleep with an angelic smile on her face.

While I was contemplating pinching her or handing her over to the agent, I felt a strong arm reach over my shoulder and heard a firm voice say, "Excuse me, but check your book of conduct," he boomed as he helped himself to a thick volume on the desk.

Then he turned to me and introduced himself. "I was on the plane from Moscow and I've also adopted a few kids. It can be tough. I'm a Delta Pilot and was planning on talking to you when we landed. TWA has a right of duty to put you on the next available plane, so I'll make sure they do that."

And he did. It looked like I had about 30 minutes to make the next flight. I would be continuing on Delta instead getting back on TWA to honor my original ticket. I was weak with relief. We stepped away from the desk and he spoke again.

"Now I don't want to interfere, but I know when you reach the US, they'll take away that visa you have (it was in a large manila envelope issued by the embassy, covered in stamps and containing all the various papers that were necessary for the adoption) and you won't get it back for about six weeks. I don't mind stepping into the offices here and photocopying them if you'd like." I meekly handed the envelope over to him, but then caught myself.

"I'm sorry sir, but I don't know you; how do I know you're coming back?"

He smiled and said, "Because you're standing here with my bag."

Off he went and within a few minutes he was back with duplicates of everything I needed. We walked a few steps toward my gate and he added, "Now is there anything else I can do for you?"

I took a chance since the copies went so well, "Yes, could you watch the (sleeping) baby while I go to the bathroom?" He nodded and off I dashed.

The trip home was another semi-nightmare, but I was getting the hang of it. At first I was trapped in the middle two seats of a five-across configuration. Marsha had woken up and was rearing to go, especially when the full food tray arrived. She ate and ate until she was chewing and spitting out food because she couldn't hold anymore.

Then the stewardess took the tray and the screaming began again. I was beginning to see a pattern. Later when we arrived home she continued this pattern until my Daddy, who I won't say was all that good with children, understood her problem. "Why don't you give her a bread roll to hold till the next meal?" If only I'd have known that sooner, the problem would have been fixed immediately.

After awhile, she still wasn't settling and from the din I could hear the stewardess leaning over the three seats to my right and saying, "Do you want me to hold the little boy for awhile?" OK, Marsha had what was called the "orphanage hair cut", a buzz about an inch long all over, (to prevent lice, I'm told), but usually when she wasn't screaming she sported the cutest little bows. Unfortunately the bow had been lost in the battle, and the stewardess could call her anything she wanted if she'd take her away.

As she exited to the right, the large Arab man to my left called another stewardess and ordered, "Bring this woman a glass of wine."

"Oh sir, I don't drink. Thank you."

"You drink."

I drank. The room began to spin and the 'boy' was back.

I excused myself, wobbled to my feet and took Marsha to the back of the plane. I locked her in my arms horizontally across my body and began to rock back and forth. She began to relax and I had two thoughts,

"Oh my goodness, this is the trip to Africa with Trevor all over again" and "True, but I'm 20 years older and she's not going to be getting the best of me this time."

She was asleep in minutes and I put her in her seat and practically fell on to her as I settled in myself. We slept the rest of the way to Boston.

Again we did the terminal walk, had a drink, went to the bathroom and boarded the next plane bound for Denver. This time we didn't even make it through dinner before we were both out cold. I laid her on the floor (you can't do that anymore) and stretched out myself.

As we were descending, I dressed her in a little outfit I'd somehow managed to keep nice, and arranged a beautiful bow in her hair. Then I stood up and my pants almost fell off. No, I hadn't lost weight, the button on my wrap around slacks had somehow come off, (imagine that) leaving me to either hold them up with one hand or search for a bobby pin in my hair. That worked fine. Now to find my shoes.

One shoe.........nope, only one shoe. I called the stewardess and she indicated that I needed to look harder. Finally, as we started our final decent, she made an announcement for everyone to be on the lookout for a black flat. It was found in the last row of the plane, having been drug under the cart the entire length of the aisle.

We were very happy to be home. To 'Papa' and to meet for the first time Nathan. He had a big stuffed dog for her and had learned the word "dog" in Russian, "Sabaka". They were off to a good start.

Now we fast forward several years to ...

Chapter 12

Hong Kong and Ethiopia

In the winter of 1995 we began to plan our scheduled furlough. It was to be for a year.

I had begun to notice a certain spirit in my children that can only be described as a sense of 'entitlement'. After all, we lived in a relatively new and comfortable house, attended schools that required tuition and acceptance to be there, we were 'foreigners' which sometimes was a detriment but usually cause for a (sometimes misplaced) feeling of laud and honor. All in all, I wasn't seeing a lot of compassion or concern for others coming from either Nathan or Nicki.

To add to this, I believe we were beginning to kick at the traces ourselves. We felt that we had done everything we could for our little church plant in Taitomi, and in the true spirit of missions, maybe were beginning to think it was time to 'cut the apron strings' and move along. At any rate, we were beginning to wiggle as if in a cocoon, loving where we were but wanting to stretch our wings.

God knew the restlessness in our hearts, and seemingly out of the blue came a proposition from our mission that we make a stopover in Hong Kong before starting our furlough and serve as interim pastor at the Japanese church there. In a few months, our good friends and fellow missionaries, Bob and Mavis Hardy, would be coming out of retirement to take on the responsibility, but the church needed someone right away. The Hardys had greatly influenced and blessed us over the years, actually helping to form us into the people we'd become, so 'filling in for their arrival' sent shivers down our spines, but we humbly accepted.

The timing of all this left about a four-month gap in the calendar, between the arrival of Bob and Mavis and taking on our "furlough role" as missionaries-in-residence at our Learning Center in Richmond, Virginia. How should we spend that time?

One day, I sat down and drafted a letter to three friends on the mission field, all in different places on the globe. Basically it said that we'd like to pitch in as a family and help them in whatever way we could. We would take care of our expenses and give them three months before moving on to Virginia.

Weeks passed. Finally one reply came in which came which left us staring at each other, knowing that if we accepted it wasn't going to be easy. It was from SIM, or Sudan Interior Mission. They were the ones who had literally saved my life back in Liberia many years before. What they needed was someone to provide support for a 22-year-old missionary girl who would be spending the summer 'alone' in a refugee camp in Ethiopia. There were five thousand Sudanese refugees there from the Uduk tribe, mostly all Christians following the conversion of their witch doctor and chief many years before. That fact alone made them targets of persecution back in Sudan and led to their packing up and relocating the entire tribe over the border into neighboring Ethiopia. It was a rough and dangerous journey, with over half of them dying along the way. Arriving in a remote area of western Ethiopia, the government allowed them to stay until the United Nations could sort them out.

It soon became apparent that the Uduks would have to be separated from the rest of the Sudanese refugees, because many of them were made up of the same people who had been persecuting them back home, particularly from the tribe known as the "Dinkas", a fierce and war-loving people.

The new camp was created just for the Uduk tribe and called "Bonga", and it was about 500 miles by dirt track from much of anything else. Claire, the SIM missionary on site, normally worked alongside other mission families, but due to furlough schedules, she would be alone. We were invited to come, primarily to make sure she was okay. It didn't take long to realize that Claire was an amazingly resourceful girl who, although happy to see us, didn't really need our "watch care" and it seemed to us often had to take care of us.

And as an "Oh by the way", the mission asked if Tony would mind teaching the Old Testament to the church elders, who didn't have it in their own language. That's not unlike pouring gasoline on a fire, and we accepted the invitation immediately.

First stop on this Great Adventure was Hong Kong and the Japanese church. Some church members picked us up and took us straight to a Chinese meal. Of course we were beyond tired, but we smiled sweetly as they served up a steaming plate of roast pigeon! We were all four taken aback, since we had a birdfeeder at home and had enjoyed our two "regulars", a couple of pigeons. We'd named them "Mr. and Mrs. Rufus". Nicki was just six and almost cried as she was dished up a big helping, but we assured her that this wasn't OUR pigeons, so she gave in and decided it was OK.

That night we settled into our two-bedroom apartment with a huge sigh of relief, excited to have begun the journey. This would be the nicest place we'd see until we reached Virginia, and we knew to be grateful. Nicki was invited to attend Japanese school in Hong Kong. This would be her first time in first grade, to be followed by three more, in Virginia, Colorado, and back in Japan.

The transition was fairly easy, though, thanks to the Japanese school system. Japan, and I assume other countries as well have "Government endorsed schools" all over the world with the assurance that the curriculum will be exactly what would be offered at home. This comes at a price, and we were much relieved that they wouldn't be charging us because we were only there for a few months. I think secretly they were thankful for an English-speaking girl and family present to help the kids and mom integrate into Hong Kong, even though we ourselves were foreigners as well.

They put her in the first grade, complete with the ceremony, which is big in Japan. Mothers and Dads attend in formal clothing, either suits and nice dresses, or if possible, kimonos. We didn't have a kimono with us, and had to settle for "Sunday best", but we were there to cheer her on. It was a great opportunity as well to meet the mothers and a big part of Hong Kong's Japanese community. Nicki was an instant hit. Being fluent in both languages as well as a little precocious meant that she had many friends almost instantly.

What I found was that the twenty or so mothers who waited with me twice a day at the bus stop were mostly in culture shock and also needed friends. The way it always seemed to play out was that when Japanese businessmen were transferred overseas, they were almost immediately swept away to work-related duties. Their wives and children were invariably left to fend for themselves, getting set up in a new apartment, new school, unfamiliar shopping areas, medical services and all the other myriad responsibilities associated with such a move. Of course there were veteran women among them who'd done this several times, but I was surprised at the number of very young ones who were still processing the fact that this wasn't Japan.

When I suggested that we get together to talk about our common challenges, and while we were at it study the Bible, most of them were quick to join in. Almost instantly we had a home group that grew to about 20 women all hungry for answers. We met in the home of Yuko Lai, a Christian Japanese lady married to a Chinese businessman. She's still in Hong Kong today, by now having raised five lovely children, became indispensible at the Japanese church and led countless young families to faith in Jesus Christ. I'm happy to still call her my friend and sister in the Lord.

The first Sunday at church, Tony preached a full throttle Japanese sermon, to be met with startled expressions. It seems that, in spite of the room full of Asian faces, many were from all over the world whose understanding of Japanese was limited. They preferred to hear

English, while the Japanese (especially the newcomers) were anxious to hear their mother tongue spoken. The next week, Tony shortened his sermon by half, preached it in both languages, and everyone was happy.

Another thing that came about while we were there was the realization that we would be needing massive amounts of inoculations to be able to travel to Ethiopia. We asked about a doctor and were introduced to one of our own Japanese church members, Levi Lee. Both he and his wife are Chinese but felt led to work in the Japanese ministry. Dr. Lee indicated that our vaccinations would be free. We were humbled by this man's kindness.

But then another thing happened that I'll never forget. We were on a pretty tight budget and knew that we'd have to go downtown to get our Yellow Fever Shots because Dr. Lee was not allowed to have the vaccine in his office as it's "live". The shots would be $85 dollars each, so I was beginning to formulate how we could move things around to be able to afford such expenditure.

Then one day, out of the blue, Vivian, Dr Lee's wife, handed me an envelope at one of our Bible Studies. We were standing on the platform waiting for a train when I casually opened it up to see what it was. Inside there was EXACTLY the amount of money we needed for the shots, with the note, "Thought you might like to have some fun while you're here". She swears to this day that she knew nothing about us needing the shots or why she picked that particular amount of money. "It was just God's timing," she says. I still remember crying tears of, shall I say 'verification'?

Before we knew it, we had Hong Kong all wrapped up. It's amazing how quickly three months can pass. We will never forget the fun and faithfulness of all those Chinese and Japanese people we came to know and appreciate. We still keep in touch with many of them and visit every few years, just to be with them in a city we love.

We boarded a Cathay Pacific plane for one of the longest flights of that time, 15 hours to Frankfurt, Germany. There, we would spend a day and transfer to Ethiopian airlines to continue on to Addis Abba.

The flight went well and we arrived at our pre-booked hotel that we'd paid for with frequent flyer points. It was about an hour from the airport and the desk clerk couldn't believe that we'd come the route we had. "You should take the 'airport train' back tomorrow, it's much shorter," he chided us.

Just to verify his admonition, after we got settled in the room, we walked over to the train station and checked as to where and when the airport train would be the next day. All was good. And so the next day, there we were on the platform. I asked the conductor in my best German, "Airport?" to which he nodded, "Yes".

All set. And then a train arrived. What? It was about 5 minutes early! "These Germans," I thought to myself. "So efficient." We struggled on board, with our loads of luggage, including several boxes of clothes (remember we were going to a refugee camp). Off we went. After about 30 minutes, we began to wonder where the airport was. Flagging down a conductor, we asked genially, "Airport?" and noticed his pained expression.

His answer stumped us. All he said was "Worms."

If you're not well-versed in the Protestant Reformation, you may not know that the city of Worms is where Martin Luther posted his famous 99 complaints against the Catholic Church. We knew that, and also knew that the town of Worms is far, far from Frankfurt and that we were in trouble.

"No worries," we thought to ourselves, we'll just get off in Worms, cross the track and come back to Frankfurt". We did that often in Japan when we made a mistake or missed a stop. By now the fact that the train arrived 5 minutes early was making sense. It very clearly wasn't the airport train! We got off an hour later in Worms and looked for the opposing train on the opposite track. There was none. Then the panic began to set in.

Suggestions were given by kind passersby. After all, we did create a distraction, four confused foreigners and a huge pile of luggage. Finally the consensus was Taxi.

We stepped out to find one rather rattled old taxi with a driver slumped over the wheel sleeping. We woke him up and said, "Frankfurt Airport?" His eyes popped to attention and we continued, "How Much?" Gathering his wits at this amazing windfall, he blinked, thought a moment and said, "One fifty" in heavily accented English. Tony nodded in affirmation and began to load the luggage in the trunk.

"Did he say 150 MARKS?" I asked. "That's all you have!"

"No," Tony assured me, "he said 115."

I begged to differ, so I shouted at the taxi driver, thinking he'd understand better if I yelled, "HOW MUCH?"

He shouted back in the same tone "One Five Zero," to which I had to counter, as I showed him Tony's wallet and the money there, "No Tip?" He smiled and agreed, started the engine with a couple of cranks and we lurched and burped onto the Autobahn.

Now every time I've ever been on the famous German Autobahn, I've been terrified. I don't believe they have speed limits and the rule seems to be 'every man for himself'. This suited me fine, as we only had about two hours till our flight left. Not this time. He drove like a spinster. Puttering along for at least 30 minutes. Finally I couldn't contain myself any longer so I leaned forward and showed him our tickets, now leaving in 90 minutes or so.

Well, I guess he got the message, because the rest of the trip was at a blistering speed. I was praying both for us and the car, which sounded like it was about to fall apart. We screeched into the departures, screaming and running for the desk. The agent looked at us in shock and said,

"I'll check you in, go get your luggage that you checked into storage and meet me back here. You two," (as she pointed to me and Nicki) "go on through security and tell them to hold the plane." So Nathan and Tony, sans passports, hurried off to collect the boxes we had left and Nicki and I dashed to immigration.

In your typical spy novel, this is perfectly doable, but not in reality. When Tony and Nathan got back to the desk with the bags, the agent had changed and no one would let them go through without their necessary passports (which the agent had given to me). They were stuck.

We, on the other hand were through immigration on the other side and weren't seeing the boys coming. Worried, I pushed BACK through immigration with a duck and a smile and started running around the airport, clutching Nicki's hand and dragging her along behind. You'll remember this was about five years before 9/11, so I could get away with it, although no one was happy. Still no sign of the guys.

I laugh now when I remember that one minute I was kneeling down to 6-year-old Nicki saying, "It's OK, Jesus will help Daddy and Nathan", and then five minutes later screaming down at her, "You're never going to see your daddy and brother again!!" Poor kid.

Finally, having gone back again back into immigration and heading for the gate, hoping against all hope that somehow they'd circumnavigated me and gotten through, I caught a glimpse of them. It looked like one of those slow motion movies, where the couples are running toward each other. I'll never forget the huge cart, loaded to overflowing, with Nathan and Tony running like mad men behind, caps and arms akimbo. Never was such a sweet sight!

We all raced through a final security point and headed for the empty gate. The stewardess shouted, "Boarding passes!" and I turned to get them and realized I'd left my travel handbag in security. That was the last straw. I just sat down and said quietly, "We're not going on this plane." I'd given up. "Just shovel me off the couch and take me to the institute," I was thinking.

As the family gathered around, wanting to poke me to see if I'd died or something, an agent came running down the hall with the missing bag. As we boarded the plane, which had now been held for quite some time, Tony whispered to me in Japanese, "No one needs to know what happened."

"Bad connection?" one of the less irritated passengers said, to which we gave a weak nod.

"You can say that again," I thought to myself while vowing never to judge that one passenger who runs onto the plane after his name has been called so many times. As we got our breath and settled in, I found that I had the energy to freak out one last time.

"Tony!" I whispered, "What if God didn't want us to get on this plane! With all this trouble, surely that's what it was!"

To which my calm and theologically in-tune husband reminded me, "If God wanted us off this plane, we'd be off." Indeed, the flight was perfect. We were able to relax and arrive rested and ready for the biggest adventure we'd had in ages.

❦

We arrived to be met by our dear friends Brian and Ruth Clark. We had made their acquaintance back in our Liberia days when she was the nurse that I helped in the Well Baby Clinic out of ELWA hospital. The hospital became famous in the early 2000's when the first case of Ebola originated there. Fortunately the doctor who first presented with the disease survived, but it was touch and go for awhile. Brian and Ruth had also been there for us when I almost died, so we could say we were pretty close.

As soon as they gathered our mountain of bags, they drove us to a missionary encampment several hours out of town for the weekend. What a lovely place to recoup from the journey. We were fascinated that they had a unique 'basket' in the lake built to enable people to swim. It was 12 or 13 feet deep and several yards in circumference. The reason for this was that the particular lake was of an unknown depth, so deep as to have never been measured. We were in Africa and no one really knew what might lurk in the murky depths so the basket was the answer for having a good time. Missionaries are ingenious, you have to say that. The kids loved it.

On the second day we took a walk with one of the missionaries. I don't know what the goal was, but it was pleasant enough, at least until we spotted some wild dogs. The missionary said calmly, "Pick up a rock and don't make eye contact no matter what". Adrenaline-based terror struck as we cast around for large rocks. We didn't want to have come this far to be ripped limb from limb by wild dogs. We continued on, trying not to panic and run for our lives, and then all became clear. Around the bend was a large dead cow, about to be devoured by said dogs.

"Whew," said the missionary. "They won't be interested in us." And we continued our walk. Back at the camp, we mentioned the cow and several commented that there'd be a mob of hyenas there by nightfall. Some of the men said from the other side of the dining room,

"Wow! If we could just get the cow up to the road, we'd probably be able to have quite a show tonight. Leave it to us!" Who says missionaries can't have fun?

At dinner that night these same guys announced, "So we went out to the spot and sure enough our arrival sparked a lot of interest with the little boys from the village. We discussed amongst ourselves, but in their language of course, about how we'd love to see hyenas but the cow is too far from the road.

After awhile the biggest boy took the bait. He piped in and asked, "Mista, how about we bring cow to road?'" So it was all set, with the promise of a real show. When it got dark, we all piled into the van and took off. Come to find out, we weren't the only ones looking for a show. When we rounded the bend in the road, we all burst out laughing, because sure enough there was the cow. But what made us laugh was the fact that it was surrounded by the whole village, come to watch the 'ferengis'(white people) watch the hyenas! We got out of the van and gave the village the 'show' that they deserved, shaking hands and telling them about God's love for them and all His creatures, even those hyenas who would be showing up soon. Best get the kids indoors for the night!

Then we got back in the van and drove down the road a ways. Soon we found a depression by a dry river bed and sure enough, there was a huge pack of hyenas, waiting it seemed, for the villagers to leave. We eased the van right up the beasts and started taking pictures. Next thing I knew, I had my window down and was leaning out slightly to get a better view. Then I saw something moving very slowly in my peripheral vision. I shrieked in surprise and yelled for everyone to get their bits back inside. There, just behind us was the biggest hyena of the pack, creeping slowly up to the van window. Some things can't be unseen. That concluded our desire to frolic with the hyenas and we headed back to the safety of camp. I'm reminded that even smart people can forget common sense from time to time.

After a few days we had bought tickets for the four-hour flight down to the refugee camp where we would begin our three-month ministry. All was going well; we were buying and packing up all the food we could carry, because apparently there was very little to be found in Bonga. To celebrate, we decided to go out on the town and try Ethiopia's national dish, Injera Wat. When they accompany it with lamb and relishes it's called something that to our ears sounded like "Injury by what?" There was a restaurant in Addis that specialized in this surpassingly wonderful dish, and we were excited to try it.

To this day if we say, "Injera Wat" to our kids, we all almost wretch. It was truly the most bizarre and (to us) unpleasant food we'd ever encountered. And believe me, we've encountered a lot! The best way to describe injera wat to my untrained palette is to take some carpet underlay, spread it on a table and then dump a bunch of indistinguishable sheep parts (including a lot of bones) on it. Then you tear the carpet underlay and using that as a spoon of sorts, dig in and enjoy.

We persevered like good missionaries, ate our fill and returned home. We soon went to bed, but in the middle of the night I woke to see Nicki standing by my bed. She looked like death, cheeks sunken in and eyes bulged out. We found out that she'd been having diarrhea since the early hours. Jumping up to help her, we found that she also was very hot.

She was the first, but certainly not the last.

To make a long story of biblically graphic proportions short, ALL of our family and the little daughter of our hosts, were so ill for the next few days, we began to think we were dying! We couldn't keep anything down or in. Brian and Ruth made pallets on the living room floor, which was only a few steps from the bathroom, but even that was often not close enough, necessitating the use of buckets and basins. It was bonding at a whole new level!

Fortunately for us, a missionary doctor lived next door and Ruth was a nurse so we were kept hydrated by sipping electrolyte solutions, but it was easy to see how people die so suddenly in Africa. They took samples into the lab and ascertained that I already had an amoeba (after only days in Africa). They laughed and told us we'd all survive this bug that they liked to call "Addis-itis".

But talk about being knocked low. We were too weak to fly, so we had to postpone for a week before we were able to crawl onto a plane headed for the great unknown. With this kind of sudden illness, depression is never far behind. After a few days, we were still sick, but recovering enough to be able to sit up. One day Tony said to me in Japanese, so no one would understand him, "We're going to die here!"

"Don't be silly," I chided him as I rolled over from my mat on the floor to face him, "Everybody says this is common, and if it's not they'll write a book about us!" He had already gone back to sleep.

Finally the day came. We were loaded to the eyeballs with food, things for the refugees, a bit of first aid medicine and mostly very weak courage. We were flying Ethiopian Airlines, which the missionaries eluded to colloquially as the "Vomit Comet". One lady had even given us four plastic bags with the sugary admonition, "You're going to need these." To that end, I forbid us all from having any food before we boarded at 8:30AM for the several hour flight.

By 11 o'clock we were getting cranky. Nathan in particular has never done well with low blood sugar and as he sat clasping his basketball to him like a life vest, glaring at me, Tony dared to approach the desk. "Can you tell me what's happening to the plane?" he asked respectfully.

Obviously startled that someone would ask such question, he thought and then said, "I think it'll leave about 2:00, sir."

"TWO?" Tony shouted without checking his protocol to be nice to this guy.

"Oh! Sorry, how about 1:30 then?" came the reply.

I can't remember when we left, but it was well after two. We were flying first to Jema where we would stop and then on to Gambella. Our plane had slings for seats and all of our luggage was tossed in the back without being secured. The solo pilot flew with the door to the cabin wide open (who would want to hijack him anyway?) and we could see he was holding a chart on his lap and leaning over to get a better look at the river below. Come to think of it, I don't know what the chart was all about; that jungle below was obviously uncharted.

I began to have to go to the bathroom, as we'd been in the air for over two hours. No worries, we were stopping in Jema. And then we stopped. I found it unsettling that everyone clapped and cheered when we landed, but I felt the same way actually. Now to find a bathroom. "Oh no," I was told as I stood to deplane. "You! Gambella". I sat back down with a shrug, determined not to be needy.

Two or three hours later, the plane landed without incident amid more clapping and cheering into Gambella. There were nine of us left, and we unfolded gratefully from the cramped seats. Now, about that bathroom …

There was no bathroom; in fact there was no airport, just a lone tree about eight inches in diameter with a windsock nailed to it. And there was no one to meet us. We had been due to land at least six hours earlier, so we felt pretty sure that our friends had given up on us. With all our bags dumped unceremoniously onto the grass, the pilot fired up the plane and taxied off. After all, he had a long way to fly alone, and he might have been worried about finding the river in the dark.

Suddenly a jeep burst out of the jungle at breakneck speed and started chasing the plane down the grass runway. I pictured armed terrorists, but instead the plane screeched to a stop (is it possible to screech on dirt?) and a lady ran up to the plane. A door opened, shut and they continued on the takeoff. The jeep came toward us.

It was a UN jeep there to pick up the other five other people who had flown with us. "Get in!" the driver shouted. I was politely waiting for the airport to be abandoned so I could make use of the tree.

Tony said, "That's OK; we'll wait for our friends."

"The only thing that's coming for you now are the hyenas!" shouted the driver. "Get in!"

And before I knew it or could plead my case for the pit stop, we were careening off toward Gambella. I had my left foot near the accelerator and the driver was shifting the gears between my knees, but we had somehow managed to get ten of us and all of our luggage in.

The driver explained the plane chase this way: "Whenever the plane is late, we just chill out at the bar and when we hear the engines we race out here. That lady was a UN doctor who needed to get back to Addis."

Eventually we pulled up to the "bar" he had spoken of. It was a simple mud-walled building with a grass roof. The driver assured us that they would have rooms for us, and that the "Bonga folks" would be back in the morning.

They did have a couple of rooms … well, two small cinder block arrangements with a bed, a mosquito net and a small hole in a far corner with a brick on either side that was to serve as the toilet. Nicki and I took one room and Nathan and Tony the other, as I didn't want to leave my kids alone. I think we were able to get some bread from our luggage and slept like babies.

The next morning before we knew it, Claire (the 22-year-old we were sent to babysit) was there to pick us up. It was a forty-mile ride over a questionable road out to the refugee camp, so we understood completely why she hadn't stuck around after dark to wait for us.

She ushered us into the SIM mission compound. Tony and I would be in one of the two bedrooms of this large concrete floored grass hut and Nicki would sleep on a camp bed in the common area. Nathan would have a grass hut all to himself. In addition to these, we had a shower hut, a toilet hut and a kitchen, which was extravagantly built out of sheet metal.

And so began our time there.

Within days Nathan was packing his bags to leave us. He was miserable. It was hot and sticky. The seemingly 'wonderful' sheet metal kitchen turned into a real oven by first light, making being in there a real chore. By the second evening, a young Uduk boy next door had died suddenly of malaria and the horror began to sink in. He had been well that morning and in fact was one of Clare's students. As the Uduks marry at 13 or 14, he already had a wife and two kids. This whole thing was becoming a reality that I wasn't sure I could handle.

I'll never forget the next morning deciding to walk through the village while it was still cool. I looked up at the sky and said, rather cheekily now that I think about it, "Lord, I know I said we wanted to 'help' you in the ministry, but I don't remember signing up for THIS!" A few steps later, we came around the corner and my eyes focused on something mammoth and white. I remember thinking, "Elephant bones?" but the gasp from Nathan told it all.

"MOM!!" he shouted. "Those are basketball goals!"

One of Clare's students who was taking the walk with us said, "Yes, the UN trucks brought them last week, but we don't know what they are!"

"I do!" shouted Nathan. "Let's get them set up!"

The boy, whose name was Yaseer, looked at him in disbelief and said, "OK let me get the guys!" Before the heat of the day set in, they had the lines marked out and were digging.

Who knew a 15-year-old boy would know ALL the required measurements?

Word went out that Nathan would be starting a basketball camp the next morning. Boys of all ages showed up, too many to count. These boys grew up playing soccer, but had never seen a basketball game.

And of course the only basketball for 500 miles was the one he had carried in his lap from Hong Kong. But they made do, using soccer balls and even scraps of rags rolled into round shapes. Nathan got them into groups according to size, found a few that spoke English, and got started. For him, his calling was clear, and he never looked back. We would take him water mid-morning because we worried about heat stroke (more about that later), but otherwise he devoted his entire time in Bonga to building his own personal Dream Team.

All the refugees had been issued one outfit from the UN… a shirt and a skirt or pants. That was it. When they washed them, they hung around in their underwear till they were dry, usually in just a couple of hours. Because of this, initially Nathan just called the boys by their t-shirts. "Hey 49er!" or "My aunt went to Ft Lauderdale!" and such. Gradually he learned their names. We had to laugh to ourselves, watching the headman of the village playing while wearing the obvious pick of the lot: a bright pink bowling shirt with the name "Alice" embroidered proudly on the front. To this day I think of him as "Alice the Chief"…….regal and all.

So with Nathan settled and actually happy, we turned to getting ourselves going. We had already succeeded with Nicki by selling her on the idea that the one hole toilet was a throne for a princess. Tony began teaching the Old Testament to people who had no written version of this half of the Bible. Looking back, it remains to this day his favorite class. They met every day at 4:00 for two hours with no break under a thatched roof. It soon became obvious that these men, brought up in oral traditions, had total recall. They absorbed absolutely everything Tony said, taking no notes. It was especially exciting to see them hear the Old Testament stories for the first time, then compare them to the New Testament references they knew already. One day as Tony was going through the Book of Jonah, the men suddenly became animated.

"That's it! That's it!" they shouted. When Tony asked what, they answered, "When Jesus said that He would be in the grave for three days, just like Jonah in the belly of the fish, that's what He was talking about!"

After each day's lessons ended, about 6:00, we would hold a worship service outside, just as the sun went down. We never knew exactly how many were standing there in darkness, but when they started singing, it was like a heavenly choir. And what made the experience even more "other-worldly" was the fact that Uduks sing according to a pentatonic music scale, which we would call rather minor tuned. Impossible to describe, but unforgettable to hear.

For me, my lot was to come up with edible food three times a day, using what we had brought along, combined with whatever the local market had to offer. We had brought a 30-pound round of hard cheese, and that helped a lot. We could sometimes get freshly butchered chickens, which was also a real treat. The other varieties of meat on offer included zebra, antelope, all manner of reptiles, and the Uduk staple: baboon. Needless to say we didn't eat much meat. Other staples existed, cereal, flour and peanuts. It was a stretch to feed 6-9 people every day, but no one ever went hungry.

Nicki fell in with a little girl her age named Rahab. She was the grand daughter of Neska, a well-built and (of course) topless woman who carried our water every day from the river, more than a mile away. Nathan could help but admire her muscular arms, even though that meant he would have to notice that they were often used to secure her sagging breasts under them as she worked.

Rahab and Nicki hit it off famously and were almost never apart. Never mind that they had no common language; they had no problems, Nicki would teach her origami from the paper she'd brought from Japan, and Rahab would teach her how to grind dried corn in a bowl cut from stone. We nearly sacrificed some of our teeth on Nicki's work, but she was learning. Within days Nicki chose the clothing option of the Uduks, something from the waist down, nothing on top. Worked like a charm and we had less washing to do.

Life rocked along, and we were happy. After that first night, no one close by died again. I think God really was teaching me something. I often tell people it's like God took His finger and wrote across the sky, "Trust me!"

Tony here. And speaking of the sky, the stars at night were the most brilliant I have seen anywhere, free of absolutely any light pollution. The corrugated tin cook shack we mentioned was our own personal observatory, cooled down sufficiently by evening to climb up and lay back on. It became a nightly ritual the four of us looked forward to, and occasionally we were joined by Yaseer, one of the boys who had become Nathan's assistant coach, translator and friend. He was fascinated with the world he had yet to see, and each night he would ply us with questions. I'll never forget one evening's discussion about the ocean. Yaseer was a boy of the desert, wise in all its ways, but everything else was a vast mystery. One night he asked me, "Have you ever seen the ocean?"

"Yes," I replied.

"Once at the river, I fell in and couldn't touch the bottom. I was so scared, I thought I would die." He paused a moment, as if re-living that experience, then asked, "How deep is the ocean?"

"Well," I started, not sure how much of an answer he was looking for, "you know how far it is to the river?" It was about a mile. He nodded, and I said, "Picture that distance, straight down. The ocean is much, much deeper than that."

From that point, I think Yaseer had a tough time trusting me, since I was obviously an idiot. But he continued. "Our headman saw the ocean." I remembered that SIM missionaries had once taken the Uduk headman to America in order to help with a final edit of the newly-translated Gospels. Yaseer's innate sense of total recall kicked in, and he started reciting the headman's story from memory. "He said the ocean is an angry thing; always trying to get to you." I could picture him watching the waves and imagining the almost supernatural power behind them. "But then the headman showed us a handful of sand. It's not like our sand from back home. It's almost white and sparkles in the sun. The headman said, 'What a wonderful God, to use sand to hold back the ocean!'"

I thought of Proverbs 8:29, where it talks about the "boundaries of the sea". I thought of sand, something I know so little of, compared to Yaseer. Sometimes, I imagine myself as a grain of sand, tossed about by every breeze. But then God comes along, and He puts me together with other grains of sand, His children, created in love and blessed with work to do. The enemy rages before us, intent upon our destruction, but God says, "Stand! Hold!" And we do.

Now to Marsha:

Time, which at first seem to stand still as we tried to count the days before we left that place, gradually picked up the pace, and before we knew it, it was approaching the time to leave. We had learned so much during our time in Bonga … so much more than we could ever have taught that band of refugees. God must have had His angels working overtime, safeguarding our steps and keeping us from serious harm. We decided as a family to climb the mountain behind the camp. It was a constant backdrop, and we felt like we owed it the honor of examining it up close and personal. We came upon a pretty substantial cave, and were tempted to go inside, but watching the hairs stand up on the dog's back, and feeling, I'm sure the hand of an angel telling us to move on, we wisely decided to leave that den to whatever creature was occupying it. We also found parts of an airplane, evidence of a crash many years previously that no one in the camp had any recollection of. We wondered what had happened, and if the people in the plane had survived.

After a couple of hours of climbing, we reached the top to find ancient ruins….evidence of a culture probably thousands of years old, but whose story will never be known. The view from the top of the hill was magnificent, and served as a reminder of just how remote this place was. As far as we could see in any direction, there was nothing but jungle. The map confirmed that by showing 500 miles of unbroken wilderness, with only Addis Ababa as a possible destination. The breeze on the top was refreshing, and it felt good to finally take off my long skirt and uncover a pair of shorts. I missed the freedom of lighter clothing as the long skirts and pants (for men) were required by tradition as well as the mission in the camp.

As is usually the case, the trip down was much more arduous, with Nathan finally carrying Nicki to keep her from crying. Our hearts smiled at this unusual show of love. Within minutes of returning to the 'comfort' of our hut, Tony doubled up in a full body cramp. While I mocked him with a "Oh, seriously, have a baby sometime!" Nicki smothered him with sympathy and kisses and Nathan began massaging his legs, which were literally jumping and twitching. I ran for the book, "Where There Is No Doctor", highly recommended for when, well, there's NO doctor. Immediately I diagnosed it as heat exhaustion (which is the precursor to deadly heat stroke) and started giving him ½ teaspoons of salt mixed in cups of water. Within 15 minutes the cramps began to lessen and he was fine in an hour or so, not even missing his much loved class.

Obviously these three months of our lives changes us forever. We can never forget these wonderful Sudanese refugees, their love for God and for each other. I have several images burned into my memory that I will cherish always: Tony, teaching his heart out to fellow pastors eager to share his Bible knowledge. Nicki, singing an Uduk song while she and Rahab ground corn together in all their topless splendor. Nathan, walking down the trail to the basketball court he had made himself, accompanied by a fellow teenager whose life experiences were, well, a world apart. Nathan still cherishes the throwing stick Yaseer had made and given him as a going away gift. In quite serious undertones, he had shared hunting tips with Nathan. "Now when you use these to hunt baboons, always carry TWO;

because baboons can count to TWO."

And finally, I cherish the memory of laying on the cool tin roof of the cook shack, watching the stars and listening to the sounds of the village. Of all people, these folks surely had their priorities in the right place. They had known the horrors of war, the inconsolable grief of loss, and through it all they loved each other and they loved God. I can still hear the sound of mothers singing their babies to sleep every night, and I chided myself for all the times I almost lost my temper when my own children fought sleep and refused to accept my discipline. I often wonder how these people's lives have changed in the 25 years since we've been back. Most were relocated to western countries around the globe. A few years ago Sandra Bullock starred in a movie called "The Good Lie" and it was an amazingly accurate account of the struggle these people faced in their search for freedom. The only difference in the movie was that the Dinka tribe were depicted as the helpless victims instead of the Uduks. In actual fact, it was the Uduks who had to be removed to a separate camp because the Dinkas were so mean to them!

A couple of years ago, Tony and I were checking into the Tucson Airport and were met at the curb by an extremely black porter. I knew at once that this man was a product of Africa. Then as I looked closer, I could see the parallel scars on his temple, placed there when he was a child. Stunned, I just asked, "Are you UDUK?"

"YESSSS!" he shouted.

We hugged, we cried, he told us he'd been in the states for 15 years and NO ONE had ever recognized him as Uduk. He was from Bonga, was a Christian and knew Claire, but was too small in 1996 to have remembered us. He grabbed our bags and ushered us to the agent shouting, "These are my brothers!" He got a big tip and it wasn't until we were on the plane that we realized that we never got his contact details.

When it had become time to leave Bonga, we were given the task of driving the mission Land Rover back to Addis Ababa. It would be a 500 mile, two-day trek. To say that the roads were tough was an understatement. We had three flat tires (two spares) and were helped along the way by ferocious-looking but actually incredibly kind men in loin cloths and carrying spears. I should mention too that the Land Rover had four seatbelts, two in the front and two in the back. I was happy to take the middle back seat, since I can tend towards car sickenss and in that position I could see the road ahead better. I was also relieved that my children would be in seatbelts. I only mention this because two weeks after we left, our dear friend Ruth, whom we'd stayed with when we were so sick, was sitting in that same seat when the Land Rover was hit head on by a large truck. Both vehicles were driving slowly, and the impact was not significant, but it was enough to throw Ruth forward into the windshield, breaking her neck. She survived the ordeal, but was paralyzed from the chest down, and has remained so in the twenty-five years since.

Another chat with God when I get to heaven.

Chapter 13

Back to Japan

Arriving in the States, we settled into our next "Stateside Assignment" as Missionaries-in-Residence at our Learning Center near Richmond, Virginia. We took some time there to reflect on all we had just experienced. Ethiopia had been a game changer, for sure.

Nathan would still declare at every meal that the Western World was wasteful and one meal alone could feed a whole village! The exercise on seeing how the other half lived apparently had succeeded.

Meanwhile Nicki and I continued to deal with insect bites that had become infected. When we left, I had done a 'quadrant' count and by the amount I had on one leg and multiplying times four, I figured I had at least 350 bites. Nicki was similar. The whole time we were there, we wrestled with rats and bugs, but the bugs seemed to like Nicki and me the most. While we never saw any mosquitoes, we figured that they were getting to me even though we slept under mosquito nets. We were all taking malaria prevention, so we weren't too worried, just itchy.

The rats especially irritated Nathan, mostly because they were erratic in their behavior and according to him, "Couldn't decide if they wanted to take the rat poison packs in or out of the holes all night long." Funny kid.

Then another 'Bear' showed up. While we were in Bonga, Nicki had been nipped by the mission dog. It was no big deal, and we washed the wound and forgave the dog. But shortly after that, the dog had died. I suddenly remembered that rabies was very prevalent in Ethiopia. We never knew what had killed the dog but …. what if it had been rabies?

We made our way to the MLC medical clinic and asked to see the doctor immediately. He wasn't in that day, so we went straight to town to a pediatrician who nodded in sage wisdom and prescribed antibiotics for her sore covered body. Our mission doctor, back on duty on campus was a little more tuned into the situation with rabies and suggested that we wait. He said that usually rabies would exacerbate fairly quickly, but it did have an incubation of up to two *years.*

"I'm going to say let's wait and see," he said, both of us knowing that IF you get rabies, it is just about 100% fatal. We agreed with the decision, but I have to say, the next two years were shadowed by the uncertainty.

Then one night as we were packing to leave MLC, there came another life-changing encounter that gave us something else to think about. Clyde Meador was our area representative for a large part of the world including Japan, the Philippines and Australia. He came by our apartment to see us, and over coffee broached a subject that would change our lives forever.

"I've got an interesting letter here from a church in Sydney, Australia," he said. "Seems a Japanese group is meeting in their building on Sunday afternoons, and they're growing faster than the Sunday morning congregation. The problem is, they can't communicate with each other very well.

Clyde paused for a moment to let us process that thought, then went on. "The Aussie pastor there is asking us to send someone to talk to the Japanese to see exactly what their intentions are. I wonder if you folks would consider stopping off there on your way back to Japan, check it out and give me a report?"

"*Would* we?" We were thrilled at the chance to do something on behalf of the mission, and honored that we would be trusted to accomplish the task. He promised us another month's extension to our time away from Japan if we'd go, and since that fit even better with the kids' school schedule, we were quick to accept. Travel arrangements were adjusted, and as soon as the final orientation session was finished, we headed Down Under.

We arrived in Australia and settled into a lovely mission house in west Sydney. We were stunned to have flocks of colorful birds right outside of our windows, and the thirty days we were there it never rained. It was almost like a dream.

On the north side of Sydney, just over the Harbor Bridge, lies the community of Crows Nest. There in the heart of town we found the Baptist church, set in an old "heritage" style building still sporting wooden pews and a pipe organ. Pastor David Jones welcomed us, and arranged for a meeting with the Japanese leadership.

This was our first real experience with Japanese outside of Japan, and it was truly exciting. Here were people like those we had been working with for several years by now, but when they opened their mouths to speak, they might as well have been Zulu warriors. They were friendly, but they spoke their mind, pulled no punches and showed a capacity for leadership we rarely came across in Japan. I had done a little homework by the time we got to Sydney and discovered that, while Japanese in Japan were about 1% Christian, among those living outside Japan, the figure approached 7%. Now I understood why. Without the cultural and spiritual bondage so inherent back home, these people were free to consider things they could not have otherwise. With no one holding them back, they readily turned to the Gospel, liked what they saw, and accepted it with joyful abandon.

Again Nicki was invited to join a first grade class at a church school near the house (her fourth for the year). They waived any fees, since we would only be there a month. We dressed her in a borrowed uniform and sent her off. She would be the thrill of the class, an American who'd just come from Africa after living in Japan. Nathan, our quiet boy, was happy to continue his home studies for the rest of the 9th grade.

The first Sunday there we were welcomed as heroes, the Japanese thrilled that someone "western" could stand in the gap with the church and still speak their language. We all fell in love with each other. We also attended the English-speaking morning service and were amazed at how different Baptists are in Australia.

There were many conversations about how and when a missionary couple would come to help with the Japanese work in Australia. At that time, we weren't thinking of doing this job ourselves, but were convinced that someone should. I began to dream via emails with Bob and Gail Gierhart, longtime friends, about how wonderful the work was in Australia. Bob began to answer that he'd always felt led towards Australia but would give it some thought. The next letter said that Gail was in no way interested.

Back and forth our discussions went and the more I tried to convince Bob and Gail to come, the more the little nagging voice began to whisper in my ear as well. Why not? If we were truly 'called' to the Japanese, why not Sydney? The kids could get their education without having to live away from us, the economy was cheaper, the weather was brighter, etc etc.

We began to seriously pray about this. We also talked to everyone we could about how this would happen. By the time we left Australia, we were about half convinced that we'd be moving down after we fulfilled our obligation to the Nagano Olympics. Nathan wasn't sold on the plan, but again, he was my child who didn't like change of any kind, even if it might give him a brighter future. He had grown up in Japan, his best friends were there, and he had no intention of leaving. That issue would come back later, but not right away.

⚮

Tony again:

Arriving back in Japan from our 1996-'97 furlough was marked by a series of conflicting thoughts. We loved our work at Taitomi, and couldn't help but rejoice in the explosive growth the church was experiencing. The fact that Trevor's death had played an obvious part was a bittersweet aspect of it all. People were coming to us from out of the blue, even total strangers, and almost before introductions could be made we were hearing things like, "I lost a son (or daughter, or spouse); I've heard about your son. How do you deal with it?"

And so it went. Meetings moved directly into relationships, and from relationships into shared grief. Grief led naturally into discussions about God and the hope of Heaven that kept our fragile sanity from unraveling. With such a foundation, it came as no surprise to see people come together with abandon, clinging to one another and calling out to God for relief from the awful pain of separation and loss. In the first year after Trevor's death, Taitomi Baptist was listed as the fastest growing evangelical church in Japan. Even years later, after the initial skyrocketing growth leveled off, it remained steady and solid, made up of men and women who knew of whence they spoke. Honestly speaking, it was not an evangelistic tool I would have chosen; even now I know in my heart that I would not choose it if I had the option.

But in spite of it all, I know, and hold onto the assurance that what we see at Taitomi is just one of those "good things" that God has worked together using the broken pieces of our hearts (Romans 8:28). I know too that one day, I will stand with Trevor and together we will rejoice to see how God has woven a beautiful picture out of everything the world would call "tragic".

That day will come, and I know that when it comes, I will turn to God with a heart filled with joy and say, "Thank you for that experience."

But not today.

Looking back now, I can see several threads that were working their way in and through our lives in preparation for the Next Big Thing: leaving Taitomi, moving to Nojiri and from there moving to Australia. I knew for example that I needed to step down from the role of pastor to the church we had started and had come to love so much. The church family would have loved nothing better than for us to stay on indefinitely. Someone even commented on the fact that parish priests often spend their whole lives in one church. Why couldn't we do that?

I'll admit, there was a part of me that was genuinely attracted to the image of kindly old Father Lonergan, looking after his Irish flock. But as I gently explained, in the first place our mission would never allow it. And besides that, our role as "missionaries" by definition meant that we would be moving from place to place. The beauty of our job was that our support did not depend on the people to whom we ministered. We could move freely into an area, settle in and work full-time toward the goal of starting a church, before that church had ever come into being. This was possible because we were supported by churches of America's Southern Baptist Convention, who prayed for us and encouraged us to "go where no one has gone, and preach the Gospel to those who have never heard." If God blessed our efforts and a church sprouted, then once enough support was available to call an indigenous pastor, we would be expected to step away and move to yet another unreached area. This was "missions"; this was what we did. I knew all this, but that didn't make it any easier to step away.

But the seed had been planted, and now I would have to revisit my understanding of just what God had called me to. No, I was reminded, my call was not to Japan, nor was it even to the Japanese people. My call was to obedience. Truth be known, even *that* perception has been tweaked in the time since I penned the first draft of this chapter. Now as I dwell on God's call in my life over the past fifty years, I'm beginning to see that His intention for me has not been primarily to serve Him as a missionary to Japan, nor to the Japanese, nor even to obedience, as vital as that is. No, today I believe that what God has desired for me all along, even from those first days while I was being knit together in my mother's womb, was *relationship*. How many times did He say it in His Word? "I will be your God, and you will be My people." Through all of the things that make up our lives, from the mountains to the valleys, from the obedient acts of service to the times of desert wanderings; through all these things, He has molded me, guided me, disciplined me and loved me in order to make me well and truly His.

I admit now what in my heart of hearts I have known all along: my life has always been in God's Hands, and in that assurance I promised to follow His call wherever it led. By 1997, that fact had defined me as a missionary, specifically as a missionary to Japan, to the Japanese people, to the precious friends who made up Taitomi Baptist Church where I now served as pastor. How could I explain to them that by that same definition I must now consider leaving them to move on to the next chapter?

Fortunately, there was a convenient break that served as a transition for us all.

We often joke that the reason we got stuck with the job of "handling" Japan's 1998 Winter Olympics Evangelistic Outreach was that when the call came to step forward, we didn't step backward soon enough. But in fact, the year and a half we devoted to the responsibility was one of the best times of our mission career, in terms of both the work and the lifestyle that came with it.

As painful as the prospect of leaving Taitomi might have been, the threads described above were moving us inexorably to that decision. And it was difficult not to see God's Hand at work when we realized that the site of Japan's 1998 Winter Olympics would be right at the heart of our favorite place on earth: Lake Nojiri. I'm sure that was a big factor in our "slowness" in stepping back when our mission asked for a person to direct the Christian volunteer teams who would be making their way to Japan over the next several months leading up to and encompassing the Games themselves. The task would require that we put our present ministry on hold, move to the city of Nagano, and from a mission house in the heart of town enlist the support of fellow mission organizations to build and oversee a program that would ensure accommodation, transportation and viable ministries for the thousands who would be looking to us for help.

This was the opportunity we had been praying for, and we knew at once that it was God-directed. By taking on this Olympic task, we could step away from Taitomi Baptist gracefully, giving them the encouragement born of necessity to seek out and call a Japanese pastor who would come and take over our work. The announcement was easier for them to hear because, first, we weren't leaving Japan, not yet at least. And underlying the prospect was the chance that once the Olympics were over, we would be coming back to Taitomi.

It was at this point that our mission helped provide an extra push that even we weren't quite ready to accept just yet. Our proposal was that we would move to Nagano with just the bare essentials, leaving our home in Taitomi intact so that we could in fact return if necessary. Our mission was not so open to the idea, however. No, we would pack up all our belongings, move everything to the mission house in Nagano and make a clean break with Taitomi.

Marsha and I argued back and forth with the mission over several weeks, but they were adamant. Somewhere during this "discussion", we slipped in one more proviso: rather than move into the mission house in Nagano, why not take up full-time residence in our cabin at Lake Nojiri? Geographically, it was closer to the Olympic site, and much, much cheaper to live in, since there was no running water, not much heat beyond a fireplace, and only enough electricity to light up a few lights. Since we'd have to move up the summer before the Winter Games began, we could take the time to winterize the place and be good to go by the Opening Ceremony.

Once again, the mission was unbending. We still cherish to this day a letter we received from Mark Edlund, the mission chairman at the time and a good friend.

He was the one to whom most of our appeals were being directed. The heart of his letter went as follows:

"Japan Baptist Mission personnel do not live in houses with no running water; they do not live in houses with no heat; they do not live in houses with little or no electricity. You will move, with all your household belongings, to the mission house located in Nagano."

The letter continued with more logistical details we would need for the upcoming move. Then, in a stroke of brotherly love and understanding, Mark finished his letter with these words: "You will move to the Nagano house; where you choose to spend your time is up to you."

So permission was given, albeit unstated, to make our home at the Nojiri cabin while we carried out the work of organizing and overseeing the Winter Olympic volunteer program. The Nagano mission house would be put to good use, first as a "warehouse" where we would be storing the tons of materials necessary for the project, such as leaflets, tracts, Bibles and "Jesus" film video tapes in many languages, logo-emblazoned jackets, caps, shirts and backpacks. The house would also serve as a "staging area" for volunteer teams working close by, as well as a place for Japan Baptist Mission personnel to sleep when they came through. And of course Marsha and I would use it as our home away from home wherever work or inclement weather required that we stay overnight in Nagano.

The summer of 1997 was spent making preparations for the upcoming Games. I contacted and set up meetings with personnel from other missions where we ironed out the details of a huge cooperative effort, each of us doing what we did best to insure that volunteers coming from all over the world would be put to the best use. Churches, schools and camps were enlisted to provide housing and accommodation. Missions were organized as transportation hubs, rostering on to help the volunteers get from place to place.

Prospective volunteers were contacted and information gathered as to the types of ministries they were preparing. International Olympic Committee individuals were contacted and presented with a list of volunteer services we were prepared to provide, from chaplaincy to entertainment, traffic and parking control and crowd directing outside the various venues. I was surprised to discover how much the IOC depended on volunteer help to get the job done. By the fact that we came to them as a unified cooperative of Christian-based, internationally-driven teams who were offering just about everything they needed, we were welcomed with open arms.

I did discover one aspect of the Olympic Committee that, unlike the mission organizations we were accustomed to working with, was not so friendly and easy-going. Testosterone ran heavy in any meeting that included Committee members, and they invariably came across as only slightly less than international dignitaries in terms of power, authority and expectations. In Vatican-like declarations, they claimed and took control of everything from sidewalk access to opening and closing times of local businesses, and woe be to the one who dared stand up against the decrees. One day, there would be a public park; the next day there would be a chain link fence and a security guard insuring that no one without the proper color-coded authorization emblazoned on his or her lanyard would be allowed inside the conclave.

As part of our mission's enlistment of volunteers, I made a website listing the needs and logistics of the upcoming Games. Then, in a move that made perfect sense to me, pasted an image of the Olympic rings on the opening page. Within days, I was inundated with responses from all over the world: "That's amazing! How did you get permission to use the rings? I didn't think anyone could do that! You guys must really be on the inside!"

I thought about the responses for a day or two, then quietly removed the rings from the website. Not long afterward, I was sitting in a meeting that included some Olympic Committee members, and casually mentioned my experience with the rings on my website. The Committee member next to me stopped smiling and pulled out a pen. "What did you say the website address was?"

I don't think I ever mentioned it, but said instead something about taking it down since I didn't want to risk a warning about the apparent infraction. "Oh, we don't warn," he said in all seriousness. "We go straight to litigation."

Meanwhile, back at the cabin, work was in full swing in an attempt to make the place suitable (or perhaps I should say *survivable*) for the coming winter. Besides the fireplace and a few kerosene space heaters, we managed to snag a big heater from a Christian school in Tokyo that was replacing their system. The thing drank kerosene like a thirsty camel, but promised to keep the cabin above freezing. Next came insulation for the walls, and we gathered up all we could find. Carefully removing the outside boards, which were at least 80 years old, we stuffed insulation into whatever spaces we could find, then nailed the boards back on.

My father came to visit that summer, and we put him to work on the project. It was then that we discovered a philosophical difference in the placing of insulation that I had not been aware of. In my father's experience, growing up in Texas, one should install the insulation with the shiny side facing out, in order to reflect the hot summer sun away from the interior. Marsha and I, recalling houses we had observed in Colorado, felt that the shiny side should face *in*, so that any heat produced inside the house would be reflected back inside. We discussed the issue for quite some time, then finally "agreed to disagree". Wherever Marsha and I installed insulation, it was shiny side in; wherever Dad was at work, it was shiny side out.

That decision, in hindsight, was probably another "God thing". The job was finished, Dad went home, and Marsha and I took a break for our August 1st anniversary, heading down to the Big City of Nagano to celebrate. Son Nathan and daughter Nicki stayed at Nojiri, with Nicki going to a friend's cabin two doors up while Nathan stayed at our place with the family dog.

That night while we were away, the cabin right next door to us caught fire and the family's 5-year-old daughter was tragically killed. She had not struggled so hopefully she died of smoke inhalation before the flames reached her. According to Nathan, the flames were so hot, the walls of our own cabin were throbbing from the heat, with everyone expecting them to combust at any moment. Our place escaped the flames however, and as we looked over the place, realized that the side of the house closest to the neighbors' was a side where Dad had installed the insulation … shiny side out.

Another winterizing task was to think through the water challenge. During the summer, there was a faucet about one hundred yards up the hill with a hundred gallon plastic tank nearby. By keeping the tank filled, water could be brought down by gravity to the cabin by means of a polyurethane pipe running just underground. Once in the house, we could access the water through a tap in the kitchen and another in the wash up room.

However, we knew that this was not a viable option when the winter freezes set in, so we worked long and hard not only to find our decades-old hand-dug well, but to access it into the house. It seemed to be working nicely, promising water for the winter, unless of course, the pipes froze.

The plan worked beautifully until one night in November when we went down into Nagano for a meeting. The weather turned cold quite suddenly, followed by a rare autumn snowstorm making it impossible to drive back up to the cabin that night. Were we ever grateful for the mission house *that* night!

The next day, we made it back up to Lake Nojiri to find the place buried in two feet of snow. After several hours of shoveling out a place to park and opening the path back to the cabin, we got inside, stomped the snow off our boots, and discovered our well and all the temporary plastic pipe we had installed during the summer was now impossibly frozen and broken in places. The water system wouldn't be thawing out until spring, so we had to rig the summer 100-gallon tank upstairs in Nathan's room and adjust all the faucets to accept the water from this source. Then we took a hundred-meter hose and filled it about once a week from our neighbor's cabin, who were blessed with a hand-dug well. We will always be thankful to our friends Jon and Becky Benedict for sharing their water. They are retired and still living in their cabin as I write this.

Finally in February, 1998, the Winter Games were about to begin. By now, our cabin was nearly buried under several feet of snow, accessible through a tunnel we maintained by the use of folded-up decking propped up along the side of the house. The other way in was by walking over the top of the snow, then climbing into the window of a second floor room. The mountain of snow actually served a useful purpose, though, by adding yet another layer of insulation over the whole structure. Our main challenge by now was to insure that there was enough ventilation coming in to keep us from suffocating. I needn't have worried about that, however. As well as the cabin was insulated, it was still an 80-year-old structure that creaked and groaned with every windstorm and earthquake, keeping plenty of air leaks opening to the southern-facing cliff side of the house. Our bedroom was at the one place where sunshine could still find its way in during the day. And besides the sunshine, many was the morning we would wake up and notice that the winds had brought in plenty of snow as well, drifted up onto our bed. Each morning, I would thank the Lord for the incomparable blessing of living and working in this winter paradise, thankful for the wonderful invention of electric blankets. Then we'd take turns shrieking with shock as we ran down the stairs to started lighting fires.

We thought we were about ready for the Games to start when one morning as I was trying to thaw out in front of the fireplace, I got a call on my cell phone (that's what we called them back then), and a man introduced himself as the leader of a Youth With a Mission (YWAM) team on their way to the Games. "We've arrived in Tokyo and are about to get on a train for Nagano," he said. "Where would you like us to go?"

"Uh," I stumbled, "How many of you are there? Three hundred, you say? What do you plan to do while you're here? Oh, anything at all?"

I was hung somewhere between angry and incredulous, but managed not to blurt out, "Where were you last year when we were organizing all this?!?" Instead, I said,

"I don't know of any accommodation that hasn't been booked up for several months now. There's really nothing at all here ...." Then I stopped and thought a moment. "The *only* place I can think of is a church camp just down the hill, but it's buried under six feet of snow."

"That's no problem," he said excitedly. "We're young and energetic. Do you think we could borrow some shovels?"

Against all reason, they pulled it off. Other volunteers met them at the station, shuttled them to the camp, the owner of which had by now given his permission to use it, and gave everyone a digging tool. By the end of the day, they had scooped out enough of the facility to move in and have a prayer meeting. All during the Games, we would see them downtown, passing out tracts and having a great time. The only other time we met was when one of the girls had to be taken to the hospital with a case of appendicitis. But somehow, I suspect even that was part of God's plan for them, and wouldn't be at all surprised to learn of doctors, nurses and patients having been blessed by their presence and willing to give it all for the Kingdom.

Eventually, the time came for the Games to begin. We were as prepared as we could be, although no amount of preparation could take into account all the unforeseen circumstances that would transpire, such as the car wreck during the first few days.

In addition to the hundreds of volunteers from all over the world that we were caring for, we were also blessed to welcome many local missionaries who were able to take off brief periods of time from their own work to come and help out. These folks were invaluable, since most of them had the language enough to jump in as translators where needed. Many also came with their own vehicles, so we assigned them transport jobs, helping to move the volunteers from place to place.

One young man arrived with his very own mission-assigned four-wheel drive Toyota van, a real gem in light of the fact that a recent snowstorm had left the roads icy and treacherous. A small group needed to make their way down the mountain into Nagano, so we gave him the job, with Marsha going along to lend a hand.

Unfortunately for the young man, while he was driving a top-of-the-line four wheel drive, his experience in snow driving was a little limited. One of the first rules of maneuvering along ice-bound roads is that four-wheel drive is a great advantage when going *uphill*, but not much help when going *down*. It was almost inevitable that he lost control on a sharp curve and continued straight on, off the road and down the mountainside. The van sailed through an apple

orchard until finally meeting a steel telephone pole head on……..
right on the edge of a cliff.   Thankfully, injuries were minor, but it
was decided that one girl should be checked out for a possible head
injury, and Marsha was in quite a bit of pain from the seatbelt doing
its job. Everything was sorted out, though, and we were grateful once
again for God's protection.

The Games themselves were a great success. Marsha and I were
able to serve on a chaplaincy roster, helping to staff a chapel in the
Olympic village. This gave us some wonderful opportunities to meet
the athletes, and we were able to invite many of them to speak at our
local churches.

We encountered a surprising blessing at the end of the Games,
when everything was re-done to accommodate the Paralympics.
In many ways, these events were identical to the Olympic Games,
except for the fact that some of the skiers were missing arms and
legs. There were also a few games that were designed especially
for the Paralympians, such as Wheelchair Rugby (talk about your
blood sports!) and Blind Dodge Ball. The most impressive aspect we
noticed though was in the hearts of the athletes themselves. They
seemed to be driven not so much by a "victory at all costs" attitude
but more by a sincere thrill for the competition itself. Many of the
participants had already overcome so many challenges just to be able
to compete; we were left humbled and awestruck. We also noticed a
significant increase in the number of overt Christians in the group,
both among the athletes and the coaches.

Listening to their testimonies of courage, Marsha and I had to take
another look at our own lives. Yes, we had met the Bear, just as these
young men and women had. Some had emerged from the encounter

unscathed while others were left with physical and emotional challenges that would plague them for the rest of their lives. And we couldn't compare one person's grief to anyone else's. Which was worse: to lose a son to cancer or to lose your arms and legs to a tragic accident? Everyone's tapestry is unique, we decided. Each thread is being woven into place for a purpose, and if allowed, will become a thing of beauty that will bring blessing to many. As we shared stories and prayed together with these amazing men and women, one thing became clear: the Bear is not the Weaver, nor does he have any authority to make a person's life anything other than what God has intended. Understanding that truth has helped many a soul come to terms with the grief, the joy, the hope, the disappointment, the victories and the defeats that we must all face. The key to real joy as Christ has promised us lies not in our circumstances but in what we choose to make of them.

Chapter 14

Move to Sydney

Sydney

The Nagano Games were over, the crate packed up and headed for Australia. With one last visit back to our church in Taitomi, we cried our eyes out as everyone gathered around us and sang,

Til we meet, til we meet,
til we meet at Jesus' feet.
Til we meet, til we meet.
God be with you til we meet again.

Words cannot describe the emotions that ran rampant over our hearts that day. After battling with the questions concerning our call, and just where God wanted us, we had finally accepted that this move was okay in His eyes, but looking into the eyes of loved ones with whom we had shared every joy and every grief, in some cases for more than 25 years was almost too much to bear. Intellectually, they understood this decision and accepted it, but I couldn't shake the debilitating sense of guilt, especially as I looked at those to whom I had promised, "Yes, I will bury my bones here." Our parting words to them included a reminder of that promise, and the assurance that, God willing, our children will bring our ashes back to the land we love, and we will be laid to rest alongside those of our firstborn son.

That was the promise, and we still intend to keep it; but who knows what the future will hold? That question comes to mind and adds a fervor whenever I pray, "Lord, hasten the day! May neither I nor our kids have to deal with that issue. Please come quickly!"

The grief at leaving Japan was almost a palpable thing, and I feared for awhile that it would keep us from moving confidently into this next chapter of our lives. But a thought came to mind somewhere along the way: a memory of our son Nathan when he was a toddler. Whenever his world fell down around him and he seemed inconsolable, all we needed to do was say, "Oh look! A doggie!" and his grief evaporated. On more than one occasion, when Marsha and

I felt ourselves slipping into a punk, one of us would call out, "Oh look! Australia!" and the moment passed.

And it was true. Australia presented itself in such new and exciting ways, it was impossible to dwell on anything else for long. The country itself beckoned as a true "land of opportunity", with more rich and as yet undeveloped land than you could imagine. Any young person with half a passionate bone and not threatened by the prospect of hard work would undoubtedly find a place to call home here on these shores. Inland, away from the shore, might prove a different story, as one glance of a map will show. Australia's Outback rivals any place on earth for its sheer desolation. Did you know that the longest overland missile testing range operates in southwestern Australia? That means you can fire off a rocket and it can go until it runs out of fuel and is never in danger of falling on anyone.

Marsha and I met a few surprises upon our arrival in Sydney, however. The first was the discovery that although everyone thinks they're speaking English, we remain divided by a common language. Vocabulary and accents team up to make the simplest conversation an experiment in terror. Case in point: I stepped into a MacDonalds (although here they call it "Mackas") and asked for a cup of coffee. Without looking up, the harried lady at the cash register asked, "What?"

I raised my voice a notch and said again, "Coffee."

"What?"

"Coffee."

It was at this point that we discovered our first challenge to living in this country. What the lady was saying was, "White?" meaning did I want cream in my coffee. Between the accent and the unfamiliarity with the vocabulary, I failed my first test. And here's the thing: had this happened back in Japan, the girl would simply smiled behind her hand and thought, "Oh! A foreigner! How cute!"

Aussies don't operate that way. The lady raised her eyes, looked at me with a stare that could melt steel and said, "Look Mate, do you want milk or not?"

And that was just the first of many culture shocks. The second came on subtly but surely, expressing itself in the growing realization that, regardless how things may look, this was not America. In Japan, we Americans were known for speaking directly and to the point. For us, it's a mark of good character; for the Japanese it's a sign of poor upbringing. If Americans are considered by the Japanese to be "straight shooters" when it comes to conversation, compared to Australians we're Mumbling Mike Milktoast. Walk down any Sydney street, and you can strike up a conversation with anyone, on any topic. They'll be only too happy to let you know exactly their stand, why it's the right one, and why you may be looking for a punch up if you don't agree.

Some have said this is because of Australia's convict roots, something in which Australia's man on the street takes great pride. Some can even tell you the name of the First Fleet ship that transported their ancestor here, and what crime they were charged with. There does seem to be a correlation to the country's aversion to authority in any form, including the church. We even found traces of it among the Japanese living in Australia, which resulted in a few shocks.

For example, at the Japanese church where we settled in to help, we were having a business meeting one afternoon. I can't remember now what the issue was, but I offered a suggestion that might help solve it. The Japanese didn't even pause to consider it, but just said "No", and moved on to the next topic. I was dumbstruck. In 25 years of ministry as a missionary in Japan, no one but *no one* had ever contradicted me. Oh, they disagreed plenty, but being well-versed in Japanese culture and politeness, they would smile, compliment me on my wonderful idea, *then* move on to the next topic.

I had to say something. "Wait a minute," I cut in. "Did you understand what I was suggesting?"

"Yes of course."

"Then why aren't we considering it?"

"We did already. It's a bad idea. Next."

I have to say, once I recovered from such a rebuff, I concluded that I really liked these guys! For once in my career, I've found people who will tell me what they think without going off talking about red dragonflies and the clouds over Fuji .... Something that to them would speak volumes but to me would mean absolutely nothing.

While I was finding my feet with this whole new way of doing ministry among Japanese outside of Japan, I was also finding myself involved with the Australia Baptist Convention. They were the ones, after all, whose formal request made our move possible.

The request had been prompted by the pastor of Crows Nest Baptist Church in North Sydney. He had allowed a small group of Japanese Christians to begin using the church facility on Sunday afternoon, and before long the tiny group had flourished and was beginning to surpass the Aussie morning worship service.

By now, Both Bob and Gail Gierhart and our families were here in Australia.

Australia is very strict about who can and cannot come into their country, and would never allow us in if an Australian citizen could do the job. Wanting to follow proper procedure, the Australia Baptist Convention advertised in the local paper for a person to come to work for them. He or she, they pointed out, must be proficient in the Japanese language, have at leave 25 years experience working with Japanese Christians and have a working knowledge of America's International Mission Board, with special emphasis on their participation in Japan. After two weeks, the Convention contacted Australia's Immigration Department and said, "Look, we really need someone to fill this position, and no Aussie has come forward. We'll just have to request overseas. Oh look! Here's a qualified applicant right here!"

So with Convention support, our initial work visa was granted, paving the way for step two: permanent residence. It seems that work visas are only good for three years and are not renewable. To achieve permanent resident status, one must be sponsored by an Australian (i.e. Australian Baptist Convention) and show "exceptional talent". After long and hard consideration, it was decided that our exceptional talent was our proficiency in Japanese. This is a matter we keep quiet about, since our Japanese friends would laugh their heads off if they knew.

The third and last step was optional, but we decided to go ahead and get Australian citizenship as well. We're allowed to keep our American passports (which is good because our pension still comes from America) and there's no conflict of interest, unless of course the two countries go to war, in which case we would have to intern ourselves.

∽

All that is to say, we spent a lot of time in the offices of the Australian Baptist Convention, made some great friends and discovered a new ministry that led to my beginning blood pressure medication. I was enjoying a "cuppa" with them one morning, when one of the men turned to me and said, "Say Tony, weren't you in charge of the Nagano Olympics?"

"Well, not exactly," I clarified. "I just helped organize the Christian volunteers who came to serve."

"Answer to prayer!" he nearly shouted across the room. Grabbing a pen and paper, he dashed of the name and number of a man called David Willson. "Go see this guy as soon as you can. He's connected with Quest International, the group that's doing the Summer Games in 2000. They need a Baptist representative on the committee." I was happy to hear that "Quest" was in Sydney. David and I had worked together in Nagano. I could hardly refuse; these folks had been so kind and accommodating to enable us to come to Australia. And besides, Nagano was fun. This should be great!

I met David and some others the next day, and that's when I began to realize just what I had signed on for. Whereas at the Nagao Olympics we had organized about a thousand volunteers, Sydney was expecting 50,000. As leader of the Quest team, David was definitely was the man for the job. He had already been involved in several sports ministries including the Nagano Olympics), and even as we spoke was putting together a "Dream Team" of sports celebrities who would be the image we would be bringing to the International Olympic Committee. Through contacts in the business world, he had secured a contract to provide the entertainment in all five Westfield Shopping Malls in Sydney during the run up and through the Games. The entertainment would be supplied by the volunteers we recruited from Christian organizations all over the world, from European boys' choirs to South African Zulu dancers. Besides those rather large responsibilities, the Quest Committee would be producing and selling Olympic pins, coffee cups, backpacks, pencils, stickers and ball caps. We would be in charge of providing chaplains for the Olympic Village, organizing "Sports Days" in hundreds of public parks and for accommodation and transportation for … how many did you say?…. 50,000 volunteers.

My personal responsibility was to convince Australia's Baptist churches to get on board and help support the project nationwide. I was the poster boy, and with my Texas accent never failed to draw a crowd. Churches were enthusiastic to help, opening their doors to help accommodate both athletes as well as volunteers.

The first snag came when those volunteers began to understand how far away Australia actually was. Face it, the "Lucky Country", as they call it here, is not on the way to anywhere. Just about any journey to Sydney would involve a trip halfway around the globe.

Then there was the Hemispheric Confusion. By definition, these were to be the *Summer* Olympic Games. Had anyone pointed out that summer and winter are at opposite poles Down Under? July and August, the natural times for such an event, would be mid-winter in Sydney. They finally compromised by moving the date to September 15th. "Wait a minute!" the volunteers began to respond. "School has already started by then. We can't possibly come that late!"

Along with other issues that gradually made themselves known, by the time the Opening Ceremony came around, our volunteer force of 50,000 had been reduced to just over 7000. Still a formidable force, mind you, but not nearly enough to make good on all our commitments to churches, businesses and Olympic Committee members. The project packed a double punch, considering that we had worked so hard to set everything up, then had to try desperately to either make good on our promises or else back away with a modicum of self-respect.

All in all, I believe it was still a great success. Many thousands were blessed by the work of the volunteers, and relations between churches of all denominations were deepened, thanks to the huge challenge. I'll close with just one vignette, to give you an idea of what we were facing on a daily basis:

Churches in Papua New Guinea were excited at the chance to participate, and offered to send a dance troupe who would not only typify their nation's culture, but also share the love of Jesus through their personal testimonies. This was fantastic, and it wasn't long before their schedule was filled with appearances in churches all over greater Sydney and even a slot in the Opening Ceremonies.

The troupe arrived at Sydney airport, and it was soon obvious that their attire was problematic. Aside from the fact that the ladies were topless, their clothing was made primarily of grass native to their homeland. Customs officials were the first to step up. "You can't bring plants into Australia. Those outfits have to go." The folks were quite willing to remove them on the spot, but that brought the attention of the local police. Finally, after a stack of emergency blankets was produced, the happy dancers were allowed into the country and soon led out of the city, where they could find suitable attire among Australia's native grasses.

Next issue was the fact that, well, they were still topless. When the folks at the first church where they were to appear collapsed into apoplexy, it was pointed out that these were the people for whom they had been praying for many years, after all. If we refuse to let them share their testimonies, then what does that say about our love and concern for them?

Finally, they were allowed to come into the church and perform. And although I wasn't there to see it myself, I hear the congregation was thrilled. One lady was even heard to remark, "At first I was just horrified. Then as I listened to them, I was ashamed at myself for being so judgmental. By the end of the evening, I was amazed to find that I had forgotten all about the reservations I had held at the beginning.

The next challenge came as the dance troupe was lining up to enter the Olympic Village to perform and testify of God.

"This is completely unacceptable!" one event organizer was heard to exclaim.

After a few tense moments, one of our leaders pointed out the fact that there had been topless Aboriginals in the Opening Ceremonies.

Finally a compromise was reached. They could proceed with the performance provided the ladies "covered up". "With what?" they were asked. Grass was scarce, and the show was about to begin. Someone suggested paint, and the issue was settled. It was an unfortunate choice of color, I suppose, since all the crowd seemed to notice was the display of bright red breasts against a backdrop of brown native grass. Everyone agreed that it was unforgettable, though, and just as the church folks had done, the athletes soon forgot the attack on their senses and left with a new appreciation for the Papua New Guinean culture.

The Olympics were finally over, my blood pressure medication was adjusted and working, and we could now get serious about the thing that brought us here in the first place: ministry to Japanese outside of Japan. It wasn't long before we had made contact with groups of Japanese Christians all over the country, managing to introduce a few new programs that are still evident today, such as a nation-wide network of Japanese language ministries including Sydney, Brisbane, Perth, Adelaide, Melbourne and Canberra. We even branched out and found eager participants in New Zealand, Hong Kong, Singapore, Peru, Brazil and America.

The key to the network's success, I believe, lies in the commonality among Japanese living outside of their homeland. After hundreds of years of isolation, broken only after Commodore Matthew Perry and a couple of cannonballs persuaded the nation to open their borders to trade, an ever-increasing flood of Japanese began leaving their shores and discovering new opportunities in lands where their own language and culture do not prevail.

Known as the Japanese Diaspora, these folks spread to every corner of the globe, bringing with them new innovations and new ways of doing things. Things like this made our work in Sydney such an exciting opportunity that we never regretted leaving Japan, even though we still miss our friends there. It also resulted in a growing determination to branch out. After many years in Sydney, we started looking at one of the most responsive areas along our "Japanese Ministry Network", now known as JAMN. It was the Gold Coast.

Situated roughly 400 miles north of Sydney, the area known as the Gold Coast is truly a slice of paradise. At a higher latitude, it's on average about 10 degrees warmer than Sydney, but not so far north as to feel uncomfortably tropical. Best of all, it's just below the "croc line" so that you can feel reasonably safe when swimming in the rivers (unless of course a rogue shark, box jellyfish, blue octopus or a sea snake doesn't happen by).

The main area of Gold Coast centers around Surfers Paradise, a world class tourist destination filled with miles of sandy beaches, restaurants, souvenir shops and even a wax museum. Think "Hawaii" with not so many people. It's interesting that the town was not nearly so popular before sometime in 1930, when the city planners decided the change the name from "Elgernon" to Surfers Paradise. Go figure.

Primarily due to its popularity as a destination spot, Gold Coast is also the home of a thriving tourist business, including a significant number of Japanese. As we began to develop our Japanese Ministry

Network, Gold Coast quickly became our number two place of ministry after Sydney. Contacts were made, resources and ideas were shared, and before long Marsha and I were making regular trips north to encourage the folks there. We had also started, with a young doctor and his wife, a Christian Japanese Fellowship that still meets monthly up in Brisbane, just an hour north.

Eventually, after we'd been in Australia about eight years, it was decided that the Sydney-based work could continue quite well under the capable leadership of Bob and Gail Gierhart, who had also come Down Under six months before us. At the approval of our mission, they continued immersing themselves in Crows Nest Japanese Church while we pulled up stakes and moved to Gold Coast.

Here's Marsha: After receiving the permissions needed to pursue the move, we decided to call one of the Christian schools there that we had noticed. We were interested in enrolling our daughter, Nicki. In Sydney waiting lists for private schools were long, and as she was scheduled to begin in just 8 months, we held our breath as I dialed up Hillcrest Christian College.

I explained our situation and the registrar said without hesitation, "Why don't you come up and see us? The school is putting on their annual play and I'll set aside two tickets for you, complementary to your application."

Since Nicki was profoundly interested in drama and music, we made the plane reservations and were on our way. By noon we'd, arrived, rented a car and had the interview. They accepted her for the next school year on the spot. Somewhat stunned, we left and began to think about housing options. There would only be three of us as Nathan was well into seminary by now and would be staying in Sydney. I went to a realtor and asked to see some rentals in the vicinity of Hillcrest. We would be happy with an apartment, as we were downsizing. The realtor looked at me as if I were asking to rent the Taj Mahal. "There's nothing anywhere near that area as there are five prestigious schools in that area. You'll have to look elsewhere."

I need to include here that a year or so earlier we had received an inheritance from my parents and had some money to invest, so buying something was an option, but we were thinking of doing this only as an investment, not to live in since we never knew when the Lord and the Board might move us to a new place. To that end, we had looked around casually in investment properties in Sydney and just couldn't find anything; even a studio apartment that we could afford. Our thought was to house Nathan in something while he finished school but that wasn't working out and he was eying the dorm anyway.

Jokingly, one time Tony said, "If we ever come across something that's a number 47, we'd know it was from God! The reason for this casual comment was that the only thing we'd ever owned was a cabin/shack on a lake in Japan (see above about "Nojiri"). My kids still refer to it as our 'home town'. And......our cabin was Number 47. And of course we can't discredit the fact that the mission house we were assigned to live in when we spent that life changing month in Australia on the survey tour was also a "47". We are not superstitious, but it was a 'happy' coincidence, hence Tony's quip that if we ever found a '47' that'd be a sign.

Back in the car after being thrown out of the realtor, I told Nicki we were going to drive in concentric circles around the school till we saw something. Passing the school we started up a slight hill. We passed a home with a basketball net on the garage whereupon Nicki said, "Do you think God will give us a basketball net?"

"Such childish faith," I mused to myself. "I'm not even sure He'll give us a roof over our heads"

Then there it was. A very large 'For Sale' sign made me slow to a stop. I looked over and down the hill. It was a full-sized house and a bigger lot. I figured it was worth asking about and reached for the phone to dial the number posted on the board. As I was waiting for the agent to answer, Nicki started punching my arm and saying "MOM!" There, under the tree, attached to the garage........was the basketball net.

Absorbing that information and still waiting for the agent to answer, my eyes caught something else. There, on the mailbox were two large numbers, ...You guessed it, "47". When the agent finally answered, I was able to feign casualness and ask about the property. We made an appointment to go through the house in a couple of hours. When I pulled away, I drove to the bottom of the hill and called Tony. By then I was crying. "God has given us a house!" I blubbered into the phone to Tony. The asking price was less than we could have imagined and even though I hadn't seen the inside, I knew this was the house.

Later we laughed that at the inspection, neither Nicki nor I went into the kitchen, happy to just shout "Huge!" from the front door and move on. Now thinking back of the thousands of happy hours we've spent in that kitchen, and the house as a whole, makes me thank God again and again for loving us and providing for us so.

Chapter 15

Back to Japan, by way of Thailand

We were rocking along happily. The year was 2007. One morning we were out driving looking for a place to baptize some new Christians. A lot of Australians prefer to gather together with friends and have their baptism at the beach. In some ways it might be more appropriate since most of their lives are centered around the beach. Sometimes it's a good witness to all the non-Christians who are watching as well. The phone rang and the name of the caller was one of our bosses in Japan.

Tony said he'd prefer not to answer it, so I took the call. "Hello," a stern voice on the other end said with no preamble. "I've got some unsettling news for you, you have to leave Australia as soon as possible!"

I thought he was joking and laughed back, "Ha! Not going to happen. Nicki just started her senior year!" He wasn't joking. In terse language with just a hint of 'you better not defy me' thrown into his intonation, he 'explained' that the Board had just yesterday been made aware of a tax agreement with most first world countries that US employees would not stay in said countries more than 5 years without a 6 month break.

Later we found out that not only was he telling the truth, but we, the Woods, had been 'out of compliance for over 10 years and stood to lose our Social Security if we didn't act immediately.

The more we talked, the more angry we got. Not because of the oversight and the facts, but the delivery. He saw no solution than to take Nicki out of school and return to the States immediately, making her either revert back a full grade (school terms are off by 6 months in the southern hemisphere because of the seasons), or else going into the last two months of her senior year without the course work and in a new school.

To make a long story short, we had two weeks to deliberate, panic, appeal and research the situation. We also got some comforting words from others in authority, Don Dent, who was in charge of our mission area and a good friend who said,

"How about you go to Bangkok and teach English at the Baptist Student Center for 6 months? We'll take care of Nicki so she can stay in Australia and do her senior year."

Tony soon got over being angry as we realized that the Board was not set to destroy us or our family, so seeing the light at the end of the tunnel, in two weeks, packed up the house, settled Nicki in the basement apartment and got visas and plane tickets for Thailand.

A couple of things came from this, and that is why I'm even including it in our story. Firstly, not all 'bad' things are bad. We would have never volunteered to up and move to Thailand, but necessity demanded it. We realized that six months would pass quickly and we'd be back in our home before we knew it.

We also came to be reminded that the Board had our best interests at heart and would do whatever was needed. They went out of their way to take care of Nicki, and assured us of their love and respect.

We bid everyone goodbye and boarded a plane for the unknown.

Nicki had just learned to drive and with her little car and her 'own' apartment, she matured immediately into a grown up. It was sweet to see that she could cope on her own. Little did she know that the entire church was watching her every move and would email us if she as much sneezed. Through the wonders of the internet, we spoke often as well.

We landed in Bangkok and were met by two missionaries who would become good friends, Linda and James Rediker from Oklahoma. They'd been in charge of the English program at the Baptist Student Center and with the casual aplomb of an Oklahoma farm couple (actually he was also a highly educated high school administrator), we learned to enjoy the craziness of all things Thai. Starting with the first night.

"You're going to love your place," they drawled. They didn't see my jaw drop when they brought us to our door and opened it onto a small two-room apartment. It had a couch, a desk, a TV, a BIG bed, bath and alcove kitchen. A lady appeared at the door and we were told we'd be paying her $20 a month to clean, wash and iron all of our laundry.

We CHOSE to be happy and we were. That's something else we learned again after many years. Stuff doesn't matter, loving life, each other and especially GOD makes the difference. We had a ball in Thailand as a result.

So much so that by the time the six months were over, we were fairly open to the idea of moving there permanently. We'd had time to dip our toes into the Japanese work there and could see the potential for much needed ministry. The mission had been on the fence for years about downsizing the number of missionaries in Australia, so we broached the subject with the powers that be and made plans to move back 'permanently' after our furlough in 2009.

With 80,000 Japanese residing there, it was not enough to be considered for a full time assignment (100,000 was necessary), so we would be focusing on Bangkok's International community instead. For reasons that we've never been able to understand completely, our mission at that time was not inclined to recognize the importance of working with Japanese outside of Japan, in spite of growing evidence that it was replete with advantages. We held our tongues and accepted the role of "International workers" and everybody was happy.

We went directly into language school with the admonition that we would achieve a 'level 3' category in Thai before commencing full time work. The rationale was that we needed to be able to get around with at least enough language to shop, pay the bills and hold basic conversations with nationals. We were okay with that, but admittedly less than motivated when most of our daily dealings were with the Japanese living there.

Finally after eight months of gut-wrenching study both in formal schooling and with the use of tutors, we were both able to reach level three. I have to say, it wasn't really an honest assessment. We used a lot of props and crutches, and Tony even chose to sing a song in Thai at the end of his proper exam, ostensibly to wow them with shock and awe!

Moving into full-time ministry, we began by helping two groups of Japanese who were meeting for Bible study and worship. The timing was good, because the leader of one of the groups, a retired Japanese pastor, had to go back to Japan rather suddenly for health reason, and Tony was asked be their interim pastor until a replacement could be found.

I also found several opportunities to get involved with Japanese wives, teaching the Bible and helping them settle into Bangkok life.

Back in Australia, our kids were doing well. Nathan was married to a sweet and talented girl named Kylie, and their little boy, Isaac Trevor was born on born February 5[th,] 2010. Nicki had also met the love of her life, a brilliant I.T. programmer named Chris, and they were engaged to be married. We were excited beyond belief to watch our children grow in love with the Lord and with each other, even if we had to watch from a distance.

Life in Thailand was easy; the work was fulfilling and we enjoyed lots of new friends. There was also the added adventure of moving north to the town of Chiang Mai for a few months in order to cover for a Japanese pastor who hadn't had a home furlough in twelve years. It was good to be back in the "pastor role" and the church couldn't have been more supportive. So you can imagine our shock when an email came in one morning from our mission boss that said simply, "We need you to move back to Japan".

Stunned, we looked at each other. Tony picked up his phone and called the boss for verification. He talked rather vaguely about the numbers of "veteran" missionaries who had left Japan, with the result that the mission there was quite young, and most in fact were still in language school. "We need someone ol….. someone with experience," he said.

As perturbed as we were to be uprooted again, just like Ethiopia, we felt that God was saying, "Trust me". Finally, after a few days of kicking around and trying to pray, we decided to trust "the Lord and the Board" and started packing.

We finished out the commitments we had in place, moved from Chiang Mae back to Bangkok and took six months to tie things up. In late January 2011, we bundled up as best we could and took a Thai airways plane to Narita, Japan.

Mark Busby, who was to be our on the ground supervisor, met us at the plane and took us to the guest house to wait for our apartment to be finalized. He explained, with some embarrassment, that he would be acting as our boss. "But we both know that your are my "sempai" (honored elder), and I will respect that. We worked well together and are friends and confidants even today

Within a few weeks, we had moved into a very nice apartment in the northeast section of Tokyo, an area in which the mission had never worked. It looked in many ways like and rather dilapidated community, but was in the process of being "gentrified" by an influx of younger Japanese professionals. Our apartment was in a modern building with very lovely fittings. After Thailand we felt like we were living in the Ritz. And then, just as we were settled and looking around to begin work, the infamous 3/11 Dai Shinsai Higashi

Nihon Jishin struck: a 9.1 earthquake followed by a record-breaking tsunami.

The day of the earthquake, Tony and I were in Yokohama, visiting some of the places we'd lived in when we first went to Japan, over 30 years before. We were stepping out of a chandelier store in a ritzy shopping street where we used to enjoy window shopping. At first I felt my stomach turn and thought I was having a dizzy spell or something (I don't do this) but then I began to hear screaming and as my eyes saw the undulating street and my mind made the cognitive synapses, I grabbed Tony's arm and tried to run back inside. People pushed me out onto the street where we stood frozen as things accelerated. Finally we were clutching each other and freezing in terror. While we didn't make any sound that I can remember, the Japanese were screaming. I'd experienced so many earthquakes with the Japanese before and they'd never even seemed concerned, but we all knew this was the mother of all of our nightmares, like riding on the back of a bull. The lady next to me screamed out for "Kamisama!" (God). Later we learned that the epicenter was 350 miles north, in our hometown of Sendai. I can't imagine what it must have been like there; here, it was a nightmare. Cars were dancing across the street like toys, Buildings, several stories high, were snapping back and forth, touching each other at the top and throwing things off the roof.

It's hard to describe the feeling of thinking you're about to die in the next moment. Perhaps that's how I would have felt that night in the tent with the bear approaching. The earthquake lasted over four minutes, plenty of time to give me a chance to ponder the question.

When it finally seemed to be stopping, Tony pulled out his phone and immediately texted the kids in Australia, "We're OK". He'd read enough to know that the phone signal would not be lasting long. He was right, as every phone was dead within a minute. We did a quick look around to see if anyone needed help, then started to move toward the park nearby. We knew there would be aftershocks, and didn't want to spend another minute in the middle of this jam packed area surrounded by lots of things that were sure to fall soon.

We no sooner arrived in the park than the tsunami warning started sounding. We looked up and saw that we were standing right on the edge of the harbor. People were shouting,
"Get to higher ground quickly!" And where would that be? I wondered. Downtown Yokohama is built almost entirely on landfill.
At any rate, we didn't have long to think about it, since the crowds became a solid mass of humanity, with us in the middle moving with the flow. We looked ahead and saw that the crowds were disappearing right in front of our eyes, then realized that they were being directed in a subway station. Tony said, "What? If a tsunami's coming, the last thing I want to do is go into a hole!" But we had no choice, and were pulled along with the crowd, down into the bowels of the earth. I had the presence of mind to be very careful, as I knew this is how people are needlessly trampled. If anybody could fall down, it would be me, but by the grace of God I kept my footing with Tony right behind me and we headed for a pinpoint of light that we figured would be outside. We finally maneuvered through and got out the door. Still no high ground in sight, but there was a Sheraton hotel which we figured would be pretty well built.

We got in the door and discovered at least 2000 other people had the same idea. Finding a spot along the wall, we sat down on the floor and waited for the next six hours. There was no tsunami, but there were thousands and thousands of misplaced people. We began to chat with our fellow strandees, who showed us a pictures on their phones of a huge tsunami sweeping over an area near Sendai, inundating people, cars and anything else in its path. Our insides churned as we thought about everyone we knew up there, and said a quiet prayer for them.

Finally, we were told to make our way to a nearby sports center that was being converted into a temporary shelter. On the way, we commented to each other how quiet everyone was. Tony said, "Yeah, if this were in just about any other part of the world, it would be chaos, with looters taking over the place." As if to underscore that observation, we passed a Seven Eleven and thought we'd better try to find some food. There was a long line stretching outside, but we took our place and shuffled politely along with everyone else. By the time we got inside, we were able to buy a sack of potato chips and a boiled egg. Everything else was gone.

We got to the shelter to find almost every spot in the huge stadium taken. I remember just seeing a sea of black. Black hair, black clothing; this is Japan. Finally we settled in on a landing in the stairway. It was cold and windy but it was safe and we settled down to eat and try to get some sleep. We were glad it was early enough in the spring that we still had coats on.

The hours drug on. Once in awhile we would hear an announcement over the PA system, but were unable to understand what was being said, mostly because they were using such formal Japanese. My imperturbable husband would stand up, lean over the stair rail and come back saying, "No one's running, so it must be OK."

Finally in the wee hours of the morning, Tony came back to say that he thought the announcement said there'd be a train running back up to Tokyo. We jumped up and made our way to the station and again were pushed and shoved onto a train going north. The station master told Tony there were over 15,000 in the Palisade stadium that night.

There was no heat, but we were so crowded in the train we were warm. The girl next to me was crying so I just took her hand. I didn't think she needed the dumb foreigner trying to understand her problem at that moment.

Then the train came to a stop and we thought maybe we'd get off and try to get to some friend's house, but we couldn't exit from the press of the crowd and were literally swept onto the next train. Fortunately it was traveling the way we wanted to go so we just stayed on till it stopped for good. We were about six miles from our house.

The sun was coming up by the time we got to our apartment. We were delighted to find that, first, the power was on and we seemed to have access to water, heat and even internet. Second, even though everything in the apartment had been thoroughly "shaken and stirred", there was very little breakage. Our building was one of the newer structures in the area, and had been built with just such disasters in mind. Down in the basement, the foundation was set on huge shock absorbers, meaning that the place did move around a lot, even with relatively small tremors. But by doing so, the building maintained its integrity and very few cracks could be found.

Outside, it was a different story. Even 250 miles from the epicenter, the strength of this monster could be seen everywhere. Railroad tracks were bent at impossible angles. Roadways were raised and lowered at random, and even though no bridges fell in Tokyo, they were all closed until they could be inspected. The bottom line: over 39 million people were stuck together in an area no larger than Fort Worth/Dallas, a place where just under seven million call home, by the way.

But it is times like these that the Japanese show their true colors. More than greed, more than fear, the nation rests on its sense of honor. Before the debris had even stopped falling, Japanese were everywhere, helping in any way they could. During our long walk home that night across Tokyo, Marsha and I were cold, hungry and exhausted. About 2:00 am we passed by a restaurant. It was closed of course and almost completely dark inside. But looking through the front window, I could see that the place was packed with people, all standing together silently. I said to Marsha, "Let's see if we can stand inside and warm up a bit." Opening the door, we were met by a solid wall of humanity. We started to turn away, but the crowd shuffled and rearranged themselves, allowing us to squeeze in. I'm taller than the average Japanese, so I was able to look over the crowd all the way back to the double doors leading to the kitchen. And there, blocking the way to any further access was a man who was obviously the manager. He was looking in my direction, giving me a confused face and

I said to Marsha, "I think we're about to be asked to leave." A minute later, here he came, working his way to the front door. When he got closer, I could see that he was carrying a big tray. When he reached us, he lowered it a bit and said quietly, "Dozo" (here). Heaped on the tray were dozens of "onigiri" balls of rice wrapped in seaweed.

We each took one, bowing as deeply as the crowds would allow. We were truly grateful. We were moved to the core of our being as he made his way thru the rest of the crowd, distributing all he could find in the kitchen.

 But on further reflection, we were not especially surprised at the manager's treatment of this crowd of refugees. He was Japanese, and he served out of a sense of honor. To do any less would have been unthinkable. I thought with a twinge of sadness, this is the same sense of honor that drove the nation to such extremes during World War II. Honor was, and is everything. Life without honor is no life at all.

During the first week following the earthquake, we stayed inside our apartment with the only real fear that of aftershocks of which there were many. I packed pillows around my computer to protect it and we tried as best we could to "pad" our bedroom with couch cushions, mattresses and anything else that might offer some protection. We were on the fifth floor, so that presented a conundrum. Statistically in an earthquake, most injuries happen to people running outside, so we determined that no matter how big the aftershocks, we would remain indoors and hope for the best. On the one hand, being in a building designed for earthquakes meant that we stood the best chance of survival; on the other hand, we knew that an "earthquake building" in the face of overwhelming movement, is designed to collapse onto itself, falling straight down rather than to one side, taking out a whole city block in the process. Small comfort.

We occupied our time that week trying to communicate with our dear friends in Sendai, which we knew had been the hardest hit of all. News casts were sketchy, but there was talk of a record breaking tsunami that resulted in more death and destruction than the earthquake itself. Videos began filtering in, showing a massive wave sweeping over towns that we knew well. Many of the people in the videos were not yet aware of the coming wave, but from the vantage point of the helicopter you could see that they were doomed from the start.

When we finally were able to reach the Ito family by phone, we were told that Shinkichi, grandparents and several distant relatives were still missing. Miraculously, they all survived, with stories of God's Hand on them in spite of surrounding death and destruction.

By the end of the second week, enough roads were open so that we could drive to Sendai. Loading the car with food and water, we made our way north, many times having to divert away from the main roads and sometime following military convoys. The scariest part of the journey was in the area of Fukushima, where the nuclear power plant there had been inundated and at least one reactor was leaking radiation. No one knew yet the extent of the damage, so our mission supplied us with "Rad Cards", about the size of a credit card with a strip down the middle. The strip was flesh colored, but as it picked up radiation, it turned darker. Dark brown to blue was the signal to clear the area as soon as possible. Black meant that you should find a comfortable place and make your peace with God.

Arriving at the church in Taitomi, we were relieved to find most things intact, although there was no petrol and very little water and electricity. The food and bottled water we brought were received gratefully and we were given floor space at the church to sleep. After shocks kept coming frequently, and more than once our futon mattresses were bounced all over the floor, sometimes covered with debris, mostly soft items like toys and blankets.

Meeting with the church, we talked about how we could be of the most help. They said that the major areas like Sendai and Ishinomaki were already receiving help from the military. These were crucial areas, and getting them up and running again was a top priority. The smaller areas, on the other hand were so far being ignored completely. One church member had family living out on a peninsula called "Ohshika Hanto", and so far there had been no word from anyone. Eventually we learned that this peninsula was the closest land mass to the epicenter, just off shore.

The next day, Marsha and I, along with two church members including the aunt who had told us about the place drove out to see how far we could go. On the first attempt, we only made it about half way to the end of the peninsula where the relatives lived. Bridges were down and in many places entire sections of roadway were missing. Gradually, the road was opened, although you had to check the tide charts before going out, since a high tide would leave you stranded overnight.

The first place we reached was the town of Ayukawahama. It was a fishing village, by necessity set right down on the shoreline and as a result completely wiped out. Up the hillside was a community center where the water had reached to the second floor, but because it was moving slowly by then, it did not take the building down. We were given permission to sleep on the second floor, and we made arrangements to bring a volunteer team to help clear debris.

The job we were given was to clean out a retirement home located just below the community center. It had been completely inundated, leaving no survivors. Every day we prayed for the strength to deal emotionally and spiritually with the carnage all around us. In that way, we shared a bond with the few townspeople who had survived. I spent a lot of time talking to a man who had worked at the post office. He told me, "As soon the earthquake hit, I knew there would be a tsunami. I dropped everything and ran as fast as I could. The tsunami was there before anyone saw it coming. Anyone who hesitated died. I didn't hesitate."

Another community center nearby had been set up as a shelter. We stopped in to see what we could do, and they were very gracious but seemed to have things in hand. "You might look over at the crematorium," they suggested. "We've heard that some people are staying there, but no one has visited." It was located higher up the mountainside, so had avoided the tsunami, but was far removed from the rest of the disaster relief efforts. We made our way to the front door, and were met by about a dozen elderly ladies. Marsha took the lead, asking them how they were and how we could help.

"We're okay," one lady offered. "The power is off and the furnace is broken, so no one will be wanting to use the place any time soon. Thank you, but we have everything we need."

Marsha pointed back to our van and said, "We have supplies of clean underwear."

"Please come in, won't you?" Her polite face turning into a big smile" We'll make some tea." We were able to make friends and go back for visits often.

Just across from the peninsula was the town of Onagawa, sitting right at the river mouth on the edge of the ocean. It was surrounded on three sides by steep mountains, so when the tsunami came in, it had nowhere to go but up. Five story buildings were completely submerged, with two falling onto their sides. The highest building in the town was the local hospital, sitting up on the mountainside. The water rose all the way to the first floor, then mercifully receded. One of the tallest structures downtown was the bank building. When the earthquake struck, the five employees closed and locked the doors, then, bound by honor, determined to stay at their posts. The wave came and rose quickly. The five employees keep climbing until they were on the roof. One by one they were all swept away, only one surviving by clinging to floating debris.

Eventually, the road was opened all the way to the end of the peninsula, and we were able to make it to a church member's family. Before going, we loaded up with fresh fruits and vegetables and several pallets of bottled water. Pulling into their place, we found everyone working in the garden. They were up high, and so missed the wave.

As for drinking water, the area's main water line had broken and they had an unending supply flowing just down the road. They accepted our gifts with good grace, offered us tea, and sent us home with more vegetables than we had brought.

The owner told a remarkable story. About a mile offshore from the tip of the peninsula was a small island. After the earthquake, he stood in amazement as the ocean receded, leaving a strip of dry land all the way to the island.

"Just like Moses," I whispered.

Then the wave came, setting all records. The family had front row seats and shared with tears the experience of knowing beyond a doubt that many people were about to die, and they were powerless to stop it.

For the next four years, Marsha and I led teams of volunteers up to the Tohoku for disaster relief efforts. Some were young people who brought nothing but strong backs and a heart to serve. Others were carpenters and electricians and engineers; they were a priceless help when it came time to start rebuilding. We spent most of our time "stripping" houses that had been inundated. If the house looked salvageable, we removed everything that could be removed, from carpets to walls to wiring, then treated everything else with chemicals that would prevent mold. Finally, a building inspector would come in and examine the house from top to bottom. If it passed inspection, then the owners could rebuild, using the frame as a starting point. If not, they tore the place on down.

Volunteers slept at the Ayukawahama community center, others were invited to stay in houses and shops that were slowly rising back up from the rubble. Most volunteers, however, stayed at Yoshioka Baptist Church, where Noguchi Sensei served as pastor.

Our mission helped by adding a shower and some sleeping gear, and church people helped with preparing meals. Evenings were spent sitting around the room while Noguchi told stories of his time as a kamikaze soldier, leading to his becoming a Christian and indefatigable pastor there in the Tohoku. All together, we counted at least 4200 men and women from all over the world who came to be a blessing and in turn were blessed far beyond their expectations.

After about three years, survivors had either moved away or were settling into government housing. Our volunteer teams gradually changed their job descriptions, from cleaning up debris to helping folks find a new normal for their lives. Many had lost loved ones, businesses and hope. It was here that we could bring the richest blessings. Receiving permission from the temporary housing residents, we set up coffee shops, entertainment centers and worship opportunities. Although most of the volunteers didn't speak Japanese, there was almost always someone in the group of residents who could translate. Most important, though, was the opportunity these places provided for people to come and share their burdens with people who would listen, and pray.

Perhaps one of the most effective volunteer teams we hosted was a group of senior citizens from Hawaii. They were all of Japanese descent, but spoke not a word of the language. Their arrival was always met with incredulous wonder. Who were these people? Why don't they speak Japanese?

But the volunteers would simply smile and start unloading their boxes. Sometimes they brought food treasured by Japanese Americans but totally unknown to Japanese, such as "spam sushi". Many times, the residents would move quietly over to Marsha and me and ask, "What is this? Are we supposed to eat it?" Then they would smile, bow deeply and enjoy the new taste sensation.

Other times, they brought craft materials for making Hawaiian leis, then finish with a hulu demonstration. Finally, after everyone had enjoyed themselves completely, they shared through an interpreter simple testimonies of God's love and healing power. It was priceless.

Chapter 16

The "R" Word

Four years since our return to Japan, Marsha and I found ourselves looking back more than we were looking forward. Disaster relief was fulfilling and at the same time emotionally draining work. Both the people we worked with and we ourselves were struggling to find a "new normal" in our lives, devoid of just about everything in our personal history that made us what we were. Church planting was still on our list of options, but most of the people we encountered in the disaster areas were more concerned with survival than with new beginnings. In between leading volunteer teams up into the tsunami zone, the mission encouraged us to try and start a new work in the area around our apartment in Tokyo. But those efforts were pretty much doomed from the start. This was not church planting the way we had done back in Sendai. Years ago, we had entered the ministry as "marathon runners", settling into the community, enrolling our kids in the local schools, and building relationships that hopefully would lead to opportunities for evangelism.

Here in Tokyo, people were either at work or locked up in their apartments. There were a couple of small parks nearby, and we frequented them as often as possible in an effort to make friends. But unlike Sendai, where a foreign face never failed to draw a crowd, Tokyoites had seen it all before, and quite frankly were less than impressed with what they saw in us. We did manage to start a small bi-weekly meeting in the common room of our apartment building. We marketed it as a church, but it never seemed to catch on. After a couple of years, though, it became obvious that no one in the group was remotely interested in spiritual matters except for the one lovely young lady who tried to convert us to Sokkagakai, the aggressive branch of Buddhism.

We made the announcement that we would be finishing up unless they were interested in continuing. They all smiled and bowed and went about their business. Months later my friend, who had been faithful in attendance and seemed interested, mentioned casually, "Hey, when are you going to continue that English class?

Truth be known, I don't think we ever spoke a word of English, using the time instead to talk about life, eventually bringing the conversation around to spiritual things.

It was a disappointment that it hadn't seemed to make a difference, but we'll never know. I still have contact with several of the people, and God knows their hearts. Again, Heaven will be a wonderful place to get all the answers.

Finally the day came when I said to Marsha, "Disaster relief has been downgraded to relocation efforts, our Tokyo home group is a bust, and I miss my grandkids. Let's retire."

Even as I said it, I remembered the day my Mom and Dad had heeded the call to mission work in Africa. Over coffee one morning, Dad told me, "I've been a salesman all my life. A good one, too. I have no doubt that God is calling us to Africa, but I look around today and realize that things aren't going as well here as they used to. The Recession is going full on, customers are falling away and, well, I'm just not the Golden Boy I was this time last year. I just hate the thought of leaving a long and successful career as a loser."

We prayed together, and God heard us. A few days after his bit of melancholy, Dad got a phone call from his boss. "Great news, Buddy!" he said. The numbers are in, and you're the company's number one salesman nationwide. In appreciation, we're giving you and your wife an all expenses paid trip to Hawaii!"

"That's great news!" Dad said. "We'll start packing for Hawaii right away." He paused a moment, then went on. "And when we get back, I'll be coming to drop off my letter of resignation."

In a lot of ways, I could see myself in Dad's situation. For nearly forty years, Marsha and I had been together on a bittersweet journey following God's lead that had taken us to seven countries, precious memories and enough "success" to count the time, at least from a human perspective, as a good run. We knew of course that such standards are not those by which God would judge our lives. I had progressed in my understanding enough to know that God had not called me essentially to Japan, nor to the Japanese people wherever they might be, nor even to pure and simple obedience. What God had called us to was to a *relationship* with Him. He said so over and over in His Word: "I will be their God, and they will be My people."

With all my heart, I hoped then as I do now, that the relationship I enjoy every day with my Savior would bring a smile to His eyes. Most certainly, the relationship we have is not all it could have been. My own fears, selfishness and greed have been a constant stumbling block, and that reminder causes me to spend a lot of time in regret. But then, I believe that the relationship we have is more than it might have been. I think back to another experience Dad tells about. They were living and working in Taiwan by then, and early one morning he was walking along the beach looking for glass Japanese fishing floats. Many times they would wash up along this stretch of beach, having spent years floating down the Sea of Japan and eventually into the South China Sea. They came in all sizes, from about five inches in diameter to more than a foot.

As Dad walked, he prayed, the way a child would speak with his Father in a respectful yet natural ease. "Thank you for this beautiful morning," he said. "It's good to be alive, and I'm really enjoying the anticipation I'm feeling, that today I might find a really big glass float." Even as he spoke, his eyes were scanning the beach ahead. And sure enough, a glint of sunlight caught his attention. As he got closer, he saw that it was in fact a fishing float, surrounded by netting that must have protected it from the rocks as it washed ashore. Dropping to his knees, he began to dig around it and was thrilled to see that it was still in one piece. Pulling it out of the sand, he could see it was enormous! At least fifteen inches in diameter. His hands were shaking as he pulled the plastic shopping bag from his pocket and started trying to force the glass ball into it.

"The is fantastic!" Dad prayed aloud. "I think this is the biggest one I've even seen!" Still he struggled and stretched, but the plastic began to tear. "Thank you Lord," Dad went on. "This is a really great find … but you know, I don't think it's *quite* as big as Bill's." Bill was a fellow missionary who lived next door and who always seemed to have just a bit better stuff, a bit more interesting stories. Dad was still struggling with the bag, and was about to voice a hint of disappointment, when suddenly his thoughts were interrupted. The rest of his life, Dad couldn't say for sure if what he heard was an audible voice or else a from-the-heart message, but either way the words came through loud and clear:

"You could have brought a bigger bag…"

That story has inspired me for years, and now as Marsha and I finally said the "R" word, I mimicked Dad's experience, saying, "But I hate the thought of going into retirement as a loser."

Marsha knew exactly what I was thinking, and in a moment of revealed inspiration she said, "Let's look in the bag, shall we?" What, really had we picked up on the journey? Sifting through the items in my mind, I dug all the way down to Zambia, the beginning of our missionary career. There was Claridge Silomba, and his friend Noah: two little boys who spent more time on our porch than in their own homes. We can't claim any kind of "heavenly credit" for their lives, but we can remember in awe the way God took those two boys into adulthood, protected them patiently while they went through a time of rebellion, then called them into a lifetime of ministry as evangelists to their own people group. We still keep up with Claridge through Facebook and marvel at the reminders of the time "back then" when we didn't even have telephone service.

Zambia also was the place when our first born son Trevor was conceived, and while we can't help but grieve even now as we recall the horrific valley we walked through watching him die, we are comforted in knowing at least a portion of the blessings his life and death have brought to so many. I'm assured that, even though I don't have the strength today to do so, one day I will stand with him in Heaven and together we will say, "Thank you Lord."

And while we're on the subject, we must include our second child, the one who miscarried in Liberia. We believe that life begins at conception, so there's no reason not to think that precious child will be waiting to welcome us into Heaven. Some people take years to accomplish the "good things" that Ephesians 2:10 assures us we're given while still in the womb. Others, like Trevor, get the job done while still a teenager, and still others, like our second, take only a matter of weeks to bring about those things that will change destinies for God's glory.

Psalms 127: 3-5 tells it not in terms of plastic shopping bags but rather of quivers, filled with the arrows that are our children. "Happy is the man whose quiver is full of them," he wrote; and who could make us happier than Nathan, our solid rock "Gift of God"? He determined at an early age that he wanted to "make a difference" for the Kingdom, and that commitment has carried him into a world of ministry as a church leader, as a family man and as a policeman. As we watch his appointed "good things" be accomplished through his work and his own wife and children, we can't help but feel a profound gratitude for the opportunity to be a part of his journey.

Then there's Marsha Nicole: Nicki. Sent by God when we were in our darkest valley following the death of Trevor. One of her preschool teachers in Japan was blessed with heavenly insight when she commented to us, "Nicki has such a sweet spirit. She always goes to the children who are crying." Even now, as she has moved into her own new chapter with yet another family name given by her husband, Pennycuick, she still is a source of joy and healing. We just can't wait to see where her journey will take her.

For us, the journey has made brief stops in diverse places (Hebrews 13:9, KJV), each destination filled with experiences that helped determine the path. Liberia is one of those. It was here that Marsha "went to the edge and looked over", coming so close to death than only a miracle could, and did, save her. That experience, along with the miscarriage, will always serve to remind us of God's Sovereignty and of His never-failing love.

Ethiopia brought us to ourselves like a huge banner stretched across the skies with the words, *Trust Me* in bold letters.

Hong Kong was a first glimpse at the ministry that would define the last half of our career, working with Japanese outside Japan.

Thailand showed us that God has been with us every step of the way, even when we doubted the wisdom and motives of those in authority over us. In just a short time we made life long friends, came to love the Thai people as well as the thousands of Japanese. And let's not forget the food. Thailand will always remain as one of our 'happy places'. These were no "wasted days" of service, only days of preparation for a future about which we as yet had no idea.

Australia was and is and apparently will continue to be our training ground; a daily reminder that even in retirement, the money may stop but the work continues. As long as our hearts beat, wherever we may be, we are assured that our calling is not yet finished. That wonderful Place that awaits us, that place that "eye has not seen ......" will be there when the last job is done and we will finally hear the words we've been waiting for: "Enter into My Glory."

Japan takes the prize as far as time spent in service, claiming twenty-five of the forty years we devoted to full time ministry. In terms of the journey, we can say for certain that this was the place of our refining. Raising three children and burying one in Japan, the land cannot help but be one of the greatest sources of relationship building for us. Our friends in Australia, watching us go through the grief of separation have urged us to "put Japan behind us and move on"; but how could we do that? I think it would be easier to amputate an appendage in the middle of the race. I do understand and appreciate the advice of our Aussie friends. Our future is in Australia and the sooner we can focus on daily life here, the sooner we can stop being a "buzz kill" Down Under. What we're looking for is "Tony and Marsha 2.2", true blue Aussies with some great friends and precious family at our fingertips; but at the same time possessing a residual of the things that have made us who we are, because it is that very element that makes up the Tapestry.

I think back to that morning in Yellowstone National Park, the fourth day of our honeymoon, and in so many ways a microcosm of days yet to come. We're standing together, looking over the rubble of what had been our tent that was planned to have been our temporary home for a night or two. The Bear had come, and had wreaked havoc. That's what he does, after all. He seeks the heart and soul of a person, the home, and he tries to destroy it.

But he failed, as he always does, because he didn't understand that scrap of canvas was never our home. Our real home lies beyond the mountains, in a place where he can never reach. We stand together and look at those distant mountains, so beautifully set against a perfect blue sky. It's the morning of a new day, and the sun is just beginning to show over the peaks, its rays of light finding their way to where we stand. Another day of weaving sunlight lies ahead.

The world looks at us, much like the dear Texan we met that morning. He sees the remnants of what had been our tent, and he sees the scars. Some are still bleeding. Some seem to be healed, but the slightest touch will open them up again. He, like the world around us, looks on in horror and cries out, "Whut the *hell* happened to yew? Are you okay?"

We don't look back at him, but continue to gaze at the approaching dawn. And with a confidence born of past years, we're able to say ....

"Yeah. No worries. We're fine."

Appendix 1

Not all the stories that make up our lives fit seamlessly into the storyline of this book, but rather than discard them, we've decided to include them here in the Appendix. Consider these the ramblings of an old couple as we sit around the fire and reminisce. Pour yourself another cup of coffee, sit back and enjoy.

Clarence: The Prequel

I mentioned my friend Clarence Richardson back at the beginning, when I was trying to convince Marsha that I was a person of worth. The man will always hold a special place in my heart since he saved my life during the course of the bowling alley fire I talked about. I think he deserves a bit of an introduction.

Clarence grew up a hard drinkin', hard fightin' trouble maker in Western Colorado. He always spoke with pride of the day the high school principal beat on him all the way home from school, after which his dad beat on the principal all the way back. Together, Clarence and his dad worked on a vein of coal in a mine they had dug themselves over the course of several years outside of Carbon City, Colorado. Our paths would probably never have crossed had it not been for the career crisis they faced one day.

They were working about 300 yards into the mine when the mountain quite literally started closing up. They looked up and saw the huge railroad timbers placed crossways along the tunnel cracking then breaking in half like toothpicks. Dropping their tools, they started running for the entrance. Clarence said with a confused look on his face, "I don't remember my dad passing me on the way out, but I *do* remember passing *him* three times."

Father and son made it to the entrance just as the mountain came together, effectively finishing the mine, every tool they owned and their livelihood. Moving east in the direction of Denver, Clarence found work as a bowling machine repairman, and about that time he found Jesus. The summer I worked for him (as described above) was a constant buffet of wild stories (mostly true, he insisted), wisdom that could only be gained at the coal face of life, and a look at what God can do with any of His children. Clarence was a changed man after his conversion, without a doubt; but there was something in the man that still drew trouble like a magnet.

I remember one day as we were working at a bowling alley (the same one that was destined to explode and burn to the ground soon, by the way), a bunch of bikers elbowed their way inside, scoped the place out, and were immediately attracted to Clarence. He was sawing a piece of wood, and smiled a greeting to them as they approached. The obvious Alpha Dog of the group picked up Clarence's hammer, swung it around a few times then said, "I think I'm going to beat you over the head with this."

Clarence kept sawing til his board was cut, then stood up, smiling all the way. "Why don't you do that, son," he said. "In fact, you take that hammer, I'll take this saw, and we'll see what we can build." Then he just stood there, smiling and waiting, until the guy put the hammer down and left the building. "Too bad," Clarence said as he watched them go. "I was hoping I'd get a chance to tell him about Jesus."

A Little Light Romance

As I look over this book, I realize that you might not know how much FUN Tony and I have had over these 50 years.

For our 45th anniversary, I gave Tony a framed list. I called it "45 times I loved you more" and it lists that many times when we doubled over laughing, or smiled and gave each other a little kiss, or........

Most of these instances would mean very little to you, the reader, because that's just what they are: nothing much in particular, except times when we were glad that we had each other.

I think that's very important to a good life, having someone to share it with. Phrases that have no meaning to anyone except the people involved. Even as I write this, I'm thinking of the words, "I'm up to my duck!" and that says it all. To be surrounded by all that life throws at us, not to mention the unknown things that lurk just beneath our feet. The phrase actually goes all the way back to a time when our precious niece, Jinja, was swimming in the deep end of the pool with us, clinging to the inflatable swim ring in the shape of a duck that held her fast. Now when the rising waves of life start to threaten, one of us will say simply, "I'm up to my duck!" and the situation is immediately made lighter.

Tony the Airplane Pilot

During my university days, I joined the Air Force Reserve Officer Training Corps (ROTC). I'd like to say it was out of a sense of duty, but truth be known, the handwriting was on the wall. The Vietnam War was raging, the draft was right around the corner, and I figured if I had to go to Vietnam, I wanted to go as an officer, flying over the mess instead of wading down in the mud. As it turned out, by my third year, they discovered gunpowder in my eye, the result of a shotgun accident when I was 14, and concluded neither they nor any other branch of the service would be needing my assistance. But that's another story.

What really attracted me to the ROTC program was their Sabre Drill Team. It was a squad of 16 highly trained cadets who marched with M1 rifles fixed with 18-inch bayonets. They were amazing to watch, and I tried to join up. Unfortunately, they weren't taking any new cadets, I was told, but if I'd like to come to practice and observe, a place might open up. I went to every practice, marching on the sidelines with a broom handle until I could match them move for move.

And before long, a place did open up and I was part of the team.

We spent a lot of time on the road, traveling to drill meets all over the country. We were pretty good, I have to say, although it was hard to compete against the Navy's drill team. Instead of our heavy M1s they used lightweight carbines that could be thrown around a lot more.

Whenever we went on long trips, we traveled via an old C47 "Goonie Bird", a two-engine prop job that sits down on its tail when it's not flying. We loved that old bird, even though we had to wire the outside door shut with a coat hanger. We all sweated a bit when she blew a piston while trying to muscle her way over the Continental Divide on the way to Salt Lake City. Oil was going everywhere and we were losing altitude. The valley we were in became a box canyon, and I swear I could see squirrels in the tops of the trees just before we cleared the pass and were able to coast on in to Salt Lake. We had the experience of landing on a "foamed up" runway and watched as two fire trucks sprayed water on us all the way until we rolled to a stop.

The piston repair was simple, but the engine's prop needed replacing, and that meant waiting for three days until a cargo plane big enough to carry one was able to bring it to Salt Lake.

After a week, we were finally ready to go home. The weather didn't look good, but the powers-that-be decided it was good enough. The plane held together as we bumped and bounced back over the Divide, but we started getting airsick after watching our 1000 pound crate of rifles break its mooring and levitate in front of us before settling back down. Nobody bothered risking a trip back to the head; we just vomited where we were.

Then the cockpit door opened and the copilot came staggering out, vomiting on everyone as he passed. I was sitting at the door closest to the cockpit, and the pilot caught my eye. "You! In here!" he ordered.

I let go of the harness I'd been clinging to and made my way in. "Sit down," he said, pointing at the right hand seat. I sat.

With the combination of instrumentation lights in the darkness and his obvious condition, the poor pilot looked positively green. Giving the panel a dismissive wave, he said something to the effect of "Keep it at 5000, airspeed 180; head for the big flashing light on the horizon." Before I could say anything, he started vomiting, but to his credit missed any important instruments. Finally he settled back in his seat, mumbled an embarrassed "Thanks", then asked, "How many hours do you have?"

"Are you kidding?" I practically yelled. "I'm no pilot!" I thought he was going to vomit again. "I thought all you guys were pilots." He sat there for a minute, then asked, "Wanta give it a try?" For the next half hour or so, I actually flew the Goonie Bird. Later the guys in the back said it was a rougher ride than we'd had during the storm.

As I got up to leave, the pilot looked me in the eye and said, "If you tell anybody about this, I'll kill you." I wasn't sure if he was talking about me flying without a license or the fact that he vomited in the cockpit. I opted for total silence on both counts, at least until now. I figure he's a few years older than me, so certainly no longer a pilot. Still … I hope he doesn't find this book.

Ambulance Mystery

Working for the ambulance company was fulfilling, and it was exciting, and sometimes mysterious. I remember one night going to the home of a family. The wife lay dead on the living room floor, shot through the head and a pistol lying nearby. The husband was next door with the neighbors, his left hand wrapped in bandages. Examining him, I found a bullet hole in his palm, and could see the outline of the bullet just under the skin on the back of his hand. He told me he was cleaning the gun, it went off, and well.....

The house itself was a mess, with the phone ripped out of the wall, broken beer bottles all over the place and furniture tipped over. Two young daughters were asleep in a bedroom, and my partner and I managed to get them out of the house without then seeing their mother.

I followed the story over the next few weeks and was appalled to read that it was judged to be an accident, just like the husband had told me. No way was that an accident, I thought; but I was never given the chance to testify. Then …. 25 years later… missionary career in full swing, our own two children swinging from the rafters….. we were in the States on furlough, visiting in the home of my Dad. The TV was on in the living room. No one was watching it, but suddenly I heard the words, "Fort Collins, Colorado," the town where we had gone to college and where I had worked as an ambulance attendant. I went over and turned up the volume and saw that it was one of those "reality crime shows". They were talking about an event that took place back in 1972 in Fort Collins and the narrator was saying, "Police were called to the home of a couple. The wife lay dead on the living room floor, the husband had a bullet lodged in his left hand." It was that guy! I was there that night as an ambulance attendant!" The program went on to say that the two girls had been sent to foster homes and had grown up. One was doing well, but the older sister could never get over the belief that her father had killed her mother and tragically, had committed suicide. The younger sister made it her life's goal to find the truth, and eventually her father was convicted of murder and sent to prison for life.

Thinking back to that night, I wondered if there was anything I could have done that would have brought justice to that family sooner rather than later. I don't think there was, but still…

Appendix 2: Discovering Fire

Below are listed a few of the things we encountered through life that left us with the same emotions I'm sure were felt by those who first discovered Fire, such was the impact on just about everything else.

For example:

Television

...had been around for quite awhile by the time we were in our formative years, but commercially-produced television sets didn't make the scene until around 1954. Even then, it was a rare commodity with not a lot of programming to make it interesting. Still, it was a fascinating concept to think that a camera located clear across the country could broadcast its pictures all the way into our living rooms.

Grandma and Grandpa Woods were the first family members I knew who took the leap and bought one sometime in the late 1950s. As I think about it, I don't believe what they had was a new set, and so definitely not "state of the art", but I can still remember the tiny round screen set inside a handcrafted wooden cabinet. The picture was never very clear, and only became somewhat so after what seemed like hours adjusting the "rabbit ears" antenna that sat on top, often with the addition of a few creative strips of aluminum foil twisted onto critical places. The sound was not bad, however, since radio had already come into its own, so we gathered around the set a few times a week, just like our parents had done, but not to listen as much as to watch and try and imagine what we were seeing. Color television didn't begin showing up until the early 1960s, and our reaction to that was much like that to the first tvs. The picture was even more blurred and distorted than the black and whites, but hey, it was in color!

Transistor Radios

Probably of more significance than television during those days was the tiny transistor, and the exciting applications that came with it. Now, instead of plugging in a big wooden box and waiting for the vacuum tubes to warm up, you could pick up a small plastic device (That's right; plastic was a brand new invention in the 1950s), and thanks to a specially-designed battery, turn a button and instantly have access to radios stations all over the area. This was a major boost and defining moment for the young people in that generation. Now you could take your music anywhere ... at least the music the radio station chose to broadcast. In the early days of the transistor radio, it was advertised mostly as a survival device, for use in the bomb shelters when those Russians dropped their nukes in our laps. In the meantime, it was good for listening to farm reports, which served as an acceptable reason for buying one. It didn't take long, though, before the local radio stations began to see the potential among those youth who were accumulating more and more disposable income. Rock and roll stations were on the rise, along with a whole new generation who wanted what they offered.

Tube Testers

With great technology comes great need for maintenance. Pre-transistor radios and tvs were still the norm in the 1950s, and the vacuum tubes that ran them were quite fragile. A hard knock, a slight power surge or just short shelf life meant that repairs were needed frequently. The rich called the repairman, but most of us relied on the local "tube tester". This was a machine about the size of an ATM (something BTW that wouldn't make the scene for many years to come), and usually located in a convenience store or gas station.

First, you would remove all the vacuum tubes and place them carefully in a paper bag. This did NOT include the big tube where the tv image actually appeared. It carried a residual charge and people who failed to "ground" it first with a screwdriver had died coming in contact with it. Anyway, if the problem was there, you needed more than the tube tester could provide.

On the top of the tester were about 20 plugs of various shapes and sizes. Taking your tubes one and a time, you found one that fit, plugged it in, waited til it warmed up, then pushed a small button, usually on the right side. A meter display at the back, behind the tube, would react by sending a needle up and over. All the way into the red was a good sign; tube okay. Anything less was a worry, and no response was a sure sign that the tube was defective. With all the tubes tested, you then opened up a door down below where there would be hundreds of tubes stacked and marked. Pick the ones you needed to replace and take them to the cash register.

Electric Typewriters

For years, the standard manual typewriter was the default for everyone from secretaries to students to the Pentagon. You want two copies? Place a sheet of carbon paper between two pages and insert them into the carriage. Want to write in red? Some models came with a typewriter ribbon that was black on the top, red on the bottom. To go from one color to another, there was a button on the keyboard that raised the ribbon so that it would strike red or black. Want to erase? You're out of luck, especially if it's an important document. There were "typewriter erasers" that were particularly tough, and usually created a hole in the paper before completely removing the errant type. "Liquid paper" was another solution that was nothing more than white paint meant to cover your mistakes. But in spite of the advertising, it was never invisible, especially to finicky professors who insisted on perfection.

It was the golden age for professional typists, who would guarantee perfect typewritten copies – for a price. With the coming of electric typewriters, we gained enough confidence to try and make it on our own. The keys were easier to strike, and going from one color to another was more than simple. AND the newer models had "automatic correction" features, which when you looked at it, was basically the same process as liquid paper, but done more precisely.

Marsha and I both went through university and pre-doctorate seminary work on typewriters, and would like to conclude therefore that our degrees *must* be more valuable than today's.

Computers

Without a doubt, this spelled the death knell for typewriters, although there were many "hold outs" who insisted on staying up close and personal with their work.

We were convinced of the times though in 1983 while serving as missionaries-in-residence at the orientation center in Pine Mountain, Georgia. One of the staff was quite proud of her "personal computer", an Atari about the size of two cinder blocks and at least as heavy. It took forever to boot up and the tiny green screen reminded me my Grandparents' first tv.

But our sneers turned to praise the night of the graduation ceremony. Included in the event was the distribution of a list of all the missionaries, in alphabetical order. When the staff person printed the list a few minutes before the program began, we were horrified to discover that one person had been omitted. And of all people, this girl had a pretty low self-esteem. To pass out a list without her name on it, or worse, one with her name at the bottom almost as an afterthought seemed too cruel for words. We would have to type the list over, and there was simply not enough time.

"No problem," smiled the staff person, who placed her cursor on the line where the missionary's name belonged, hit return and typed in the needed information in the now magically-appeared space.

Today of course, such tasks are laughingly simple and vastly overshadowed by the range of possibilities we see now. But in 1983, on that night of crisis, it was like discovering fire.

Video Player

Back up a couple of years. We were in Japan, still in our first term, around 1980. Missionary life was a daily challenge, but we were surviving quite nicely. After all, we didn't *need* a television that spoke English and there were plenty of friends, missionary and otherwise, who were happy to swap English books around whenever we needed to "step out of the culture" for a moment.

Then we went to Osaka to visit a missionary family who ran a student center. They were hoping we would come and join them after language school and so were showing us all that could be ours if only we would move to Osaka. We enjoyed a fabulous meal with them, thanks to their ready access to a grocery store that featured "American" food items such as corn flakes and dill pickles. "Won't get this up in Sendai," they smiled in a way that sounded more like a threat than an observation.

After the meal, we retired into the living room, where our host turned on the tv, then turned on another machine with the letters "VHS" on the front. He hit play and I stood mouth agape, cave man before the flames. There was an episode of "The Dukes of Hazard". In color. In English. When I was again restored to mostly consciousness, I understood that this was called a "Video Tape Player", and it could play anything our families back in America could copy and send to us. It wasn't long before the entire mission was hooked and organized into a cartel of sorts, exchanging everything from John Wayne movies to Billy Graham sermons. The latter, by the way, served as ample reason for buying into the system for the "evangelistic" opportunities it created.

I can't be certain, but I strongly suspect that it was precisely this kind of technology that cut into missionary effectiveness over the next several years. As much as we wanted to be forward-thinking spiritually, the temptations were just too great. We justified the time spent by saying that it made our schedule more flexible, but in fact it took away time that we might have spent actually talking to people about Jesus. I might get some push back if I took this to the next logical step, but I think it bears long and careful consideration: are the amazing technological advances we're seeing on the mission field now helping or hindering the cause for Christ? It's not a simple issue, I will admit, and there are no easy answers. But still the questions must be raised, and take it from one who has been singed repeatedly over the years: fire is not always your friend.

www.ingramcontent.com/pod-product-compliance
Lightning Source LLC
Chambersburg PA
CBHW020742100426
42735CB00037B/171